Praise for

Time to Write

"If you're a Boomer who's giving thought to writing as a pastime, as an occupation, or simply as a new challenge, do yourself a favor and get this book."

—Ken Dychtwald, Ph.D., author of *The Power Years: A User's Guide to the Rest of Your Life*

"If you have something to say (and who over fifty doesn't?), you can say it to the whole world by writing. This book gives you all the information you'll need to start a writing career or resurrect one that you had years ago. Milligan tells you how to start, how to get better, what to write, when to write, and how to sell what you write. In short...how to have *fun*."

—Gene Perret, Emmy award winner and author of *The New Comedy Writing Step by Step* and *Unleashing Your Creativity After 50!*

"Frank Milligan hits the nail on the head with precision, artistry, and enough how-to information to put every Prime Timer (retired adult) on the road to the late life pleasures of writing. Step-by-step information is enlightening and never intimidating. I have proven his theories with publication of articles, short stories, a novel, and two nonfiction books since age seventy."

—Willma Willis Gore, author of *Just Pencil Me In: Your Guide to Moving and Getting Settled After 60* and *Long-Distance Grandparenting: Connecting with Your Grandchildren from Afar*

Time *to* Write

Discovering the Writer
Within After 50

Frank Milligan

Sanger, California

Printed in the United States of America.

Published by
Quill Driver Books/Word Dancer Press, Inc.,
1254 Commerce Way, Sanger, CA 93657
559-876-2170 / 800-497-4909
QuillDriverBooks.com

Quill Driver Books' titles may be purchased for educational, fund-raising, business or promotional use. Please contact Special Markets, Quill Driver Books/ Word Dancer Press, Inc. at the above address or phone numbers.

Quill Driver Books/Word Dancer Press Project Cadre:
P.J. Dempsey, Doris Hall, Linda Kay Hardie, Christine Hernandez, Dave Marion, Stephen Blake Mettee, Cassandra Williams

First Printing

ISBN 1-884956-76-9 • 978-1884956-76-8

**To order a copy of this book, please call
1-800-497-4909.**

Dedication

This is dedicated to my mom, Catherine Milligan, who made me believe I could do anything, and to my dad, Frank Milligan, who worked nights to make it possible.

It's also dedicated to my wife, Isobel, and to my sons, Brian and Craig, without whose love and support nothing would be worth doing.

And finally, it's dedicated to my brother, Scott, for his example as someone who risked it all to follow his dreams and won.

Library of Congress Cataloging-in-Publication Data

Milligan, Frank (Frank R.)
Time to write : discovering the writer within after 50 / by Frank Milligan.
  p. cm.
ISBN-13: 978-1-884956-76-8 (trade pbk.)
ISBN-10: 1-884956-76-9 (trade pbk.)
1. Authorship. 2. Older authors. I. Title.
PN147.M6214 2007
808'.02—dc22

2007036754

Contents

Introduction vii

How to Use this Book xi

Part I
Becoming a Writer

1. Writing in the Second Half of Life 3
2. Writing for Many Reasons 8
3. Learning to Think Like a Writer 14
4. Making Your Writing Dreams Come True 23
5. Building Your Writing Tool Kit 29
6. Establishing a Time and Place to Write 36

Part II
Getting Ideas from Your Mind onto the Page Without Losing Either

7. Overview: The Writing Process 42
8. Planning: Step One of the Three-Step Writing Process 47
9. Drafting: Step Two of the Three-Step Writing Process 56
10. Revising: Step Three of the Three-Step Writing Process 61

Part III
Grammar and Usage Refresher

11. Spotting and Fixing Problems 70
12. Building a Foundation of Good Writing 83

Part IV
Writing Techniques

13. Constructing a Page Turner 101
14. Developing Characters 114

15. Determining Point of View 121
16. Crafting Realistic Dialog 126
17. Revealing Character Thoughts 133
18. Creating the Setting 138

Part V
Forms of Writing

19. Writing Fiction 151
20. Writing Nonfiction 168
21. Writing Poetry 179
22. Writing Drama 192

Part VI
Publishing, Freelancing, and Going On From Here

23. Publishing Your Work.. 202
24. Freelance Writing as a Business 214
25. Going On From Here 222
26. A Final Note 227

Interviews with Professional Writers 231
Resources 261
Annotated Bibliography 274
Manuscript Format 282

Index 283
About the Author 287
Acknowledgments 287

Introduction

In many ways I owe my writing career, and this book, to a fellow named Doug. No, Doug wasn't an inspirational high school English teacher, or a writing coach, just a guy I knew at the office whose retirement in the mid-1970s had an unexpectedly profound effect on me. At his retirement gathering, obviously uncomfortable as the center of attention, his voice quivering yet firm with conviction, Doug told the crowd how thrilled he was to finally have the time to get to all of the writing he'd put off over the years. His long deferred dream of writing essays, opinion pieces, and maybe a novel verged on becoming a reality. While I had never given writing much thought, what Doug said that day gave voice to a dormant dream inside me. I decided right then to be a writer—if Doug could write in retirement, then some day, when my time came, so could I.

But Doug never did. He found writing more difficult than he'd expected. He couldn't decide what to write about, and, when he did, he had trouble getting started. If he got started, it didn't go anywhere. He could see it in his mind but couldn't get it onto the page. Reluctantly, he gave up his dream.

Determined not to let that happen to me, I set out to learn to write in my spare time, around raising kids and building a career. Now some thirty years later, after an odyssey that began with buying a used typewriter and included taking various credit and noncredit writing courses, reading loads of how-to-write books, earning a M.A. in fiction writing from the Johns Hopkins University, accomplishing my initial goals of publishing short fiction and nonfiction, and making some money doing freelance writing, I'm now developing and teaching courses in business writing and creative writing.

Along the way I took some great classes and some not so great classes; read some really terrific books about writing and some really poor books about writing; made use of some good writing software and some poor writing software; produced some good writing and quite a bit of bad writing. And frankly, a lot of it was wasted time.

Many of the classes were workshops where students submitted writing for critique by the instructor and classmates. As a result, the topics were introduced not in a comprehensive and logical fashion but by learning to fix what wasn't working in the manuscript currently under consideration—useful, but so much more useful after I had learned the basics.

Many of the writing books I studied demonstrated techniques by including examples from the great masters like Hemingway, Faulkner, Carver, Proust, and Shakespeare—beautiful and inspired writing, enjoyable to read but often discouraging, because I had no hope of producing anything like these literary giants.

On top of that, I found both classes and books very segmented: how to write a novel, a short story, a memoir, a poem, a play, and so on.

Eventually I discovered that there are elements and techniques common to all creative writing that apply to whatever form you are writing in, whether poetry, drama, or fiction and nonfiction prose. That small changes like using concrete nouns, strong verbs, and active voice can immediately elevate your writing to the next level. And that although everything you write is based on use of the English language—there are substantial differences between grammar and usage as we learned it in English class in the 50s, 60s, and 70s with its focus on taxonomy instead of communication, and the visceral understanding and ear for language a writer needs to communicate information, emotion, mood, and vicarious sensations to the reader. And finally, that an array of easily mastered tools existed to help get your thoughts on the page, organize them, and perfect them. To all of the problems that kept Doug from realizing his dreams there were solutions; the trouble was finding them in one easily accessible place.

As I began to contemplate my own retirement, it occurred to me that Doug and I were not alone in wanting to begin writing at this point in life; most people feel that they have at least one book in them. Using Doug as my model, I began looking for a reference book for my creative writing classes that described all of these features in a straightforward and direct manner, was written in plain English, and included easy-to-follow examples that novice writers could emulate in their own writing. One that included straight-from-the-shoulder advice from successful writers who would share their experiences, insights, and writing tips and provide advice specifically directed to writers beginning in the second half of life. I wanted a book that would have given Doug all he needed, in one place, written in such a way that he could read it end to end, or skip around to follow his interests because after all, this is supposed to be fun. I couldn't find such a book so I decided to write one. This is the book I wish had been there for Doug when he finally had the time to pursue his dream. I hope it will help you in the pursuit of yours.

How to Use this Book

At midlife, our learning process changes, and I've kept that in mind. This book is constructed so as to optimize your learning experience.

- You can start anywhere. You can begin at the beginning and work your way through to the end in a linear fashion. Or, you can skip around the book to follow your developing interests. If you're pressed for time, whenever you have a few minutes you can read a segment.
- You can proceed at your own pace.
- You can easily find the help you need with a detailed index.
- The exercises are designed to help you practice the concepts, so that you can incorporate them into your own writing.

To Get the Most Out of this Book

Take advantage of the opportunity to make this book as useful to you as possible. Having an actual project or projects in mind as we progress through this book will help focus your attention from the theoretical to the practical. It's far better and a lot more fun to apply the techniques we'll be covering to real-world writing projects than to simply read about them.

How this Book Is Organized

The book is divided into six parts that present the writing process in the way that I've found novice writers best understand the overall process of writing from beginning to end and the relationships of the individual parts to the whole. Also, for someone with no writing experience it parallels the logical development of a new writer from learning to think like a writer to publishing a finished product and learning the options for taking her writing further. The six parts are as follows:

Part I: Becoming a Writer—Introduces you to the writer's world; explains why the second half of life is actually the best time to begin your writing career; and shows you how to think like a writer, how to find and develop topics you want to write about, and how to build your writer's tool kit.

Part II: Getting Ideas from Your Mind onto the Page Without Losing Either—Shows writing to be a three-step process of planning, drafting, and revising while keeping the needs of your readers in mind and reveals the insider secrets to getting the words from your mind to the paper in the easiest and quickest way possible.

Part III: Grammar and Usage Refresher—Helps eliminate one of the biggest obstacles to writers beginning writing in the second half of life: lack of confidence in their grammar and usage skills and explains why it's much easier than you may think to write well and to spot and eliminate problem writing.

Part IV: Writing Techniques—Describes the basic elements of story, theme, and plot as well as how to keep your reader turning pages in both fiction and nonfiction. It will show you how to build believable characters (both real and made-up); use setting, dialog, and interior thoughts; identify and develop conflict and suspense; and determine the best point of view to tell the story.

Part V: Forms of Writing—Guides you through selecting the best form for your writing: fiction or nonfiction, poetry, or drama, and describes the various genres of fiction. It includes writing short stories, novellas, and novels as well as structuring various types of nonfiction such as articles, essays, memoirs, and books. It describes how poetry and drama differ from writing prose and why writing in these forms can be a good choice.

Part VI: Publishing, Freelancing, and Going on from Here—Explains self-publishing versus commercial publishing, the role of agents, editors, and publishers, and how to give your written products the best chance in the marketplace. It covers freelance writing, and concludes with a discussion of the resources and options available should you decide to take your writing further.

Resources

The "Resources" section at the back of the book includes:

• Interviews with professional writers including: Robin Hathaway, award-winning mystery writer, who began writing novels when she was fifty years old; award-winning literary novelist Richard Bausch; highly successful freelance writer Donna Boetig, who literally wrote the book about writing for the women's markets; Emmy Award-winning (*The Sopranos*) television and film writer James Manos, Jr.; and, award-winning journalist, fiction writer, and associate chair of the Master of Arts in Writing Program at The Johns Hopkins University, David Everett.

• Lists of wordy, redundant, and grandiose words and phrases to avoid.

• An example of a query letter proposing an article.

• An annotated bibliography to help you find additional information on the topics covered.

Online Extras

You will find additional tools, articles, and enhancements to the material in this book at WritingAfter50.com.

Exercises

To become a writer you must write. At the end of most chapters you'll find a "Making It Real" exercise, like the one below, that will ask you to employ what you've learned in a piece of writing. Please complete the exercise below now.

Making It Real
Putting Your Words to Work

Develop three ideas to choose from, for a writing project you want to work on while reading this book. They can be existing projects or new projects. Write a paragraph covering what the subject might be and what form it would take. Some examples of projects might include:

- A poem about your mother
- A short story about a rescue
- Your autobiography
- A nonfiction book about how you built your business
- An op-ed piece for the editorial page of your newspaper
- A novel you've thought about writing
- A magazine article for a trade magazine about one of your interests or hobbies
- A memoir about a turning point in your life
- An essay about someone who helped to form the person you are today

Part I

Becoming a Writer

Chapter 1

Writing in the Second Half of Life

Congratulations! You've decided to spend some time doing what you've wanted to do for a long time—to finally scratch that writing itch you've felt all these years. Like most of us, you've thought: Someday, when I have the time, I'm going to write that book, that story, that essay or poem that's been in the back of my mind. But your responsibilities—the need to earn a living, to raise your kids, to take care of your parents, or for some of us, all of the above—got in the way of your writing. Responsibilities filled the majority of your hours and there never seemed to be enough time.

But now, it's time for you. You've decided to set aside some time in your life that wasn't available before and you're going to fill it with writing. Whether you can write full-time or need to squeeze in your writing around your continuing obligations, this book will show you how to realize your dreams.

You probably feel you've missed out by not being able to write until now—and there's some truth in that. Writing takes practice, and yes, you've missed some practice time. But that's not going to hurt you because, as we'll discuss later in this chapter, the second half of life is actually the best time to start writing, and I'm going to show you several ways to make up for that missed time.

But how to get started? Sure, you could pick up a pencil and paper or fire up MS Word and just begin—but at this stage in your life you've been around the block a time or two. You know that every field has its tricks of the trade: things you can do to make the work easier and to make the results seem more professional, more competent, and above all, not amateurish—tricks and techniques that make the pro stand out from the amateur. That's as true of writing as of any other art or trade. The goal of this book is to teach you the techniques, shortcuts, and insider secrets that will have you up and running as a competent writer in the shortest possible time no matter what kind of writing you plan to do.

Why the Second Half of Life Is the Best Time to Write

You could not have picked a better time to begin writing because writing is an art where age and experience actually trump youth and ambition. While other arts have their child prodigies who can, at a very early age, produce a finished piece with a very high degree of quality, writing does not. In writing, the finished piece benefits from and is informed by the maturity and experience of the writer.

In her book *Invented Worlds: The Psychology of the Arts*, psychologist Ellen Winner, in contrasting painting, music, and the literary arts, says: "The attainment of such high levels of skill at an early age is less often found in literature. Unlike painters, composers, or musicians, poets and novelists often write their best works toward the later years of their lives. While one might conceivably mistake a preschooler's drawing for a Klee sketch, it would be hard to confuse a six-year-old's story with one by Tolstoy.

"Hence, one cannot write a great poem or novel until one has lived through—or at least had the opportunity to observe and reflect upon—a number of important experiences. And this most often comes with age. It is difficult to imagine a fifteen-year-old Tolstoy writing Anna Karenina for someone so young could hardly have gained so much insight into life."

The bottom line? Age and experience are an asset to beginning writers, not a liability. It's never too late to start writing and midlife is a particularly good time to begin.

At midlife you've got twenty or thirty years of writing ahead of you. More than enough time to learn how to write, become good at it, and even launch a writing career, should that be your desire.

The Baby Boomers Are Ready for Prime Time

Our generation, the approximately seventy-seven million people born between 1946 and 1964, has changed every institution with which we've come into contact, at every step of the way, and we're going to do the same in the second half of life.

Apart from sheer size, what distinguishes our generation is that we were the TV generation. TV influenced us and we influenced TV, so for the purpose of this book, rather than call us Boomers, or refer to our stage of life as midlife, I'm going to use the more accurate and descriptive term: prime time.

Prime time in the TV industry is the best time slot, the coveted time when the best shows run and the most expensive commercials air, so it's the most rewarding time for viewers, stations, networks, producers, and sponsors.

Likewise, prime time is the best time in our lives, a time of financial stability for most of us, and the time which holds the greatest potential to be the most rewarding in terms of self-actualization and personal fulfillment.

Writing Can Help Answer Today's Questions

By prime time, we've achieved at least a modicum of personal and financial stability. With our lower order needs of food, shelter, and security met, we can focus on our higher order needs: the need for self-expression, for self-fulfillment, and to take stock of where we are now and where we want our life's direction to turn next. Our first half of life questions have been replaced by newer, deeper, closer to the bone questions, such as:

- Is this all there is to life?
- Am I satisfied with what I've done with my life and where it's going?
- Am I happy?
- Who am I, really, and what do I really want out of life?
- What have I not yet done that I want to do before my time is up?
- What do I want my legacy to be?
- Am I good in bed? (Some things never change.)

Writing can help in that process of discernment, because as we write, whether it's fiction or nonfiction, poetry, or drama, we inevitably learn more about ourselves in the process. That is not to say that all writing has to be heavy or laden with deep insight. It can simply be fun and satisfying and as uncomplicated as it is for one of my former students, Maria, who simply writes stories to entertain her fourteen grandchildren. She loves the process of writing, finds it fulfills her need for a creative outlet for her vivid imagination, and brings her closer to her grandchildren who revel in listening to her read the stories they know were written just for them.

Ten Benefits of Being a Writer in the Second Half of Life

1. Writing gives you an opportunity to vicariously remake your life, to consider things that might have been, had they been done differently.

2. You can use writing to transport yourself back to a time and place you once enjoyed, or to a place where you've always wanted to be.

3. Writing gives you an opportunity to express truths you've learned in life through fiction, nonfiction, drama, or poetry to help others realize those truths.

4. Writing about a subject makes you an expert on that subject in the eyes of most people. This can be particularly important if, like many of us, prime time is a time for you to change careers or open your own business.

5. Being an author earns you the respect of others.

6. Writing is one of the pathways to inner tranquility and gives you a way to work out your thoughts on paper to achieve inner peace. It can be a path to enlightenment and an aid to self-discovery.

7. Others can benefit from your unique life experiences by understanding the challenges you've faced and how you've overcome them, so that they can too.

8. Writing is something you can do when you want to. It can fit in anywhere, even in a busy schedule. You can write at home, or on the road, or even while waiting to see the doctor, and you don't need anything more than a pencil or pen and some paper.

9. Writing helps to reduce stress by allowing you to express feelings you might not otherwise be willing or able to express.

10. Writing is an excellent way to keep your brain young and toned while accomplishing something worthwhile at the same time. Recent studies have shown that the brain functions like a muscle: Use it or lose it. Unless we use the brain it will atrophy. The market is responding with games like Sudoku and video games targeted at the prime time generation.

A Journey of Self-Discovery

Creative writing is a journey of self-discovery. No one but you can express what is in your heart and what is on your mind. But there is help to guide you and make the journey a little bit easier.

Lewis and Clark didn't set out on their journey without a knowledgeable guide who knew the way, and neither should you.

Ultimately, it's your journey. You must choose the destination and the route, just as Lewis and Clark did; but just as Sacagawea did for Lewis and Clark, this book will keep you from making the big mistakes that can discourage you and cause you to quit your journey too soon when you might otherwise have been successful. No false promises: It will take time. But this book will save you the time of researching and discovering by trial and error, the who, what, when, where, why, and how of writing so that you can spend your time concentrating on what you want to write, not worrying about how to do it.

Let's begin our journey by being honest with one another: There is no magic elixir, no silver bullet that will instantly turn you into a writer. It takes hard work and effort to be a good writer. What this book will do is show you how to work smart and write smart, how to get the most out of your writing time with the least wasted effort, and how to make the most of your talents and abilities in the shortest possible time. This is the book I wish had been available to me when I started writing.

You can take the trial and error route; most people do, but at this point in your journey, I'm sure you'd rather take the more direct path. By working together, we'll avoid the many blind alleys that can waste your time and sap your creative energy.

Chapter 2

Writing for Many Reasons

Each of us has a story to tell. We all have something worth saying. We grew up and lived through interesting times. Some of us were hippies, some of us preppies. Some became soldiers, others politicians. Some went into business, others into government, religion, politics, or teaching. Some were successful, others not so successful. What we have in common is that we've led our lives in interesting times and we've learned quite a bit about life along the way.

Maybe you want to write about growing up or your military service. Or maybe you want to pass on what you've learned in a cookbook or a textbook or a how-to book. Maybe you want to share the wisdom you've acquired in an essay or an op-ed piece or a book. Maybe you're an expert and want to pass on your knowledge or make known your opinions about your trade or field. Maybe you've read novels or seen movies and thought: I know I can do better than that. Or, if you've been very successful, perhaps it's time to give something back, to pass on your knowledge to the next generation, or even to brag a little about how you achieved what you did. Maybe you simply want to try to make sense of it all by laying it out in a personal journal, never intended to be read by anyone else.

The Perfect Midlife Pastime

Writing is the perfect midlife pastime. It's a hobby you can take with you when you travel. It requires no special equipment; a pen and paper will do nicely if you don't want to carry a laptop. It enables you to vicariously go anywhere in the world, do anything you want to do, and be anyone you want to be.

We each have a unique perspective and a unique way of seeing things and expressing ourselves. We've had children (or seen our brothers and sisters or friends have children) and marveled as we watched them grow and become people separate and apart from us.

At midlife you've put some miles behind you. You know if you're on track for success or disappointment and you've had your share of both. You're not as naive as you once were. You've seen war times and peace times and the market rise and fall.

You've also reached a point in life where writing might actually make financial sense. Younger writers usually have to teach or do something else in addition to writing to support their families. At prime time we are free to write because we want to and you may be one of the lucky ones who can actually make a few bucks doing it.

But more than that, people who begin writing at midlife already have the stories; they just need to learn how to write them. This is a chance to do what you've dreamed of doing and on your terms.

Will Reading this Book Turn You into a Writer?

Ready? Cue the trumpets. Drum roll. Writing is what makes a writer a writer. Writers write. They don't dream about writing; they don't spend a lot of time talking about writing. They don't obsess about becoming a big star, or making a fortune (well maybe just a little). They simply write.

If you are writing regularly, and you are seeking publication but have not yet achieved it—you're a writer.

If you are writing regularly and publishing it yourself to an audience consisting of only your family or a small group of friends or associates—you're a writer.

If you are writing every day and don't know what to do with it—yes, you're entitled to call yourself a writer.

If you're striving to reach your writing goals, whether you achieve your goals or not, you are a writer every inch of the way.

Remember, you're the one who decides what being a successful writer means to you. You don't have to achieve some goal, pass a test, receive a degree in writing, or even be published to earn the right to call yourself a writer.

How Do You Define Writing Success?

Only you can define what writing success means for you. Below are the most common goals expressed by my students:

- Publishing with a large scale publisher to create national sales leading to fame and fortune.
- Writing the novel or a nonfiction book burning inside you that you simply must write; publication is icing on the cake.
- Publishing with any recognized publisher, small or large.
- Passing on a record of your accomplishments or your life to a limited audience.
- Getting paid for your writing.
- Feeling content to write a journal that no one else will ever see.
- Self-publishing a how-to book to pass on a particular skill, a cookbook to preserve local recipes, a chapbook of poetry to sell at local readings, or a novel.
- Writing a children's story for an audience of one.

Stop reading right here, for just a minute. Grab a pen and a sheet of paper. At the top of the page write the date. Under that write: "The following are my goals as a writer." Set a timer for five minutes and write your goals as quickly as you can. Don't stop to think about it. Write whatever pops into your mind.

The objective is to do a mind-dump to collect the thoughts lurking just below the surface, thoughts of which you may not be consciously aware. When the time is up, take another three minutes to review and tidy it up. If your goals are vague and general, like "writing a best-seller," clarify them to the extent you can. Try to be more explicit, like "writing a best-selling cookbook." Feel free to add anything you forgot the first time through. Now simply fold the paper in half and put it in a safe place, one you won't forget. We'll use it later in Chapter 4.

You Don't Have to Be a Pirate

Hemingway ran with the bulls; Eudora Welty stayed pretty close to home. It's all right to do either or both. If you've lived an interesting and exciting life and want to write about your experiences, by all means please do. But remember you don't have to have been a pirate to write about pirates. Write what you know; research what you don't. That's what experts, libraries, and the Internet are for.

To the best of my knowledge, Agatha Christie never murdered anyone, except the characters on the pages of her mysteries. And Sebastian Junger made clear that he weathered the perfect storm on shore. But both sure knew what they were writing about.

Writing for Fame and Fortune

If your primary reason for wanting to write is fame and fortune, you're probably going to be disappointed.

The writing business resembles show business: A few big stars make all the money, and a lot of talented performers share what's left. In the performing arts, for everyone who makes it to the top, whether in Hollywood movies, in television, in the music business, or on the Broadway stage, there are literally ten thousand talented people who don't make it to the big time. It's the same in the writing business.

Have you ever taken a cruise or seen the performers at Six Flags, or Disney World, or any one of a number of amusement parks that have live entertainment, and seen how talented the young people who appear in those shows are? We know, as do they, that most of them will never make it to the big time. But that doesn't mean that they are unsatisfied. They love what they're doing and who knows, maybe one day with a lot of perseverance and a little luck they will become that one in ten thousand. There's nothing wrong with having big dreams.

I want to be realistic with you. It's very difficult to make a living at writing, particularly without devoting years to paying your dues, unless you're extraordinarily talented or lucky, or somehow become famous or infamous.

While writing may not make you rich, it can make a financial difference. Once you become good at it, a few bucks here and there for publishing an article or a short story, or providing writing services to local businesses can provide some spending money, maybe even enough for a vacation. While your chances of becoming the next Stephen King or Frank McCourt may be slim, fame and fortune aren't the only reasons to write. Writing is a terrific pastime with its own intrinsic rewards—and they are plentiful.

The Emotional Rewards of Writing

The greater rewards are of the emotional kind. I'll never forget the workshop at which Tanya, a bright and very intense student, about the same age as I, shared the first chapter of her novel with the class. A perfect first chapter: well written, interesting characters and setting, and several intriguing plot lines that made you eager to read the whole novel.

After her reading, she revealed to the class that she had been trying to write that novel for years, but just couldn't seem to get a handle on it until she took my class. You can't put a price on that.

And I don't think anything can ever replace the exhilarating feeling I experienced when my op-ed piece appeared in *The Washington Post*.

Another priceless memory was my first public fiction reading. How good it felt to see the audience being swept up in the story as I read, and to hear the applause when I finished. And how wonderful it felt to hear the genuine compliments of strangers, not just the compliments of friends and family who cared about me and so didn't want to hurt my feelings, but people who had no stake in whether my feelings were hurt or not, telling me they thought what I had written was good. What a blast to totally make up characters and a story and have people tell you they loved it, and were moved by it, and that it made them cry.

You have all that to look forward to, so don't let the desire for fame and fortune be your only motivation. (For more insight into achieving writing success after age fifty, please see the interview with Robin Hathaway in the "Interviews" section at the back of this book.)

It's Time to Get Started

Once again, congratulations. You're about to embark on a journey to which many aspire but few undertake. You're going to have the opportunity to know self-fulfillment, to become known in the community, and maybe to be considered an expert in your field. And it's going to be easier than you've ever dreamed. But yes, you will have to work at it. *Time to Write* will give you techniques that will save you countless hours and bring you to the destination to which trial and error might never have delivered you.

So, come on, we have a lot to do. You've got time to learn, time to practice, time to become a good writer, and time to build a legacy that will give joy to your friends, to your family, and to your children and grandchildren, a legacy that will live on long after you're gone.

Let's get started. It's time to write.

Chapter 3

Learning to Think Like a Writer

Thinking like a writer has to do with how you process the normal daily events in your life, no matter what your perspective or outlook, so they contribute to your formation as a writer. It also means arranging things in a way that makes writing as effortless as it can be, and understanding that it's unlikely that success will happen overnight.

In order to think like a writer you must:

Be Aware of Your Surroundings

Try always to be in the moment. Being in the moment simply means paying attention to what's going on around you. Every day we're so pressed by the need to get things done and the busy schedules we all keep, that we gulp the big picture as a unit. Stop and take note of specific details.

For a writer, details are the building blocks used to create and bring alive a world in the reader's mind.

At first you may have to force yourself to focus on noticing the details of the things going on around you, but after a while it will become second nature. And, as a side benefit, you'll find you take a greater joy in day-to-day living, once you start to notice and appreciate the small but telling details that make up your life's experiences.

When something strikes you as noteworthy, write it down in sufficient detail to be able to conjure the memory of it later. Don't skimp on the particulars. Specifics are needed rather than broad sketchy notes, because you may not get around to using the notes for some time. All writers have experienced finding notes that they can't interpret or can't recall why they wrote them because so much time has passed.

Focus particularly on the sensory aspects of your experiences. Record the sound, the smell, the taste, and the touch—not just your visual experiences. This will aid you in vividly recalling the experience later and make for richer descriptions when you write the piece.

As you go about your daily business be alert for interesting situations, locations, and scenery that may serve as the setting for a future story or article. Take particular note of the interesting characters you come across and be especially alert to dialog you overhear.

The best way to develop your ear for dialog is by eavesdropping on the conversations around you. I don't mean that you should be boorish in your behavior. Simply, when you hear an interesting conversation, take note of the speakers, their mannerisms, and what they say. Pick up on the word choices they use, their accents, and any interesting turns of phrase. All of this will help later when you're developing characters and dialog.

Details are important whether you write fiction, nonfiction, poetry, or drama. Let's say you're riding in a car going through the Lincoln Tunnel from New Jersey to New York. You spot the policeman stationed in the middle of the tunnel and it makes you think: I bet lots of people would be curious about what it's like to do that job day-in and day-out. What is he watching for and how does he manage to stay awake? This might make a interesting profile for a local newspaper or maybe a magazine article.

Of course if you get the assignment, you'll be back to conduct interviews and to take detailed notes, but first you'll need to write a query letter to see if an editor is interested. For now, take note of the conditions in the tunnel. What is the lighting like? How does the policeman's uniform look? Is it worn and shabby or spit-polished? What expression is on the policeman's face? Does he look bored and disinterested, or is he tuned-in and obviously on top of what's going on around him? Are the walls of the tunnel grimy or clean? How noisy is it? What does it smell like? These are all details that can add to the richness of your query, and thereby make it more likely you'll get the assignment, but details which you're liable to forget if you don't write them down right away.

Keep a Writing Journal or Note File to Capture Your Ideas

Make it a point to carry writing materials wherever you go, because you never know when a great idea will strike or you'll come across something worth making note of. Ideas are everywhere. Be prepared to capture ideas as they occur to you.

I'll give you specific suggestions on how to find writing materials that won't weigh you down or get in your way and a range of other writers' tools in Chapter 5.

Look for the Conflict

Look for the conflict even in happy stories. The essence of interesting writing, no matter whether fiction or nonfiction, is conflict. So you focus on conflict, either between ideas, between individuals, within the individual, or between the individual and something in her environment.

People tend to carp about the television news shows and newspapers always focusing on the bad news. There's a reason for that: Generally speaking, good news is boring.

Let's take the story of Antonio and Barbara as an example. The couple have been happily married for fifty years. You're not going to be able to derive reader interest for a short story about a fictional couple who are simply happy living with one another, nor be able to sell and publish an article about a real Antonio and Barbara, unless there is conflict.

If Antonio stayed with Barbara for fifty years despite adversity, for example while Barbara was in prison serving a life sentence for the murder of her previous husband, or Barbara stood by her man while Antonio suffered from agoraphobia and couldn't bring himself to set foot outside of the home during all that time, or they were both learning-disabled and had to overcome both their disabilities and the objections of their families and social services agencies to marry and live together in peace, then it's interesting and has the makings of a fiction or nonfiction story.

Finding what's interesting in the piece is usually another way of saying find the conflict in the piece. Find what it was that could have kept Antonio and Barbara from succeeding and show how they triumphed over it. That's what readers want to know. More about this in Chapter 13.

Focus on the Human and the Universal

By finding the human and the universal I mean getting to the heart of the matter. While examining the specific details, look for and portray those things that are universal to all of us. The particulars of the unique circumstances may be something that would never happen to most people, such as the struggle for an estate between a deceased ninety-year-old millionaire's children and the porn star he married six months prior. Yet, when you get to the heart of it, it's a story about defending the family against the outsider, the interloper. That's a story to which all of us can relate to.

Maintain a Clippings File

To avoid any confusion, let me first make a distinction between a "clips" file and a "clippings" file.

- A *clips file* is a collection of your published pieces: your articles, essays, stories, or what have you, that you provide to an editor or prospective clients if you're a freelancer to show that you can do the job. (You provide *photocopies* of the clips, not the actual clips themselves.)
- A *clippings file* is a file of clippings of articles, photographs, or whatever you're interested in that you clip from magazines or newspapers to keep in a reference file on a particular subject.

File Clippings for Easy Retrieval

The key to maintaining a clippings file is to be able to find the material when you need it. I generally keep two types of clippings files: one for individual stories or books that I'm working on, related to the topic of that book, and another of miscellaneous clippings into which everything not specifically designated for a project goes. I usually affix a sticky-note to the miscellaneous clippings with a few notes about what I had in mind when I clipped the story.

Periodically you'll need to cull through your miscellaneous file to see whether the items in it are worth keeping. Sometimes an idea that seemed great at the time you first read the clipping will diminish on review and you'll want to toss it.

You'll need a place to store your files. Initially a portable file box will probably meet your needs but, as you keep writing, eventually you'll want to have a file cabinet somewhere.

Read Your Local Newspaper

Your local newspaper is an endless source of ideas for stories, articles, even books. I remember one time reading a feature story about a tall persons' association. Everyone in the association is six feet and four inches or taller. They get together regularly to socialize, share resources for finding large-size clothes, and other things of interest to tall people. One of the persons interviewed for the article, a six-foot-four-inch woman, talked about how difficult it was for tall people in the singles scene. That touched off in my mind an idea for a short story.

Another project of mine is writing a novel in the thriller genre, based loosely on some of my real-world experiences as a counterintelligence special agent. During the arrest and trial of former FBI agent turned Russian spy Robert Hanssen, the press provided extensive coverage of everything about Hanssen, ranging from his childhood and leading right up to his imprisonment. I kept clippings of those articles so that when I develop the turncoat character in my novel, I'll have better insight into the motivations and life experiences that would lead a person in a highly trusted position to become a spy against his own country.

Read all Types of Magazines

Magazines often allow more space per story than newspapers and so go into greater depth on individual subjects. Also, church magazines and magazines from clubs or leagues often have articles that may strike a spark in your mind for an article or story.

Read Like a Writer

Not all readers are writers; but, all writers are readers. It's important to read frequently as well as to write if you're going to be a writer. Read widely, not solely fiction or nonfiction, and not solely long pieces or short pieces. Read in all subject areas, especially those in which you'll be writing. If you plan to write thrillers, become familiar with what's been done in that area. If you plan to write op-ed pieces, opinion pieces for newspapers and magazines, then know the various columnists who write op-ed pieces and know what's been said before about your topic.

Learn to Read on Two Levels

"Read like a writer" means that in addition to enjoying the piece itself, examine what it is that's making you enjoy it. Notice how the writer achieves his desired effect. Examine the sleight of hand he uses to evoke emotions. If you enjoy reading mysteries, examine the way the writer gradually reveals the story. Make note of the techniques, and list them in your journal or store them with your writing notes. If you find a columnist persuasive, examine the structure to learn how the column was written. How many fact statements were provided? What evidence was provided to back up the facts? Did the writer use examples? How?

At first this might sound like it's going to turn otherwise pleasurable reading experiences into work; it's not. I guarantee you that when you begin reading on two levels, first simply as a reader, and second as a writer, it will deepen your enjoyment, because now you'll enjoy and appreciate what you are reading on more than one level and you'll grow both as a reader and as a writer.

Avoid Perfectionism

Thinking like a writer also means avoiding perfectionism. Don't worry if writing is difficult for you at first. That's to be expected. It wasn't easy to hit a tennis ball or a golf ball the first time you tried. In the early days there is the excitement of making a commitment to something you've dreamed about for a long time that makes it fun, exciting, and new. But then you have to put pen to paper, or finger to keyboard, or mouth to microphone and whoops: It's not as easy as you thought. But grit your teeth and give it a chance; you'll be glad you did.

There's always a gap between the mind and the hand. The words that seemed to flow so freely and smoothly when you were thinking about them always seem awkward when you try to get them down on paper. You wouldn't expect to play the trumpet like Louis Armstrong the first day you try it, so don't expect to write like Hemingway the first day you write.

Please don't try to be perfect. It only leads to frustration. We'll talk more about perfectionism and how to overcome it in Chapter 11.

Your goal is to make your work as close to perfect as you can, given your abilities today. And understand that no matter how good you become as a writer, no matter how long you've been writing, or how many times you've been published, you'll want to do better. Writers have been known to make changes to their novel's later editions, because they found a better way to say what they wanted to say.

Also be aware that as you build on your writing skills, the writing will become more difficult because you'll want to take on more challenging writing projects. That's human nature.

All anyone can ever ask of you, and all you should ever ask of yourself, is to do your best. When you've made the piece as good as you can possibly make it, let it go. If at a later date you want to revise it again, by all means do so. But don't allow perfectionism to engender paralysis or force you to forgo sharing your work with its intended audience. The world is full of frustrated writers with half-finished novels, scripts, and memoirs stuffed in dresser drawers.

Accept Rejection as Part of a Process of Growth

There's no getting away from it: Writing requires risk. Exposing yourself to potential criticism is never easy. Whether writing fiction, nonfiction, poetry, or drama, we're afraid people will see our deficiencies.

After all, by the very act of allowing someone else to read our writing, we're saying to the world: Pay attention. I've got something worthwhile to say.

Yet our inner critic is constantly whispering in our ear, "But what if I don't? Perhaps I only think I have something that would be of interest to others."

Those of us trying to write fiction fear that people won't be interested in our story or worse, that readers will mistake us for our characters, or think that we must be just like our characters. Writers of nonfiction worry, did I get it right? Will anyone else be interested?

It takes real courage to submit something you've written to an editor, an agent, or a group of fellow writers. The very act of submission begs the question, "Am I good enough?" The inevitable wait from the moment we submit to the time we hear back can be filled with roller-coaster emotions ranging from thinking that the people reading it will be blown off their feet by the ingenious prose we've crafted, to thinking our piece is worthless and wishing we could call it back.

Sometimes receiving a form letter from an editor stating that our piece will not be used causes us to read all manner of evil things into it and confirms in our mind that our piece was no good to begin with.

Experienced writers know that rejection and the occasional case of nerves is just a part of the process. Good writers get past it and learn to take rejection in stride and to learn from it. It goes with the territory so they don't get upset by it. They know that there are many reasons a piece might be rejected that range from the writing isn't very good to it's a great piece that the editor would love to publish, but she ran a similar piece just last month. Experienced writers know to send it out again to another editor.

Learning to deal with rejection is part of a process that every fledgling writer goes through. It's part of learning to be a writer, something not to be taken personally, and something to learn from. It's worth remembering that while talent is great, persistence and perseverance are what win the day.

Stories abound about famous novels and nonfiction books that were rejected as many as forty or more times before finding the right publisher and becoming best-sellers. The same goes for queries for articles, essays, opinion pieces, short stories, and various other pieces of writing. We'll talk about this much more in Chapter 23, where I'll tell you how to submit your writing for publication.

Understand that Perseverance and Persistence Are Just as Important to Success as Talent

Some people are natural writers who can write good publishable quality material right from the first—most of us are not. But if you're interested enough in writing to be reading this book, chances are you've got some talent. To me, talent means that you have a special aptitude or affinity for words that goes beyond the norm. But most of us need to go beyond whatever innate talents we have to learn the techniques and ways of doing things that will make us successful, which is why perseverance is so important. There are people with loads of talent, but who never use it or never develop it. Someone with a little bit of talent, who takes the time to develop and refine it, can go a very long way.

Role of Talent vs. Role of Persistence

Stephen King in his essay *Everything You Need To Know About Writing Successfully—In 10 Minutes*, says this about talent: "If you wrote something for which someone sent you a check, if you cash the check and it didn't bounce, and if you then pay the electric bill with the money, I consider you talented."

So yes, talent is good to have but it's also greatly overrated. By combining the talent you do have with journeyman-level craft and regular application of the seat of your pants to your chair, you can achieve the success in writing that you desire.

Chapter 4

Making Your Writing Dreams Come True

Writing is about taking risks and about making choices. As writers, we must constantly choose what to write about, what characters will appear, how much research to conduct, what to include, what to leave out, what the setting will be, what point of view to tell our story from, and what slant to take. What's more—we risk appearing stupid, revealing too much about our personal lives, failing, and even succeeding.

One of the most important choices we have to make, however, is what form of writing is best suited to our style and personality and expertise. As you advance in your writing development and begin to specialize, these choices will become clear.

But, sometimes the material dictates the form. You may start out writing a short story only to find as the story progresses that there's such a wealth of material and interesting characters that the work demands to be expanded into a novel.

You may begin an essay or a memoir and discover that the actual events fall short of conveying the deeper truths and meaning, finding that the story lends itself more to fiction where you can control events and the characters' reaction to them.

You may realize that you have only a vignette, but one that carries a deep emotional charge that lends itself more to a poem than a story. Or, you may find that your idea for a nonfiction book lends itself to a series of magazine articles.

Writers need to be flexible and willing to try new forms. Each form has its own conventions and requirements that editors and readers will expect you to follow. Until you become established, it's particularly important to be familiar with those conventions and to observe them.

But let me make one very important exception to that advice: *If you are excited and passionate about a project which breaks all of the rules, by all means disregard the rules and go forward with it.* The last thing I want to do is to stifle your creativity. There are many stories of new writers who managed to break conventions and be wildly successful.

I'm sure many of us remember the 1970s best-seller *Jonathan Livingston Seagull*, by Richard Bach, a ten-thousand-word book about a seagull. It was initially rejected by eighteen publishers. Conventional wisdom said that an allegory about a bird had no chance in the publishing arena, but it had sold seven million copies by 1975 and is still in print today.

And, all of us who spent time with Hawkeye, Trapper John, Hot Lips, and Frank remember *M*A*S*H*. But what you may not know is that the original novel by author Richard Hooker was rejected by twenty-one publishers who didn't think a dark comedy about surgeons in wartime had a chance.

The bottom line: If you've got an idea you're passionate about, go for it. Don't worry about the "rules." But, if you're simply trying to get started, the beaten path is usually the one that leads to where you're trying to go.

Lifetime Goals Exercise

Let's spend a few moments on a planning tool that I think you'll find useful. I know I did when I first discovered it more than twenty years ago, and I've been using it ever since. The lifetime goals exercise is a powerful tool for identifying your overall goals, desires, and priorities, and developing action plans to achieve them.

Decide the Role You Want Writing to Play

What role do you want writing to play in your life? Are you going to be content for writing to be a sideline, simply one among many pastimes, or is it your new career? Will you be a writing generalist and move as the wind blows, writing a little poetry, then a short story, later a memoir, never making a commitment to any one genre, relishing wherever the breezes may lead?

Or are you determined to write a particular book or a particular essay, committed to one specific writing project after which you'll decide what's next?

Perhaps you have no specific project in mind, but you know that writing novels, or biographies, or science fiction, or a weekly opinion column appeals to you and you need only a launch pad from which to begin.

Perhaps you don't plan to publish at all, but simply want to share your work with your family and friends.

You may at this point have absolutely no idea what role you want writing to play in your life. And that's fine. The lifetime planning exercise is intended to give you a handle on that.

I hope you find the following exercise to be fun and personally rewarding as well as useful. It may even change your life. It did for me because it put me on the path to writing this book.

Having a plan with specific goals and specific objectives tied to action items provides the surest way to fulfill your writing dream. Employing a plan empowers you to capture your dream and make it a reality.

How big a role should writing play in your life? Well, how big do you want it to be? If you're retired you can probably spend as much time as you please. If you're still working, rearing kids, or taking care of Mom and Dad then it's more difficult but by no means impossible. But, for right now, let's see where writing fits in with all the other things going on in your life.

The exercise is loosely based on the process laid out by Alan Lakein in his book *How to Get Control of Your Time and Your Life*. It's the best book I've found, bar none, for managing our most precious commodity, the limited time we have for living our lives. You can find the book anywhere for under ten dollars. In my opinion, it's some of the best money you'll ever spend.

You'll need four or five blank sheets of paper and a stopwatch or kitchen timer to complete this exercise.

Step 1—Identify Your Lifetime Goals

Take out a blank sheet of paper and write at the top of it: My Lifetime Goals. Set the timer for three minutes. Now write down as many life goals that pop into your mind. Write quickly and don't overthink or censor your thoughts. Make as broad a list as you can and include not only your writing goals, but life goals including personal, family, financial, and spiritual.

You're not committing to these goals so don't be afraid to be open to such colorful goals as bull riding, losing weight, going on a safari, running for president of your neighborhood civic group, or being in the cast of a Broadway show. Simply let your mind take off. Stop when the timer goes off.

Reset it for two more minutes. Make any changes to the list that you want and feel free to list any additional items you forgot the first time through.

Step 2—Identify Your Three- to Five-Year Goals

At the top of a new sheet of paper write: What are my goals for the next three to five years?

Set the timer for three minutes to make the list, then spend two minutes tidying up as before.

Step 3—Identify What You'd do if Your Time on Earth was Limited

At the top of a new sheet of paper write: What would I do if I only had six months to live? This will focus your attention on things that are most important or deserve your attention in the short term. Assume all burial arrangements and your will have been attended to.

Set the timer for three minutes, then spend two minutes tidying up as before.

Step 4—Set Your Priorities

To set your priorities, go through each of the three lists you've created and label the three most important items in each list as numbers 1, 2, and 3 in order of importance. You should now have a total of nine goals you want to reach.

Step 5—Identify Your Three Most Important Goals

Without regard to the lists from which they came, think carefully about all nine, then decide which of the nine are the three most important goals to you.

At the top of a new sheet of paper write: My three most important goals are. Write them in order: goal 1, goal 2, and goal 3.

What Your Goals Tell You

The reason for having you look at three different time frames was to have you identify your life goals from various perspectives.

Most people find that the step 2 (three to five years) set of goals mirror or are an extension of the step 1 set, and that's fine. Some find that the step 3 (six months) goals continue the first two. But others find the step 3 exercise brings them up short because of the sudden realization that time is finite. Because we don't have time to accomplish everything we might want to, we have to focus and make it a priority to spend time on that which is most important to us.

If you're like me, you probably learned some things about yourself—maybe things you weren't aware of before. I've been doing this exercise for the past twenty years to help me make changes and set useful goals in both my personal life and my professional life. If it weren't for this exercise I would probably not have accomplished many of the things that now give me pleasure and a feeling of accomplishment.

If writing was one of your top nine goals, you'll probably want to take a writing class at a local writer's center or one offered as part of a continuing education program at a local college. You might also consider taking writing courses for credit at the college and looking around for other opportunities to learn more. You should also consider joining a writer's group.

If writing was one of your top three goals, then you probably should lay out a specific action plan to get you where you want to go. Lay out a writing schedule and stick to it. Certainly you'll want to start submitting pieces for publication on a frequent basis. Consider taking additional formal classes in writing, or perhaps earning a bachelor's degree or a master of fine arts degree in writing.

Compare Your Writing Goals with Your Lifetime Goals

Now take out the list of writing goals that you prepared in the exercise in Chapter 1. Compare the two. Did your writing goals make it onto your list of lifetime goals? Do they conflict? It's not too late to change your list of goals—hey, it's your list; put on it what you wish.

Also, if writing is one of your life goals, think about for whom you are writing. Is your goal to write a book solely for your grandchildren or is your goal to write for publication? That will help guide you in determining how much investment of time and financial resources to spend on your writing and will aid you in developing your action plan for achieving your writing goals.

Develop a Writing Action Plan

Once you've decided what you want to do, lay out short-term and long-term plans to move toward your goal. Analyze and determine the specific steps you'll take to reach both your short- and long-term goals, and the resources you'll need. Then get moving on achieving your dreams.

If you find at a later date that you're more serious or less serious about writing, change your plan.

Sometimes life events intervene: a marriage, an unexpected opportunity, a death can change our lives profoundly. Or we simply change our mind. That's why you should regularly update your plan.

Okay. Now that you have at least a rough idea of what role writing should play in your future, in the upcoming chapters we'll talk about the tools you'll need to achieve success in the various forms of writing.

Chapter 5

Building Your
Writing Tool Kit

You don't need a great deal of equipment to get into writing. If you just want to try writing for a little while, just to see if you like it, there's not a whole lot of expense or investment involved on the front end. Determination to excel and willingness to practice will take you further than a lot of fancy equipment, but you will need the basics.

Basic Writing Tools

- Pencil, pen, typewriter, or computer with printer
- Paper
- Reference books

The tools you'll need will be determined by your writing goals. If you're writing only for yourself, with no idea of ever publishing, all you need is a way to get your thoughts down on paper.

If you only want to keep a personal journal, anything from a simple lined pad, to a spiral notebook, to an elaborately bound Italian leather journal with gilt edging will do; the choice is yours. It comes down to personal preference.

But if you are thinking of submitting your work for publication— even if you plan to self-publish—you'll need a computer and printer to produce a suitable manuscript.

"Portable" Writer's Tools

Because you never know when a great idea will strike or you'll come across something worth making note of, make it a point to carry writing materials wherever you go.

The easiest thing to do is to carry a pen in a pocket or purse. Because I now need glasses not only to read, but to do any sort of close-up work, I've developed the habit of always keeping my glasses in my shirt pocket. I make it a point to carry a pen in the same pocket. Now, I won't buy a shirt, including T-shirts and golf shirts, without a pocket to hold my readers and my pen. If you haven't yet reached that milestone of midlife you can find small very thin pens that fit in your wallet. Just go to Google.com and type "wallet pens" and you'll find a number of them. A leather penholder that clips to your belt is another option. A ladies' version can be worn as a pin or on a necklace chain.

The best and easiest tool I've found to hold something on which to write is an index card case. It's a slim leather wallet that holds 3 by 5 index cards. It fits easily in your back pocket, jacket pocket, shirt pocket, briefcase, and handbag. It usually has a divider to separate unused from used cards and it will accommodate five to ten standard index cards. I prefer index cards with the lines laid out in portrait style rather then landscape style. You can find them at most office supply stores.

For a wide range of tools for writers and readers, including pens, notebooks, wallet briefcases, and writing and reading furniture, take a look at Levenger.com. Fair warning: you will love many of Levenger's tools and furniture for writers, many of which were invented by Levenger and can't be found anywhere else, but they are not inexpensive. However, they often have sales and they regularly have outlet and discontinued merchandise at good prices. You can also find pocket index card holders, some made of leather, some of vinyl, at Wal-Mart, Target, office supply stores, and some pen, leather, and luggage stores.

Reference Books

Since none of us knows or can remember everything, a good basic reference library is essential for everyone who writes.

There is a trick I like to use when I'm shopping for a new dictionary or a new thesaurus: Choose a relatively complicated word and look up that word in each of the books you're considering. See how well the dictionary explains the word. Is it something you can immediately understand and put to use? If not, return the book to the shelf and look at another. This also works for choosing between writer's guides and grammar guides. Look up something like "parallel structure" or "passive voice" to see which book describes it best and gives the most useful examples. For specific recommendations see the bibliography at the back of this book.

Dictionary

Invest in a good dictionary. Get one of the mid-priced printed dictionaries that has fairly thorough explanations of words and their origins. Sometimes while browsing through the dictionary you'll get other ideas, ideas that would not have occurred to you if you use a digital dictionary. Keep it conveniently within reach.

Often a good mid-priced dictionary will come with a CD-ROM, that way you have the best of both worlds. The CD-ROM is especially valuable if you travel a lot. Just take the CD with you or load it onto the hard drive of your laptop and it's the equivalent of lugging the book with you, without the lugging. Sometimes the CD will have an audio feature so you can hear the words pronounced, which can come in handy if you're doing a reading.

Thesaurus

A thesaurus should be used when a word is on the tip of your tongue, or you've repeated a word a couple of times and need some variety. But beware: Don't use words with which you are not familiar unless you thoroughly check the primary and secondary meanings in your dictionary. Too many new writers make the mistake of using a thesaurus-found word that sounds correct but is a shade off the meaning. Especially don't be tempted to look up a more complicated, more polysyllabic word to make your writing sound more important. This never works, as we'll see in Chapter 11.

Desk References

Have a small one and a big one—the small one for quick lookups and the big one when there's a less common issue to research.

Computers and Printers

Prices have dropped to where computers have become a commodity. You can set yourself up with a name-brand desktop computer with printer for as low as $300 or a low-end laptop computer with printer for less than $500. High-speed Internet access, depending on whether you get cable or DSL, runs about $30 per month. Dial-up access costs around $10 per month, more if you want a separate phone line.

If you haven't used a computer before, there is nothing to be afraid of. Many libraries and high schools offer free or very low cost training on basic computer use, keyboarding, using the Internet, and common word processing programs like MS Word.

If financial resources are holding you back from the digital age, you can get around that problem. Virtually all libraries now have available computers with print capability (usually at minimal cost per page) but you'll probably have to wait in line to use them.

Preparing the Manuscript

Learning to Type

If you're ready to learn touch typing (now called keyboarding) there are several low cost ($25 or less) typing instruction programs that you can load on your computer. The programs will teach you to type and measure your progress.

If you're not interested in learning to type, for about $170 or so you can get speech recognition software that will do most of the typing for you. The software that I use comes packed with a headset and microphone. You simply speak into or read into the microphone and you'll see your words showing up on the screen as you speak.

Don't worry if you have a regional accent; you train the program to recognize your voice by reading passages the program displays on the screen. Over time it learns your unique way of speaking.

The latest versions of the Microsoft Windows operating system come with speech recognition built-in, but I've found it is not as good as programs dedicated to speech recognition. The best program, without doubt, is Dragon Naturally Speaking (preferred edition). Make sure you get the latest version.

Dictation Services

Okay. There's still a way to come out with a finished typed manuscript without having to learn how to type. Two ways, in fact. You can subscribe to a local administrative support service where you can send or deliver microcassette tapes and have the manuscript prepared for you by administrative professionals who will return the tape, often within twenty-four hours, with your typed copy and your manuscript saved on a computer disk (so you can send the disk to the publisher if they request it). Look in the yellow pages under secretarial services, typing services, or transcription services for local businesses that can meet your needs.

The second way is to sign up with Idictate.com, a web service where you simply dial a toll free number and read or dictate your material over the telephone. I haven't tried this myself yet, but their site says you'll get the manuscript sent to you in a day or two. It only costs $.125 per word, and they've been around for several years, which is a lifetime on the web.

Tools Beyond the Basics

There are many tools which, while not necessary, can make your writing time easier and more productive.

Dictating Machines

If you spend a lot of time on the go, a dictating machine may be a worthwhile purchase for you. They're so cheap now you almost can't afford not to have one. Carrying a dictating machine with you is great for long trips because it allows you to dictate any thoughts that come to mind. I've also used a portable dictating machine for on-site research, because it allows me to dictate my observations as I'm exploring the site. Some now come with a camera built in so you can take pictures to supplement your spoken observations.

Digital vs. tape—Unless you're sending microcassettes out to be typed, or dictating very lengthy passages of text, I recommend using a digital voice recorder. You can get very good ones for less than $100 (often much less). However, if you'll be doing a lot of direct-from-dictation transcribing, microcassettes have the advantage because you can add a microcassette transcriber with a foot pedal and earphones. The foot pedal allows you to forward, reverse, and stop the tape without having to take your fingers from the keyboard. Those run about $200 and up.

Digital machines frequently come with a USB port that will enable you to move your dictation from the dictating machine directly into your computer for use with speech recognition programs. However, my experience has been that when using a portable dictation machine, as opposed to speaking directly into the microphone hooked up to the computer, accuracy falls from about 95 percent to 80 percent or less.

Whichever type of machine you buy, remember to transcribe your notes as soon as possible so you don't forget the context of the notes you dictated.

Lighted Pen or Paper Holder

If you are the kind of person who has "Eureka!" moments in the middle of the night, then get a lighted pen or a lighted paper holder with pen and have it at your bedside.

File Storage

You'll need a place to store your research files and copies of manuscripts. As I mentioned earlier, initially a portable file box will probably meet your needs but, as you keep writing, eventually you'll want to have a file cabinet somewhere.

Computer Software

There is a wide assortment of software designed for writers, some intended to help you with writing fiction, others to help you with formatting.

There are some you might find useful, particularly if you're new to word processing software and its capabilities. Some programs offer writing advice as you go. However, I find that most of the advice that's offered is stuff you can just as easily read in a how-to-write book.

The good thing is that for many of these software programs, you can try'em before you buy'em by downloading a demonstration program that works just like the real product. I strongly recommend doing that before you make a commitment to any of these programs.

Word Processing

For straight-up word processing the industry standard is MS Word. There are some cheaper programs, some that come preloaded with the computer, and some free programs available on the net, but stick with the standard. When agents and editors request you to send digital files most will expect them to be in MS Word format.

Microsoft OneNote

One of the most useful programs I've found is Microsoft OneNote. What I really like is that if you get a sudden inspiration while you're in the middle of writing something else, you can instantly call up OneNote, make a quick note, and go right back to what you were doing without missing a beat. OneNote even has an automatic save feature. The files can then be sorted and stored under different tabs that appear on the screen like pages in a loose-leaf notebook.

The feature I find most useful and use most often is the one which enables you to copy data from websites, and paste it onto a page in the OneNote file. The OneNote program automatically notes where the file came from and builds a link to the site.

Sources for Writers' Software

The following are reliable sources for learning about and purchasing writers' software:

- The Writer's Digest Book Club at writersdigestbookclub.com
- The Writers Store at writersstore.com
- The Writers Super Center at writerssupercenter.com

Making It Real
Putting Your Words to Work

Make a list of the equipment you'll need: pens, pencils, writing pad, writing implements to carry with you, reference books, computer and printer, and so on.

Chapter 6

Establishing a Time
and Place to Write

Most writers I know have established a regular place to write: a niche, however small, that they can call their own, where they can leave their writing things, be somewhat comfortable, and hope not to be interrupted. I don't feel that establishing such a place is critical to writing. Nor do I feel you should train yourself to write in the same spot at the same time each day. The theory there is that over time you will subconsciously and consciously respond to being in your writing place by writing. If that works for you, great. Just don't become addicted to it.

I am, however, a firm believer in using whatever works for you. We're all different, with different likes and dislikes, so my recommendation is to try that and see if it works. It didn't for me. I have an office in my home, equipped exactly the way I want it. I have a desktop computer, a printer, a large library of reference books, a view of the garden from my window, and a door I can close but seldom do. I love writing in my office, but I also love to write at the kitchen table, on the back porch, and in the gazebo outside. I installed a Wi-Fi network so I can write and have Internet access from anywhere in and around the house.

At your home it is likely that everything is convenient: your reference books, supplies, the phone, anything you could possibly need is right there. But, you know what, you don't need conditions to be perfect. As long as you have a pencil and piece of paper, you can write to your heart's content.

However, even if you use a computer, with the convenience of a laptop, you can write anywhere: on airplanes, in the food court at the shopping mall, in the coffee house section of bookstores, in hotel lobbies, in a bar on a pier overlooking the beach, in fast-food places, at a Denny's, or anywhere else you happen to be.

Bottom line: Train yourself to write anywhere. Flexibility is the key. Especially if you're not yet fully retired and must fit writing into and around the rest of your life. Don't let yourself get into a mode where everything has to be perfect, the planets in alignment, the weather just right. You'll never get any writing done.

Making Time to Write

Once you become known as a writer, people will inevitably tell you that they too would love to write if only they had the time. If you feel this way, recognize that there are choices that must be made in order to make time to write.

Don't say you don't have time to write if you're sitting in front of your television—you do have the time, but you're making the choice that watching television is more important to you, at that moment, than writing. And that's fine, so long as that's the decision you intended to make.

However, if you choose to write, and you find that your other responsibilities don't allow for it, there are some tricks that you can use to free-up more time for writing:

- Always carry something you're working on or something you need to read. For example, carry with you what you wrote the day before; if you find yourself with a few minutes to spare use that time to edit the work you've done.
- Get up a half-hour earlier each morning (if you're a morning person) or stay up a half-hour later every night (if you're a night owl) to get some more writing in.
- Instead of going out to lunch, brown bag it. Find a quiet space where you can get some writing or revising done while you eat. This also works for coffee breaks.
- Take your latest project with you when you take the kids or the grandkids to sports practice.

- Write with a dictating machine while exercising, taking a walk, or driving. Of course you need to use common sense and pay attention to the road and not get wrapped up in the movie playing inside your mind.
- Use your bus or train commute to write, edit, or do some research.
- Make the best use of your time in the doctor's waiting room to write or edit your work. All it takes is one emergency call to knock a doctor's schedule off by a half-hour or more for the remainder of the day.

Interruptions

Phone calls and family members—even the dog—can all demand your attention when you are writing. Put your phone on auto-answer, feed the dog, and ask the indulgence of the people you live with so you can remain uninterrupted during your time to write.

Write Every Day

Writing is like exercise in that the more you do it the easier it gets, the more you do it the better you get at it, and, the better you get at it, the more enjoyable it is and the more successful you'll be with it.

Some people can write just a few days a week and not lose momentum. If that works for you, fine—but for most of us it's important to write every day, because doing so helps to build your skills.

If you're trying to fit writing in around your day job or your familial responsibilities, you'll have to be flexible and schedule around those.

Eventually, you'll get to a point where if you don't write every day, you'll miss it.

Making It Real
Putting Your Words to Work
In order to deal with the practical issues of time and place:

- Designate a place to write and stock it with any related necessities such as a desk, file cabinet, comfortable chair, and book shelves.
- If you must write in an area not dedicated to your writing, such as on the kitchen or dining room table, purchase a rolling cart

so supplies, reference books, and computer equipment can easily be stored away.

• Decide how much time you'll devote to your writing each day.
• Determine when you'll fit in the time to write and, if you keep an appointment calendar, schedule it.
• Talk to your family if you feel unnecessary interruptions are detrimental to your writing time.

Part II

Getting Ideas from Your Mind onto the Page Without Losing Either

Chapter 7

Overview:
The Writing Process

There are several techniques guaranteed to get to the heart of the writing process and to make it faster and easier than you've ever imagined. But first, let's talk a little about the ultimate beneficiary of our writing, the reader.

Reader-Centered vs. Writer-Centered Writing

Reader-centered writing places the reader's needs first and has the needs of the reader as its focus. Writer-centered writing is just the opposite: It places the needs of the writer first. The best writers are reader-centered.

Reader-Centered Writing

In reader-centered writing, you ask yourself:

1. Who is my reader?

Whether you're writing a short piece or a book you should have a good idea as to the makeup of your intended audience.

2. How much does my reader already know about this topic?

The writer of a nonfiction piece intended for an audience of dentists can use a reasonable amount of dental jargon and assume the audience knows the basic tenets of the field of dentistry.

A magazine article about the latest advances in painless dentistry, intended for a general audience, can make no such assumptions and all technical terms and jargon must be thoroughly explained.

Likewise a writer of genre fiction who does not adhere to the basic conventions of the genre risks losing readers. Readers of the "Tea Cozy" genre of mysteries will be shocked and appalled if presented with the blood, violence, and gritty language that is the staple of the noir genre.

3. What will my reader gain from reading this piece of writing?

Is what you're writing intended to entertain, to educate, to motivate, or some combination thereof? The benefits to your reader should be clear.

4. What action do I want my reader to take?

If your nonfiction book's purpose is to get readers to take some action, such as to stop smoking, to be a better parent, or to subscribe to a different political belief, don't assume your reader will know what to do. Use examples and case studies to illustrate concepts, and provide clear step-by-step directions as appropriate. Avoid ambiguity and confusion by prescribing exactly the actions the reader should take.

5. Am I giving my reader enough information about this topic?

Consider your average reader's level of knowledge about your subject matter. Use the reporter's questions (who, what, when, where, why, and how) to assure you've given the reader all the information needed.

6. Will this piece of writing answer my reader's initial and most important question: What's in it for me (WIIFM)?

The primary question any reader asks herself before taking the time to read any piece of writing is the WIIFM question. With all of the electronic media and written matter vying for their attention, potential readers want to know right away whether reading your piece merits the expenditure of their time and money. Unless it's going to entertain them, educate them, enlighten them, persuade them, or meet some perceived need, they don't have time for it. If you don't answer this question early on, it's unlikely your piece will be read.

Think for a minute about how you decide what articles to read, what books to buy. Chances are you flip through magazine pages, or look at the table of contents, searching for something that catches your eye, something worth reading.

For books, we rely on the title on the spine, sometimes the front cover if it's facing out. If the title and cover catch our eye, we'll pull the book from the shelf and read the back cover or the dustcover flap for a quick impression of what the book is about. We may read the first few pages to get a feel for it. Then we make our decision, all in about thirty seconds.

The same rules apply to privately published materials produced for family, employees, or associations. While friends, employees, and associates probably will courteously accept whatever you give them, if you actually want them to read it, your writing must be interesting, polished, and focused in a way that meets their needs.

WIIFM also determines whether or not a piece gets picked up by agents or editors and, ultimately, is published. Agents and editors look for material that will sell because it meets the needs of their readers. In a nutshell: No WIIFM = no sale.

In most cases, you should lead with the WIIFM, if at all possible within the title, and certainly at the earliest opportunity within your piece. Make sure your title, your opening, and in the case of a self-published book, your cover copy, answer the WIIFM question for your target audience. (For traditionally published books the publisher's sales and marketing department usually produce this material in consultation with you.)

Writer-Centered Writing

Writer-centered writing sacrifices the reader's needs to the writer's. It's characterized by the attitudes:

1. I, the writer, have done all of this research, and have learned all of this stuff, so I'm going to dump it on you, dear reader, whether you need to know it or not.
2. I'm going to impress you with all of the big words I know.
3. I'm going to dazzle you with my style.

Over the years, I've come across authors, a few rich and successful, but very few, who will advise you to write only for yourself, without considering your audience. These writers, whom I like to characterize as representing the "writer as artiste" school of writing, will tell you that it doesn't matter if readers react positively, negatively, or at all to your work, so long as you've been true to your artistic self.

To them I say fine, write only for yourself, but recognize that there is a price for everything, and in this case the price will likely be not finding a readership. To me, with the exception of keeping a journal, writing only for yourself is the equivalent of literary masturbation. If that floats your boat, be my guest. If you're writing for others—engage your reader.

Speak to Your Reader

Knowing your audience will help you determine the level of detail to include, the tone and the voice to use, and the slant needed for a magazine piece. It helps make the writing easier. Some writers—I'm one of them—like to picture their average reader, and pretend that they are simply telling the story or sharing the information, whether fiction or nonfiction, in a conversation or in a personal letter.

Please don't mistake what I'm saying here. I'm not saying you should pander to or write down to an audience. No, I'm talking about simply communicating with your readers in the way that will best achieve their objectives for reading the piece while meeting your objectives for writing the piece.

The Three-Step Process of Writing

Although initially it may seem counterintuitive, because you'll be adding a step or two to your usual writing process, once you get used to the three-step process you'll find that you will write much more quickly and with much less effort and your writing style will improve.

In general, the ratio of time spent should be about 20 percent on the planning stage, 20 percent on the drafting stage, and 60 percent on the revision stage. This will of course depend on the length of the work, how much research is required, the sensitivity of the content, and other variable factors, but 20-20-60 is a good rule of thumb for most projects.

The three-step process includes:

1. Planning—Doing preliminary research, deciding what needs to be said, and organizing it in a way that readers can follow.
2. Drafting—Getting your thoughts down on paper as rapidly as possible without concern for editing, grammar, spelling, rules, wordiness, or redundancy.

3. Revising—Editing your manuscript to make sure you've said what you wanted to say in a way that meets your reader's needs, and have corrected any problems with organization, completeness, spelling, punctuation, and grammar. In this stage you will polish your manuscript to make it the very best it can be.

The Five Critical Cs of Writing

All good writing incorporates the critical five Cs:

1. Clear—Write in an organized logical way, using familiar words and phrases.
2. Correct—Make sure your content, spelling, punctuation, and grammar are accurate.
3. Concise—Remove all excess words, redundancies, and unnecessary information.
4. Complete—Present all pertinent information leaving no logical questions unanswered.
5. Considerate—Respect your reader's time, intellect, needs, and sensibilities.

Chapter 8

Planning:
Step One of the Three-Step
Writing Process

Planning involves deciding what you're going to write about, determining how much you know about the subject, conducting whatever research you need to write the piece, and organizing the material in a logical way so your reader can follow it.

Identify the Central Idea

Simply put, the central idea is the reason you are creating a particular piece of writing. It is the key idea that you are trying to communicate to your reader, whether you are writing a single paragraph, an article, a poem, a novel, or a nonfiction book. Some people refer to it as the key idea, the core issue, the overarching concept, the purpose statement, or the thesis statement. No matter what you call it, the concept is the same.

Taking the time to identify and develop the central idea makes your writing easier for your readers to comprehend and, a bonus, easier for you to write.

In order to identify the central idea, simply ask yourself: If I had only one thing to say, what would it be? The answer is your central idea.

In nonfiction the central idea is generally easier to identify than in fiction. For example, the central idea of this book is to teach novice writers in the second half of their lives enough about the craft of writing to make it more fun, less work, and have better results.

In fiction, the central idea has to do with story, theme, plot, and the interaction and relationships among characters. We'll talk more about that in Chapter 19.

Do Preliminary Research

Is this a subject or an issue which you have a lot of information about, or do you need to conduct research or interviews to gather background information?

For example, if you're writing fiction, an historical novel will likely take more research than a contemporary novel in a familiar setting.

For nonfiction intended for commercial publication, at the outset you need to conduct only enough research to help you focus on the central idea of your piece sufficiently so that you can form your ideas to craft a query or proposal. As we'll discuss in depth in Chapter 20, most nonfiction, whether short or long, is sold before it is written, based on a query or proposal. Additional, detailed research can be done once you and the publisher have determined what needs to be included.

Generate and Organize Ideas

After you've analyzed your reader, identified your point, and done any necessary research, planning your writing takes two final steps:

1. Generating ideas and getting them on paper and
2. Organizing your ideas into an outline.

Five Tools for Getting Ideas to the Page

I'm going to list five tools you may use to generate ideas and get your words from the mind to the page. Most people never need to go beyond the first two tools, clustering and freewriting, but I've included the others because they can provide additional perspectives and can be used in conjunction with the first two tools.

Clustering

In my opinion, clustering (sometimes called brain-mapping or bubbling) is the easiest and most effective way to generate ideas. It enables you to visualize your thoughts in a way that allows for seeing connections that might not otherwise have made themselves apparent, because instead of a list of words or a narrative, clustering results in a diagram showing how the concepts work together. It is the only tool I've found that allows the hand to fully keep up with the mind.

It can be used for any size project, from laying out a paragraph to laying out a book. It is particularly useful for people who think and learn visually because it enables you to see the entire concept on a single page. Clustering allows our creative side to operate without interference from our control side.

The drawback to clustering is that it does not appeal to people who think in a linear fashion. If you fall into this category and like to think in a neater, more traditional, more narrative way, you may want to skip clustering and go directly to freewriting.

How to cluster:

- Write the central idea of your project in the middle of a blank page. It can be a word, a phrase, or a sentence. Draw a circle around it.
- Relax. Permit your mind to go in whatever direction it chooses with regard to the central idea. Write down concepts that come to mind. Don't try to think of things to put down, let them come naturally into your mind. Circle each concept.
- Draw a line out from the center circle to each new concept.
- Jot down any additional thoughts which spring from these new thoughts and connect them with lines.
- Work as quickly as you can. Don't take time to analyze the thoughts or filter them in any way. As they occur to you, simply write them down.
- Keep going until you run completely out of new thoughts.
- Take a few minutes to review the diagram that has resulted and identify and associate like items. Eliminate any duplicates by drawing a line through them.
- Sit back and take a look at what you've got. You'll usually find that connections you were not aware of on a conscious level have made their way onto the cluster diagram.

Below is an example of a cluster for a "how-to" article.

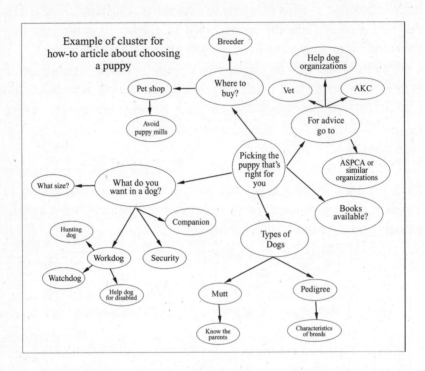

The next step will be to lay out the clustered material in an outline as described later in this chapter. In addition, take a look at the rainbowing technique below which can also help you organize your material.

Freewriting

Freewriting is a technique useful for writers who tend to think in a linear, nonvisual fashion, or who want to jump right in and begin writing.

Like clustering, freewriting allows our creative side to operate without interference from our control side. It relies on keeping the internal editor under control and out of the picture so that the writing can flow unfiltered and unjudged. Many writers find it a useful way of discovering what they know and what they think about a topic.

Here's how to freewrite:

Set a timer and write for a relatively short period of time: five, ten, or fifteen minutes. Write without stopping. Don't lift your hands from the paper or keyboard. If you run out of things to say, simply write "I have nothing to say" until you get rolling again. Just keep writing. Don't worry about grammar, spelling, or if what you're writing makes any sense. Some of it won't, and that's okay. When the time is up, stop or continue writing, it's completely up to you. When you've finished, read what you've written. You'll often be surprised at how much of what you've written is worth keeping.

Most writers will find that either freewriting or clustering will meet their needs. However, because all writers are different, and have their own ways of working, we'll discuss a few other methods.

Rainbowing

Rainbowing is a great aid that adds colors to the organizing process. Rainbowing can be used by itself or in conjunction with other techniques like clustering and freewriting.

How to use rainbowing:

You'll need four or five different colored markers to begin.

If you like clustering but don't like moving directly from a cluster chart to an outline, you can instead begin organizing on the cluster chart. Color the clusters that go together or are similar in the same color. For example, use green for things that go in the front of your piece, red for things that go last, and various shades for the paragraphs in the middle. Or you can color-code groups of clusters that go together in some other way.

Rainbowing is a particularly useful technique when used with freewriting. Color code sentences that, although scattered throughout your pages, go together, so that they can more easily be pulled together into an outline or directly into your draft.

Storyboarding

Storyboarding is a technique used in the movie business to outline the shots and the script for a movie. It's also used in developing audiovisual presentations. Each panel in a storyboard consists of two boxes: the box on the left has pictures or a rendering of the AV image; the box on the right holds the script or narration of the script. The panels can then be laid out in the order in which the movie flows. The benefit is that each panel can be easily picked up and moved around to form a different order.

How to Storyboard

Most of you won't need the pictures' side, so it's probably easier for you to simply use index cards. Put each segment on an index card. As you conceive of segments, or conduct your research, write a summary of the information on one of the cards.

For example, in an article you're writing for a magazine, you know you'll need to have an introductory hook, three to five key points, some of which will be supported by anecdotes, and some of which will be supported by interviews with experts, a summary or call to action, and a close.

While the beginning and the end are usually clear, the stuff in the middle can be arranged in different ways. This method gives you the opportunity to experiment with different structures by simply moving the cards around.

You may even find it useful to document your research on index cards which enables you to use this method without having to later rewrite your notes onto cards.

Likewise in fiction, once you have your central idea, you know you need certain scenes, and certain narrative passages to tell the story. This system allows you to experiment with different structures, simply by moving the cards around, and helps you to find gaps in your story where you may need an additional scene or narration.

For more permanence to the arrangement, you can use thumbtacks on a cork board, or sticky notes on a mirror or desk surface. This gives you a chance to visualize the final format before you begin to write, and then let it sit for a while without worrying that it may be disturbed so you can come back to it later with a fresh eye.

You can also use a variation of the rainbow method to color code the cards or sticky notes that go together or to color code them into beginning, middle, and end groups.

Heuristic Interviewing

Heuristic interviewing is a technique wherein you interview yourself as though you were interviewing a third party. The underlying concept is that we often know a lot of information about a subject that we don't realize we know.

How to use heuristic interviewing:

By coming up with a list of logical questions about our topic, the kind of questions most readers would have, and then answering those questions, we can pull from our minds the information that we need to write the piece, and also identify the gaps in our knowledge that will need to be filled. Any question that we cannot answer will become the subject of research.

You can use this method for clarifying a plot in fiction, developing characters, writing articles, essays, and so on.

Sometimes when a work of fiction isn't working, it's useful to interview your lead characters on paper. Literally, on a new page, ask them why it's not working and have them respond. Simply lay out a question-and-answer session between you and your lead character, as though you are writing a page of dialog for your story.

Okay, okay, I know it sounds nutty, but try it. You'll be amazed at what your characters can tell you if you let them speak for themselves.

Organize Your Ideas

After you have generated ideas using the techniques above, organize the material to assist you in writing your first draft. Organizing involves grouping similar concepts and then linking the resulting groups in logical order. The nature of the project will usually determine which organizational method makes the most sense.

Organizational Methods

- Chronological—In order of sequence of time
- Hierarchical—In order of importance, general to specific or vice versa
- Logical—Steps in a process, geographical layout, or analysis of data
- Compare and contrast—Comparing two or more issues, ideas, products, services, etc. using similar criteria
- Advantages and disadvantages—Weighing the pros and cons of an issue, idea, product, service, etc.

• List—A listing of useful information such as the top ten ways to grow petunias or seven ways to avoid being cheated when buying a new car

The Value of Outlining

Think of an outline as a blueprint for your writing. A builder needs a blueprint, a writer needs an outline.

Unfortunately, when we hear the term outline, most of us recall with a shudder the tedious process of outlining we learned back in Miss Strictgrammar's English class. But for your writing, your outline can be as formal as the Roman numeral outlines you learned in school or as informal as a scribbled list on a napkin—whatever works for you. It's to help you organize your ideas. Don't forget, no one but you will ever see your outline. The outline is just a guide that you can use—if the writing takes on a life of its own, you're free to deviate from it as you please. My view is, the better your organization during the planning stage, the easier it will be for you in the drafting stage; but, when the magic happens, just go with the flow.

Here's how I recommend you use the outline:

If you're writing nonfiction, always outline. It will help you to identify areas requiring further research as well as keep you focused while you're writing. In most instances an outline will be required. Except for very short pieces, nonfiction is sold before you write it, based on a query letter or a proposal. Your query will include an outline of what you plan to write and your proposal will expand that outline in great detail as well as providing additional information.

If you're writing fiction, unless you're writing a very short story, outlining will help to keep your story on track as well as keep you from writing yourself into a corner from which there's no escape but to start over.

However, it's important to understand that in fiction there often comes a time, particularly in longer fiction, when your characters become real and push the story in a different direction than you had scripted for them in your outline. When that happens it almost seems like you're a court reporter taking notes about the movie playing in your mind. Appreciate this and respect it because you'll be experiencing the true magic of writing fiction. Let your characters go and see what happens. It's rare that they'll steer you wrong.

Making It Real
Putting Your Words to Work

- Cluster for five minutes on one of the three topics you're considering for your project.
- Freewrite for five minutes on another of the three topics.
- Cluster or freewrite on the third topic.
- Develop an outline for each.
- Keep these in a safe place; you'll use them again later.

Chapter 9

Drafting:
Step Two of the Three-Step
Writing Process

Once the planning phase is complete, it's time to write your first draft. The idea is to get something on paper with which you can work: a lump of clay from which you'll sculpt a work of art. No less a writer than Ernest Hemingway is quoted as saying, "The first draft of anything is shit." Let that be your guide. The important thing is to simply get the words on paper.

Writing the First Draft:

- Turn off your internal editor.
- Get it down on paper as quickly as possible.
- Use words as simple or as complicated as you need to convey your meaning and use contractions if that makes the writing easier. You can always take them out during the revision stage.
- Don't worry about grammar and spelling.
- Use however many words it takes, no matter how convoluted it may seem, to get your vision onto the page.
- Remember that it will never, ever look as good on the page as it did when you were conceiving it in your mind.
- Never stop drafting to look something up. If as you're writing, you forget a fact like a date, an address, or a name, simply leave an indicator, like a couple of asterisks or a set of empty

brackets, to remind you to look up the information later. Likewise don't interrupt the flow of thoughts by reaching for your thesaurus or dictionary. Leave an indicator and keep moving forward with your manuscript.

- Go from beginning to end without stopping to revise anything on a short piece.
- For a longer piece or a book, allow yourself one or two minor revisions when you come to the end of a chapter or a major section, but concentrate on moving forward to the end.
- Don't let yourself fall into the "analysis paralysis" that can grip writers in the early or middle stage of projects and prevent them from finishing.

Until you have a compete first draft, other than fixing obvious minor issues like spelling and grammar, it's hard to know what needs substantive revision. But, when you see it laid out, end to end, you can better see what's missing and what needs to be revised.

You Don't Have to Begin at the Beginning

We'll talk in more detail in later chapters about the "lead" in nonfiction and the "narrative hook" in fiction. For now, all you need to know is that it's important to catch your reader's interest at the beginning of the piece with something that will pull them into the writing. Most writers realize this by instinct if not by training. Where the problem comes in is that some writers spend so much time or get so frustrated trying to develop the perfect opening lines that they never get past the beginning and give up writing the piece.

It's okay to begin your draft wherever you feel the most comfortable, wherever you're ready to begin writing. The critical thing is to begin. Sometimes, whether you're writing a short or a long piece, writing the rest of the piece will help you decide what kind of opening you need. You can start writing the thirteenth chapter in your book, then the second, and then the eighth. In your short story you can begin writing at the ending, write the middle, and then the opening. It's up to you.

To those of us in the prime time generation, this can come as something of a shock but also can be very freeing. We're used to following the rules which means beginning at the beginning and ending at the end. Murray, one of my students in his late fifties, exclaimed, "You can do that? That's great," when we covered this topic in class.

Working on your rough draft is like working on your outline: No one is ever going to see it; it's a simply a tool to help you, so write your draft in whatever order works best for you.

Beyond the First Draft

All subsequent drafts, up to and including the final draft, the one you will send out into the world, will be completed in the next and third step of writing process, revising. Why aren't all drafts completed in the drafting stage? Because the term "draft" is somewhat misleading.

For our purposes, the first draft, sometimes referred to as the rough draft, is the initial version of what will ultimately become the final draft. It follows the outline we created in step one to give it its form.

Some writers take only two or three drafts to get to the final. Most writers take more. For example, I average ten to fifteen. But does that mean I begin with the first word and write my way to the last word fifteen times? No. It simply means I go through the document and fix things, and revise things, and move things, then print a fresh copy and go through it again, and again, and so on, until it's as good as I can make it. Each time becomes the latest draft until the final draft is done.

It's easy to be confused because different segments of the writing profession use different terms. In the moviemaking business you may hear the term final draft or final script. This refers to the final script turned in to the producers by the writer. But in the field, making the movie, the shooting script, which usually reflects changes to the writer's final script made by the editor, the producer, the director, or the star is the actual script used during the making of the movie.

Style

Style refers to the way in which something is done as opposed to the content or substance. In writing, style refers to how much of your personality you show along with the material.

In nonfiction, writing styles have a wide range from technical to casual. Academic writing tends to be stuffy; writing for the Internet casual. If you're writing for the general public, your writing should never be stuffy or overly formal.

A friendly but formal style is best when you're focused primarily on the material as in a nonfiction book in which you are writing to inform the general public.

An informal style reduces the distance between the writer and the reader and is good when you want to get attention, generate enthusiasm, or win cooperation. Most how-tos are written in an informal, friendly style, as is the book you're reading now.

If you're writing nonfiction books or individual essays, that voice can change as appropriate to the material. For example the style you use to write a biography (formal, serious) will be different from the style you use to write a how-to book about finding the best bed and breakfasts in your state (informal, friendly, and light). On the other hand, if you're writing a series of essays or recurring columns, your style should be stable and consistent, or you risk alienating regular readers who have come to know what to expect from your writing. Just think if opinion writer George Will or humorist Dave Barry ever changed their styles.

Tone

Tone refers to an emotional state. Tone can be serious or humorous, friendly or hostile, supportive or sarcastic. Your reason for writing will usually come through in the piece's tone.

An opinion piece in support of a ballot proposition may be positive and upbeat; one against it may be caustic and sarcastic. In self-help and how-to books the tone should be positive and supportive. A biography may be admiring or critical. In a fiction piece the tone of a story may communicate amusement, anger, affection, sorrow, contempt or any of a wide range of emotions. When reviewing your work, make sure you maintain a consistent tone throughout. Otherwise you risk confusing your reader.

Finding Your Voice

Don't worry about developing your writer's voice. You will find your unique voice by writing. Don't try to force it; it will come. Over time the way you use language, the words you choose to use, and the unique perspective you bring to your writing will evolve into your voice. Some successful writers have very distinctive voices, others don't.

Making It Real
Putting Your Words to Work

Pick one of the three projects on which you did your clustering and freewriting in the previous chapter. Write a five to ten page first draft (or in the case of a book-length work, a narrative summary) of your project.

Chapter 10

Revising:
Step Three of the Three-Step
Writing Process

Revising is the third, final, and most important step of the three-step writing process. In this step you'll shape the piece of writing into its final form, ready to share with your audience.

In the first two steps of planning and drafting, we had a particular vision in mind, like a sculptor sculpting a horse; we've gathered words like bits of clay and formed them into an assemblage: this piece indicating a head, those several thicker pieces forming the body, long thin pieces for the legs, and finally a tail. More often than not, we've gathered and assembled too much clay, and now must trim away the excess to get to the vision which lies beneath. We may find that the piece we chose for the back of the horse works better toward the front. Through the editing process, we'll perform the fine shaping, refining, and restructuring to transform our desired creation from a fluid, imprecisely structured blob to the horse we envision.

Step Back and then Revise

As a practical matter, before you begin the revision process you should first gain some distance from your writing. Put it away for a while. How long depends on the length of the writing and your deadline (if any) for completing it.

For short pieces, overnight is usually sufficient to give you enough distance to look at the work objectively. If you can wait a couple of days, that's even better. Sometimes though, a piece of irksome writing may need to spend a week or two on the shelf for you to forget the detail of the work sufficiently that you can look at it with fresh eyes. For longer pieces, usually a week to two weeks is sufficient. Book length works may take longer.

Edit in Three Stages

I find it's best to edit in three stages: first, for completeness and consistency; second, for readability; and finally for mechanics, grammar, and spelling.

And then we will stop.

We will stop because it's possible to overdo revision to the point that you ultimately hurt the piece. This is not unique to writing. Artists, in whatever medium, have the same problem: discerning how much is enough and knowing when to stop. With practice and experience that judgment becomes easier to render.

Stage 1—Edit for Completeness and Consistency

Here you're looking at the big picture, the overall manuscript. This is the broad brush review to assure that your meaning is being communicated to the reader. It is the equivalent of using a plane with broad strokes to begin smoothing a rough piece of wood.

The goal is to make sure your piece makes sense to its intended audience, that the writing flows in a way the reader can easily follow, and that the piece answers logical questions without leaving out information important to the reader's understanding.

If you used headings, assure that they are in a logical order and are sufficiently descriptive so that if you were to read only the title and the headings, it would give you a good idea of the subject. Determine if interviews, examples, and anecdotes targeted to facilitate the reader's understanding achieve their goal.

Overall, assure that the piece achieves the purpose for which it was written. Fix or eliminate anything that does not contribute to meeting that goal.

Stage 2—Edit for Readability

Now you're examining your manuscript to assure that how it's written facilitates the reader's comprehension and does not present an obstacle. It is the equivalent of using rough sandpaper to reduce and smooth any bumpy spots left on the piece of wood after it's been planed.

Ruthlessly purge your writing of redundancies, wordy phrases, and overuse of grandiose words. Assure that active rather than passive voice is predominant and that you use strong verbs and concrete nouns. Look for opportunities to improve understanding through use of formatting such as bulleted points, numbered lists, and elimination of overly-long paragraphs.

In nonfiction, consider your audience's knowledge of your topic. When writing for a general audience, purge jargon and spell out acronyms. When writing for an audience with specialized or advanced knowledge of your subject, satisfy yourself that your text is not too simplistic or beneath their level of understanding.

In fiction, assure that you eliminate unnecessary words, sentences, or paragraphs that do not contribute to moving the story forward, improving the reader's understanding of the characters, or providing information the reader must have to better understand or enjoy the story.

Stage 3—Edit for Mechanics, Grammar, and Spelling

This is where you assure the piece is punctuated properly, spelling is correct, and that generally accepted rules of grammar and usage are observed, such as subjects agreeing with verbs and pronouns agreeing with antecedents. If you're not sure what that means, please refer to Part III of this book. This stage is the equivalent of using finely grained sandpaper to finish the wood to a smooth surface, pleasing to the eye, and with no splinters remaining to distract or annoy the reader. We'll bring our piece as close as we can to polished perfection, trimming away any remaining imperfections, removing everything that does not further our vision, all the while understanding that we will never reach perfection, but always striving to get as close to it as we are capable.

Putting the Three-Stage Revision Process into Practice

As a practical matter, the three stages overlap to a great degree. As you're reviewing your manuscript in the first phase, obvious errors that affect readability, or obvious spelling, grammatical, and punctuation errors, will jump out at you that you'll fix as you make your first pass through the manuscript.

Revising is an iterative process. By that I mean you keep cycling through the document until you are satisfied that you've improved it as much as you can. In my experience, as I eliminate or revise the big flaws, such as moving or eliminating sentences or paragraphs, the finer, more granular flaws become evident that I didn't notice on the initial pass through of the document. That process occurs until all the flaws have been fixed or eliminated.

Read Your Text Out Loud

At any stage in the revising process, and definitely when you think you've finished your final draft and your manuscript is ready for publication, a good technique is to read the piece aloud with a highlighter in your hand. Wherever you stumble, or it doesn't sound right, mark it to fix later.

Your ear can often hear errors that your eyes gloss over. If it doesn't sound right, it warrants a further look.

Also, sometimes when you've read the same words over and over through multiple drafts you can become what writers refer to as "snow blind." You've seen the error so many times that your eye doesn't notice it, and your mind subconsciously corrects it as you read. But, if you read your piece aloud, you're more likely to catch these errors.

Make Sure Your Writing Answers the WIIFM (What's in it for me?) Question

As we discussed in Chapter 7, WIIFM is the question on every reader's mind before deciding whether or not to read a written piece. WIIFM also determines whether or not a piece gets picked up by agents or editors and ultimately for publication. Agents and editors look for material that will sell because it meets the needs of their readers.

Don't Rely on Spell-Check Alone

Spell Czech is a grate tool, butt bee wear of miss takes wan ewe right sump thing fore udder pee pole two reed.

The previous line graphically illustrates why you should never completely trust the spell-check function of your word processor. Try typing this line into your word processor and then run the spell-check function. I guarantee that this obviously incorrect sentence will pass muster every time, because each word is spelled correctly.

Spell-check is one of the greatest tools ever invented; however, spell-check does not read words in context. So, if you spell a word incorrectly for the context, for example "*two*" or "*to*" instead of "*too*" as in "*It was two hot to run,*" spell-check doesn't know the difference.

I recommend that you use spell-check to catch the obvious errors, but then carefully read the piece yourself to make sure nothing has slipped through. This is particularly important if you're using speech-recognition software. Until you have the software properly trained to recognize your voice you will see a lot of "sounds-like" words.

Check and Recheck Your Research

There is never an excuse for getting your facts wrong. The review stage is the time to recheck to assure your facts and details are accurate. This is true of fiction as well as nonfiction.

Don't have your detective tuck a Sig-Sauer, 38 Special revolver into his waistband, when no such gun exists; and don't have your heroine driving downtown on Tenth Avenue in New York City, when Tenth Avenue flows one-way uptown. Your readers will call you on it and you'll lose credibility.

Obtain Feedback

Over time, as you gain experience and confidence in your judgment as a writer, you'll rely less on external feedback and more on your internal compass to determine if your piece is on target. But when you initially start out, once you've satisfied yourself that the piece is as good you can make it, it's useful to get confirmation and feedback from someone else.

Family and Friends

Is there someone in your family or circle of friends who will give you an honest opinion on your work? Be cautious because friends and family can be either too praising or too damning. It's a difficult call because while most people are willing to tell you when your work is good (sometimes even when it's not) it's difficult to find people who will tell you when your work needs help. You'll have to make your own judgment on whether friends and family are a good place for you to look for feedback.

My wife is my first reader because while she may not know exactly how to fix a problem, she's great at spotting problem areas where things aren't working. She knows that the only way that she can hurt my feelings is by not giving me her honest opinion.

Writers' Workshops

When you're starting out a writers' workshop is an excellent way to get feedback, assuming that the workshop has a group of sensible writers who will give you the feedback you need. Writers' workshops can be a great source of reaction to your work because the members of the group are trying to do the same things you are. They know what's involved in trying to write a good piece, and because of their varied experiences in writing, can often offer useful suggestions on how to fix whatever isn't working.

While you must always be the final judge of your own writing, if two or more of the group find the same problem, you should look at that section again. However, recognize that you're never going to please everyone. After a while you learn who the better reviewers are for your work and you can dismiss the comments of the rest.

There are two things to beware of with writing workshops: dysfunctional groups and dependency. Dysfunctional groups are not well led and devolve into needlessly tearing into one another's work or the opposite: becoming mutual admiration societies. Avoid these types of groups because both are destructive to your progression as a writer. Unfortunately, you usually won't know if a group is any good or not until you join. If you find your group is dysfunctional, find a new one right away.

The second danger is becoming dependent on the group. The object of belonging to a writer's workshop is to get feedback for a limited time, until you can progress on your own. Over time, it's quite possible to learn what pleases this particular group and as a result, subconsciously or consciously, you learn to write things that will please the group. Pleasing the group becomes your source of reward. Don't let that happen to you.

Peer Writers

Often in workshops you'll find one or two of your fellow workshoppers who seem to "get" what it is you're trying to do, and consistently provide useful editing and feedback advice. There's nothing wrong with asking one of them to read your piece and provide comments outside of the workshop. Of course, you must be willing to reciprocate.

You Are the Final Judge of the Quality of Your Work

The review stage is your opportunity to put your stamp on your writing; to make it as good as you are capable of. Believe in yourself, follow the techniques in this book, and enjoy what you're doing. I guarantee if you keep practicing, keep learning, and persevere, you'll become the writer you want to be. Remember, in the final analysis, you are the one who makes the decision on what if anything needs revision.

Part III

Grammar and Usage Refresher

Chapter 11

Spotting and Fixing Problems

The goal of this chapter is to give you the tools to quickly and easily spot and fix the most common writing problems you're likely to encounter as a new writer. In essence, the idea of this chapter is not to cover everything there is to know about grammar, but rather to give you most of what you need to know to be a successful writer.

This is a book about writing—not English. That's an important distinction because we're concentrating on communicating with readers rather than spending time describing, memorizing, and enforcing grammatical rules.

Fear that our grammar skills have gone rusty can be a real discouragement to those of us who start writing later in life. Most of us were taught in English class that there was only one correct way to do things and God-forbid-if-you-screw-up because you'll be confirming to the world, now and for all time (or for however long the piece of writing lasts), that you're nothing but an ignorant lout who uses substandard English.

But there's good news: Good grammar is neither as difficult nor as strict as you may remember from your school days. With a little effort, a good reference book, and applying the techniques we're about to cover, you need have no fear about your grammar and usage.

Substance Over Form

Things have changed for the better since we were in school. Grammarians recognize that the language is evolving and should continue to evolve and that grammar should be descriptive (reflecting how people actually speak and write) as well as prescriptive (prescribing rules for proper usage).

This does not mean anything goes, however. There are still rules, but there's a great deal more flexibility. And, while some readers will continue to be sticklers and will think less of you if you don't follow what tradition dictates, most recognize that grammar is a matter of choice and that even the grammar experts don't always agree on proper usage.

Grammatical Terms

Here are the only grammatical terms you need to know:

- *Noun*—A word or words that name a person (Cynthia), a place (Washington, D.C.), a thing (pencil), a concept or idea (technology), an action (writing), or a quality (innocence).
- *Pronoun*—A word that takes the place of a noun, such as *he*, *she*, *it*, *we*, *us*.
- *Verb*—A word or words that express an action, such as *walk*, or a state of being, such as *is*.
- *Subject*—The subject does the action described by the verb. "John (subject) threw the ball."
- *Object*—The object receives the verb's action and sometimes answers the questions what? or whom? after the verb: "John threw (what?) the ball."
- *Modifier*—A word or group of words, such as adjectives, adverbs, and prepositional phrases that restrict, qualify, or expand the meaning of another word: "The hot (adjective) water (adjective) heater empties quickly (adverb)."
- An *adjective* modifies nouns and pronouns: "We had a *quick* dinner." Here *quick* is an adjective modifying the noun *dinner*. It tells what kind of a dinner.
- *Adverbs* modify verbs, adjectives, or other adverbs and answer such questions as how, when, where, and in what way. They typically end in *ly*: "We ate *quickly*." Here *quickly* is an adverb modifying the verb *ate*. It describes the way we ate.

- A *prepositional phrase* is a group of words beginning with a preposition (usually short words such as *to, of, about, on*) and containing a noun or pronoun that shows the position or relationship of one thing to another and usually does the work of an adverb or adjective: "John went *to the store.*" In this case the prepositional phrase *to the store* functions as an adverb modifying the verb *went* by telling us where John went.

The New Rules of Grammar

I've always found it amazing and contradictory that some of my favorite people, English teachers, the same people who admonished us against using jargon in our writing, should have, in apparent conspiracy with the grammarians, developed their own jargon and then required the rest of us to embrace it. Form triumphed over substance. More emphasis was placed on how we said things than on what we had to say. For too many of us, red pencil marks decorating our English homework, and regular quizzes on the definitions of arcane technicalities of grammar transformed writing from an opportunity for self-expression to something to be avoided and even feared.

Fear not: We will not be covering dangling participles, split infinitives, gerunds, or other esoteric grammatical points that you may have been forced to memorize in Miss Strictgrammar's English class.

In fact, I encourage you to ignore some of the things you were taught by Miss Strictgrammar because they don't make sense in today's writing. The following are some examples:

- If you want to end your sentences with a preposition, go ahead. What are you afraid of? (Doesn't this sound better than, "Of what are you afraid?")
- And if you want to start a sentence with *and*, go right ahead.
- Don't be afraid to use contractions (like *don't*) in your informal writing. In formal writing, you'll probably feel more comfortable writing first drafts using contractions. You can always take the contractions out in the final draft.

This is not to say that correct grammar is unimportant. As we discussed in Chapter 5, you should have access to adequate reference materials so that when you have a question about grammar you can quickly look up the answer.

The Flip-Side of Poor Grammar: Perfectionism

Perfectionism, trying to write perfectly, immobilizes many new writers and is one of the primary reasons why many people write poorly. This results from the belief that we are required to affect a more formal and fancy style when we write than when we speak. We feel that when we commit ourselves to writing it has to be perfect, that it must stand for posterity. This might sound like a noble goal, particularly if you're trying to create great literature, but it's just plain foolish.

Accept the fact that you will never achieve perfection in writing. Professional writers will tell you that the words will seldom read as well on the page as they sounded in your head. So please, decide now that you're going to do the best you can, to write as well as you can, to the best of your ability, right here, right now, today, and then you're going to let it go.

Becoming a Fearless Writer

Immobilizing fears about rusty grammar or an unhealthy drive for perfectionism can be quickly overcome when you focus on the following:

If You Can Talk, You Can Write

Problems arise when people try to write much differently than they speak. This is caused by a combination of the following:

- What we were taught in high school
- Emphasis on following rules instead of communicating with a reader
- Textbooks that relied on the detached, academic style of writing
- What we were taught on the job, often using go-bys from years gone by

One qualifier: I'm not talking about the regionalisms and colloquialisms that we employ in joking around with our friends, although those have a place, particularly in fiction. Right now, I'm talking about how we speak in more formal conversation, like when we talk with our clergy, our doctor, or when we conduct business.

We'll talk more about regionalisms and colloquialisms in the next chapter, and we'll consider the problems they can cause with subject-verb agreement and with the way we use pronouns.

It's Easier to Write Well than to Write Poorly

- Poor writing involves poor organization, overuse of passive voice, wordiness, use of grandiose language, jargon, and smothered verbs. (Don't worry, I'm going to show you how to recognize and eliminate all of these in this chapter and the next.)
- Good writing gets the message across more effectively with fewer words.

For example, it's much harder to write:

When interviewed with regard to his findings, the senior auditor indicated that based on a careful consideration of the audit findings, it was recommended that the ABC Company endeavor to enhance its ability to facilitate location of its personnel files by recruiting and hiring individuals possessing the requisite background and experience to affect a positive change for the better within its filing operations and facility.

than it is to write:

The senior auditor, based on his findings, recommended that the ABC Company hire qualified people to work in the file room.

We can laugh at that first sentence, but I'm sure we all recognize it. The first sentence is written in passive voice, and uses wordy construction, redundancies, and grandiose words. The second sentence uses fewer words, delivered in the more dynamic active voice to make the same point.

The Plainer and Simpler You Write, the Better Your Writing Will Be

Plain and simple does not mean that you write down to your reader or that you cannot write in your own unique style. Plain and simple means you make yourself understood by using ordinary language as though you were conversing directly with your reader in your living room or office.

Your Reader only Reads What You Actually Wrote, not What You might Have Written

Sometimes the exact word or phrase you want is just a hair's width from your grasp, tantalizingly close, yet unobtainable. A thesaurus may help. If exactly what you want remains elusive, simply reword the phrase, sentence, or paragraph so it still gets the point across, even if it's not written as elegantly or powerfully as you know it could have been.

This is particularly important when you're working on a deadline. Write it as well as you can, right now. Your audience will never miss how great it could have been.

Likewise, don't let grammar or usage conundrums stand in your way. If you're away from your reference guide and encounter a problem, write whatever it is out as best you can, then underline the problem area as a reminder to check it later. If you'd rather not bother looking something up, simply write around the problem by rewriting the sentence. No one but you will ever know the difference.

When you're writing your first draft, do the same for facts you can't remember. Simply write what you can and leave an underlined notation to yourself, like "insert cost of a pound of butter here." The important thing is to keep going.

The Ten Commandments of Grammar

While a few grammar purists resist the evolution of our language and insist on labeling any diversions from traditional English grammar as serious errors, most grammarians recognize that such deviations are inevitable.

There is consensus that some rules, such as never using a double negative (*don't* use *no* bad grammar) must be observed. To do otherwise brands you as one who uses substandard English. Other rules such as using *can I* instead of *may I* to ask permission, or splitting an infinitive (*to boldly go* instead of *to go boldly*), have evolved to the point where the writer can choose to use either presentation. Naturally, when writing fictional dialog or even when quoting something someone has actually said when writing nonfiction, grammar rules go out the window.

Most people speak and write good grammatical English, so trust your instincts and don't drive yourself crazy analyzing every word you write. Just be aware of and avoid the more common, serious grammar errors which I've listed below. I call these the "Ten Commandments of Grammar." Break any of these in your writing and there is no forgiveness.

1. Don't mix-up homophones (words that differ in spelling and meaning but sound alike).

Not: Their going to the store.
But: They're going to the store.
Not: Do you want to go their?
But: Do you want to go there?

2. Don't use a double negative.

Not: I haven't got no money.
But: I don't have any money.

3. Don't use redundant subjects.

Not: Those bees, they can sting you in a hurry.
But: Those bees can sting you in a hurry.

4. Use the correct verb form in the correct tense.

Not: I swum from one end of the pool to the other.
But: I swam from one end of the pool to the other.
Not: We had swam from one end of the pool to the other.
But: We swam from one end of the pool to the other.

5. Don't use a double comparison.

Not: That horse is more faster than mine.
But: That horse is faster than mine.

6. Don't confuse contractions with possessives.

Not: Whose up next?
But: Who's up next?
Not: Who's glove is this?
But: Whose glove is this?
Not: Did the cat lose it's collar.
But: Did the cat lose its collar.

7. Distinguish between adjectives and adverbs.

Not: The children played the game good.
But: The children played the game well.
Not: He did it easy.
But: He did it easily, or He easily did it.

8. Do use the correct form of pronouns. Use subject pronouns for subjects and object pronouns for objects.

Not: She likes he.
But: She likes him.
Not: Between you and I, . . .
But: Between you and me, . . .

9. Do be sure the verb and subject agree.

Not: One of the boxes are open.
But: One of the boxes is open.

10. Don't use "of" for "have".

Not: We could of gone to the game, if you only would of bought the tickets.
But: We could have gone to the game, if you only would have bought the tickets.

Non-Grammatical Problems

As you now know, when writing your first draft the critical thing is to keep going. It doesn't have to be pretty; it just has to be there. Now, in the review stage you're going to locate and fix all of the problems. The following are common problems that you'll most likely encounter in your draft, but relax: they're easy to fix.

Don't Be Redundant

Somehow, a large number of redundant phrases like those listed in the box below have crept into our vocabulary so insidiously that we don't notice them any more. See "Redundant Phrases" in the "Resources" section at the back of this book for a more complete list.

Redundancy	Short Form
few in number	few
he is a man who	he
absolute necessity	necessity

Go through your writing and ruthlessly search out and eliminate redundant words, phrases, and sentences. After you think you're finished, repeat this process until you're satisfied you've eliminated as much redundancy as possible. For example:

To avoid redundancy, don't repeat the same thing over and over again.

Surely we can get our point across with fewer words and less repetition.

To avoid redundancy, don't repeat the same thing ~~over and~~ over again.

There. We've eliminated two words. Let's see what other words we can eliminate. In the context of our sentence, *over* and *again* mean the same thing. Time for more trimming.

To avoid redundancy, don't repeat the same thing ~~over~~ again.

Another word bites the dust. But let's not rest yet; there's more to be done. The word *repeat* means to say something again. So let's take out a bit more.

To avoid redundancy, don't repeat the same thing ~~again~~.

Much better, but can you spot the debris still to be eliminated? That's right. You've got it. What else are you going to repeat—something different? If so, you wouldn't be repeating. Let's make the final trim:

To avoid redundancy, don't repeat ~~the same thing~~.

Now we have it:

To avoid redundancy, don't repeat.

Don't Smother Verbs

You smother verbs when you change the verb into a noun with modifiers.

Smothered: The council will take your idea under consideration.
Better: The council will consider your idea.

Smothered: The director has come to the decision staff must be cut.
Better: The director has decided to cut staff.

To avoid smothering verbs, avoid the words: *make, give, take, come* and the endings: *-ive, -sion, -ment, -ization.*
For example, when we add:

• *-ive, support* becomes *supportive*
• *-sion, convert* becomes *conversion*
• *-ment, improve* becomes *improvement*
• *-ization, customize* becomes *customization*

Not: I want to be supportive of my employees.
But: I want to support my employees.
Not: When you get to France, obtain a conversion of your currency.
But: When you get to France, convert your currency.

Not: Please make an improvement in your performance.
But: Please improve your performance.

79

Not: We completed the customization of your automobile.
But: We customized your car.

Eliminate Wordy Phrases

Like redundant phrases, wordy phrases have crept into our language and should be sought out and removed from your writing. As a general rule, whenever you can get rid of a word without changing the meaning or the emotional content of what you are writing, you should do so. See "Wordy Phrases" in "Resources" at the back of this book for a more complete list.

Wordy Phrase	Preferred Short Form
a great deal of	much
a large number of	many; several
a limited number of	one, two, a few, etc.
a majority of	most
a number of	several

Avoid Grandiose Words

Writers who overuse complex language to impress others usually achieve the opposite effect: They come off sounding pretentious and foolish rather than impressive. Instead of trying to impress readers with an inflated vocabulary, impress them with the clarity of your communications. For instance:

A mass of concentrated earthly material perennially rotating on its axis will not accumulate an accretion of bryophytic vegetation.

This is just an overly pretentious way of saying:

A rolling stone gathers no moss.
Here's another, found on the Internet:

It has come to our attention that herbage, when observed in that section of enclosed ground being the property of an individual other than oneself, is ever of a more verdant hue.

Translation:

The grass is always greener on the other side of the fence.

Being able to use a broad vocabulary makes writing more interesting and informative, but excessive or exclusive use of long, complex, polysyllabic words sounds pretentious. This pretentious style of writing is referred to as gobbledygook or governmentese.

Below are a few potentially pretentious expressions and their alternatives.

Pretentious	Alternative
aggregation	total
onus	burden
contiguous	next to
pestiferous	troublesome

I call these "potentially" pretentious because any of them are fine when used occasionally. It's when used unnecessarily that these words make our writing appear overweening. (See? *Overweening* means *presumptuous, arrogant, immoderate, exaggerated*, any one of which would be more appropriate.)

Don't Misplace Modifiers

A modifying word or phrase misplaced in a sentence results in lack of clarity, sometimes with humorous results:

Burned to a crisp, the waiter took the toast back to the cook. (The waiter was not burned to a crisp; the toast was.)

The zoo visitor laughed at the monkey wearing sunglasses. (The monkey wasn't wearing sunglasses, the zoo visitor was.)
Tired and grouchy, the bus full of tourists finally reached the hotel. (The bus wasn't tired and grouchy, the tourists were.)

To fix misplaced modifiers, rearrange the sentence and add or omit words as necessary to place the modifying phrase next to the word or words it is modifying:

The waiter took the toast, which was burned to a crisp, back to the cook.

The sunglass-wearing zoo visitor laughed at the monkey.

The bus full of tired and grouchy tourists finally reached the hotel.

Don't Be Tricked by Tricky Word Pairs

To feel confident in using tricky word pairs such as *affect* and *effect*, *less* and *fewer*, *farther* and *further*, you must either memorize the correct usage or at least be aware each has a tricky-twin and look it up.

Making It Real
Putting Your Words to Work

• Grab a pencil or a highlighter and go through the list of redundant phrases at the back of this book. Highlight or circle the ones you recognize as those you use. If you borrowed this book from a library, make a copy of these pages and mark on the copies. It's important to do the exercise on paper, not just in your head. The idea is to become conscious of redundancies you use subconsciously so you can rid your writing of them.

• As you did with the redundant phrases, go through the "Wordy Phrases" list. Again, highlight or circle those you recognize as ones you typically use.

Chapter 12

Building a Foundation
of Good Writing

In this chapter we'll talk about how to keep your reader with you, every step of the way, using proper punctuation and transition words, eliminating confusion, in your writing, and banishing boring, turgid prose.

Although we are decades removed from our last class in English grammar, we prime time writers have a distinct advantage over much younger writers: We are probably the last group that actually diagrammed sentences in school. Diagramming sentences taught us how words work together structurally, giving us a strong sense of what makes writing good, even when we can no longer remember how to identify a split infinitive or a gerund. So, with a little brush up on the fundamentals, you'll be ready to build on that firm foundation.

Punctuation: The Traffic Signs

Just as we use traffic signs (such as stop, yield, slow, and my personal favorite, soft shoulders) and directional signs (Rt. 66 Next Right, Rest Area 1,000 Feet), we use punctuation as signs to help readers stay with us from the beginning of our piece to the end.

The Importance of Proper Punctuation

For our purposes, I'm only going to cover a couple of points concerning punctuation, those where I've seen inexperienced writers have some difficulty. When you have a question about punctuation, you can always look it up. Many good dictionaries include style guides which will answer most of your questions about punctuation. Looking it up is the best way to learn it.

Punctuation Makes a Difference

An English professor asked his students to punctuate the following sentence correctly: "A woman without her man is nothing."

All of the males in the class wrote: "A woman, without her man, is nothing."

All of the females in the class wrote: "A woman: without her, man is nothing."

Punctuation makes a difference.

I once had a student named Ernie in one of my creative writing classes who was an absolutely delightful man in his seventies. Ernie, a member of the greatest generation, had enlisted in the Navy at the age of seventeen, just before the end of World War II, and he wound up making a career of it. He told me that for many years he had rolling around in his mind, what he called "My great Russian novel." What he meant by that was that his novel was vast in scope, with a great many characters covering much of the world, including many of the places he had visited while he was in the Navy. Now, he felt, was the time to get started on it. He was an interesting fellow and quite a character, who added a great deal to the class with his engrossing questions and witty comments. I couldn't wait to read his first chapter.

When I saw it, I was dismayed. Other than some paragraph breaks, it contained absolutely no punctuation.

My initial impression was that his writing was gibberish but I decided to try to insert punctuation, as best I could. I thought I'd simply do the first page to give him an idea of what needed to be done.

But as I got into it, I was fascinated by the story that unfolded. I "translated" four or five pages, enough to know that this had great potential as a novel. It was full of compelling characters, the dialog was spot-on, the story laid out several intriguing plot and subplot lines, and the narrative voice was interesting and engaging. All this within the first five pages.

I told Ernie that he had wonderful potential as a novelist because he understood the hard part: having something to say and saying it well, having a good ear for dialog, and a good feel for setting and characterization. But now he had to learn the easy part, the mechanics of punctuation, because his great Russian novel would never see the light of day unless he learned to use punctuation. Readers are willing to work moderately hard for a good story, but they're not willing to work that hard.

The Period and the Comma

The period's primary use is at the end of a sentence. It is also used after initials and at the end of most abbreviations.

The comma tells us when to take a brief pause, as compared to the longer pause of the period. Use a comma between items in a list (such as lemons, apples, and pears) and to create a break between the component parts of sentences.

Some new writers have a tendency to put commas where they don't belong, such as between two independent clauses. Independent clauses are parts of a sentence which, if separated, could stand on their own as a sentence. Using a comma to separate independent clauses is generally referred to as a *comma fault* or a *comma splice*. Here's an example:

> "I'm going to hit every bar in this rat-hole of a town, I'm going to drink myself someplace else."

To fix a comma splice between two independent clauses you can insert a period at the end of each clause to make two separate sentences, or you can include a conjunction to join them:

> "I'm going to hit every bar in this rat-hole of a town. I'm going to drink myself someplace else."
> "I'm going to hit every bar in this rat-hole of a town, and I'm going to drink myself someplace else."

This sentence could also be rewritten to eliminate the comma splice and the redundancy:

> "I'm going to hit every bar in this rat-hole of a town until I drink myself someplace else."

For additional information on resolving a comma fault when the two independent clauses are closely related, please see the section on semicolons below.

When attempting to set off a clause with commas, a common error involves inserting the first comma but forgetting to insert the second.

Another problem with commas can occur when writers omit the final comma, called the serial comma, separating items in a list. Some writers hold that the serial comma is not needed, as in the following:

I went to the store to buy bread, eggs, bananas and cheese.

That's true in many circumstances. Eliminating the serial comma in the example above causes no problem in understanding. The reader is clear about where the writer went and what he planned to buy.

But let's look at a different series of items in a list:

I owe this prestigious writing award to all of the members of my fan club, my mother and my sister.

Eliminating the serial comma in this sentence appears to change the meaning, and, while the reader will probably recognize that the writer's mother and sister are not all the members of his fan club, there is that momentary pulling of the reader out of the piece to sort it all out. Had the serial comma been used it would have been clear that the writer was thanking his fan club, his mother, and his sister:

I owe this prestigious writing award to all of the members of my fan club, my mother, and my sister.

Avoid the confusion by always including the serial comma.

The Semicolon

The semicolon is a relatively sophisticated punctuation mark that most inexperienced writers don't know how to use properly. Unlike a period, a question mark, or a comma, which are required punctuation marks depending on the sentence, the semicolon is never required, so you may never have to actually use one.

The key to making the semicolon work is to remember to use it in situations like the following:

1. To separate two parts of a sentence that are closely related and could otherwise stand alone (independent clauses) as individual sentences or be joined by a conjunction:

It's raining; we can't play outside.
It's raining. We can't play outside.
It's raining and we can't play outside.

2. To separate a list of items that already includes commas:

On my vacation, I plan to visit Phoenix, Arizona; Seattle, Washington; and, Honolulu, Hawaii.

3. To separate long clauses in complicated sentences:

Many new writers dream of becoming full-time freelancers; before making that jump they would do well to make sure they have a reliable customer to provide a regular source of income; and to ensure a cushion of money in the bank to get them through the spare periods, because there are no guarantees.

Exclamation Point

Exclamation points are often overused by inexperienced writers who tend to rely on them, rather than language, to introduce excitement. If your writing does not convey a sense of wonder, drama, or excitement, no type of punctuation will help. Avoid using exclamation points.

Transitions: The Directional Signs

Transitions are words and phrases that work like highway signs to keep the reader from getting lost or mixed up as they move through a story. Transitions can be used to move within or between sentences and paragraphs.

Transitions in Sentences

Let's say we are writing an article about the few businesses in our locality that realized their participation goals for the United Way Campaign. The following sentence provides the facts but has no transition:

> Most businesses didn't make their United Way Campaign participation goals; Writers of Main Street, Inc. had ninety-three percent participation.

The sentence consists of two complete thoughts with an implied relationship between the two, but fails to make clear the relationship. Unless the reader has independent knowledge, it's impossible for the reader to know if Writers of Main Street, Inc. made its goal or falls under the umbrella of "most businesses" that didn't reach their goal.

Using the wrong transition word, as in the following sentence, can result in more confusion.

> Most businesses didn't make their United Way Campaign participation goals and Writers of Main Street, Inc. had ninety-three percent participation.

In this case the conjunction *and* works to join two correct facts together, but in a way that is confusing and misleading. It sets up the false assumption that the second part of the sentence reinforces the first part of the sentence.

We need a transition word that takes us in the right direction.

> Most businesses didn't make their United Way Campaign participation goals; however, with ninety-three percent participation, Writers of Main Street, Inc. did.

The transition word *however* indicates a change in direction, a contrast to the concept that comes first in the sentence. It tells the reader something different is coming. Other transition words we might have used include *yet, conversely, on the other hand,* and *in contrast.* Any of these would have pointed the reader in the right direction.

Transition within Paragraphs

Transitions are equally important for guiding the reader within a paragraph. Let's say we're writing a how-to article on obtaining a job with the City of Washington, D.C. The following illustrates how this works:

> There are several ways people go about entering information on the D. C. Standard Form 2000. For example, many people begin at the beginning and answer each question completely before proceeding to the next. Conversely, a lot of people skim through the form, filling in only what they know with certainty, preferring to come back later to questions they're unsure of.

In the above example, the transition words *for example* and *conversely* make the writing smoother, guiding the reader between sentences. If you reread the paragraph, leaving out the transition words, the text becomes awkward and disconnected.

Another way to transition is to use similar words to establish the connection. In the example below, *some* and *others* do this work.

> There are several ways people go about entering information on the D.C. Standard Form 2000. Some begin at the beginning and answer each question completely before proceeding to the next. Others prefer to skim through the form, filling in only what they know with certainty, preferring to come back later to questions they're unsure of.

Transitions between Paragraphs

Smooth transitions between paragraphs enable the reader to immediately identify how the current paragraph relates to the one preceding it. There are several ways to do this. For example, you can:

- Use the main idea from the preceding paragraph in the opening sentence of the current paragraph.
- Repeat a key word from the preceding paragraph in the current paragraph.
- Ask a question related to the preceding paragraph.
- Use a phrase to connect the main ideas.

- Indicate to the reader you are transitioning by using an obvious connector like *on the other hand* or *despite that*.
- Divide the paragraphs with numbers, bullets, or other devices.
- Say things like, *"The first type of investigation is...,"* and then, *"the next is...,"* and so on.

Seven Types of Transitional Words and Phrases

The following are seven types of transitions, each with examples of various words and phrases that help accomplish the particular type of transition:

1. *Physical proximity*: above, across, adjacent, alongside, around, behind, below, beneath, beside, between, beyond, by, farther, in front of, in the middle, inside, here, nearby, next to, on the far side, opposite, outside, throughout, under, upon, within

2. *Hierarchy*: above all, best of all, equally important, especially, finally, first, first of all, in a similar vein, in fact, in the first place, in particular, indeed, initially, least important, more important, most important, just as important

3. *Comparison and contrast*: also, although, as long as, at the same time, but, contrary to, conversely, despite, equally, even though, however, just as, in contrast, in a similar vein, in like manner, in spite of, in the same way, likewise, neither, nevertheless, notwithstanding, on the contrary, on the other hand, otherwise, similarly, still, unlike, yet

4. *Cause and effect*: accordingly, and so, as, as a consequence, as a result, because, causes, consequently, for, for this reason, hence, produces, results, then, therefore, hence, in short, otherwise, since

5. *Chronological order*: after a short time, afterward, as soon as, at the end, at last, at length, at the moment, at the same time, at that time, at this point, before, during, earlier, eventually, finally, first, following, formerly, immediately, in the beginning, in the meantime, later, lately, meanwhile, next, now, presently, prior, second, soon, shortly, since, sooner or later, temporarily, then, thereafter, thereupon, until, when, while

6. *To add on or to summarize*: again, also, and, and then, as a result, besides, consequently, equally important, finally, first, further,

furthermore, in addition, in brief, in conclusion, in short, in the same fashion, last, lastly, likewise, moreover, on the whole, second, third, to conclude, to sum up, to summarize, too, yet another

7. *To elaborate*: as an illustration, for example, for instance, in other words, in any case, in fact, in particular, namely, one such, specifically, to illustrate

Transitions Tie a Work Together

Let's say you're writing a freelance piece on behalf of your client, an audit firm. The client has requested a white-paper for use as a sales tool, a piece that outlines the benefits to potential clients of auditors and identifies high-risk areas of corporate financial operations, and then suggests several types of proactive reviews be implemented to determine if the risks are being exploited.

You might spend several paragraphs on the types of reviews the auditors have conducted in the past and how they met their clients' needs by identifying problems of which they would otherwise be unaware. But you also want to talk about how important the deterrence value is to the client, because when auditors are proactive, employees are more afraid of getting caught, so less internal crime occurs. To tie these together you might finish the section describing the past reviews with the following sentence:

As you can see, our auditors have a good track record in identifying and resolving emerging problems before they become major problems.

Then begin the next paragraph:

Equally valuable to corporations is the deterrence effect of the audit reviews, which helps prevent problems from happening in the first place.

You could then go on for several paragraphs explaining the details and virtues of deterrence before coming to the next major transition, the summary and conclusion, which might begin as follows:

In summary, a thorough audit review will both detect emerging problems and prevent others from getting a start. Our clients benefit from...

Parallel Construction

Parallel construction refers to presenting a series of words or phrases using the same wording format. Parallelism makes your writing more rhythmic and fluid. Just as a sour note on a musical instrument grates on the ear, or a cockeyed picture frame in a row of pictures will seem discordant to the eye, a lack of parallelism disrupts the flow of what we're reading.

Use Parallel Word Construction in a Series

When dealing with words in a series, decide what form of the word you want to use and stick with it.

> Not: I like swimming, fishing, and to hunt.
> But: I like swimming, fishing, and hunting.
> Or: I like to swim, fish, and hunt.

Regional Dialect and Colloquialisms

I don't know if this happens to you, but whenever I spend time in a different part of the country, I tend to pick up the pronunciation and colloquialisms that are common to that area.

Regional dialect and colloquialisms serve the same purpose as jargon does in the workplace. They are a means of communicating among people who share a commonality of experience. But when we bring regional dialect and colloquialisms into written materials intended for a general audience, they can lead to confusion. Let me give you an example.

At one point in my career as a federal agent, my job was to review reports of investigation coming in from our field components in the southwestern United States. I was reading a report and came across a sentence I couldn't make sense of. It said: The subject and his partner just couldn't gee and haw.

I thought it must have been some sort of a typographical error, you know, the kind where your fingers are on the wrong keys. I telephoned the investigator to ask him what he had meant to say. He told me, in a bit of a huff, that the way he wrote it was the way he had meant to say it. So I asked him what did "gee" and "haw" mean? He explained to me that "gee" and "haw" are the commands given to a team of mules or horses so they turn in the same direction. "Gee" means turn right; haw means turn left. If a mule team can't "gee" and "haw," it means they don't work well together. So what he meant was that the subject and his partner couldn't work well together.

The investigator and I both learned something that day: He learned a bit about communication, and I learned a bit about team-driving.

One area in which using regional dialects and colloquialisms works well is when you're writing dialog. In both fiction and nonfiction dialog, accurately capturing dialects and colloquialisms adds to the authenticity of what you are writing.

Subject and Verb Agreement

Intervening Words

Intervening words between the subject and the verb can lead to confusion. For example, which of the following two sentences is correct:

> The box of cookies are on the table.
> The box of cookies is on the table.

If you chose the second, you're correct.

The subject of the sentence is *box*. *Box* is singular so it takes a singular verb. Don't be confused by the prepositional phrase *of cookies,* which comes between the subject and the verb.

Compound Subjects

Another source of confusion is compound subjects. Which is the correct verb below?:

> Claudia and Tom (is or are) going on a trip.
> Claudia or Tom (is or are) going on a trip.

In the first sentence, the correct answer is *are*. Claudia and Tom are both going on the trip, so the subject is plural and takes a plural verb.

In the second sentence, the correct answer is *is*. Either Claudia or Tom, one or the other, is going on the trip, so the subject is singular and takes a singular verb.

Sometimes a compound subject will have both a singular and a plural noun or pronoun joined by *or* or *nor*. In that case, the word that is closest to the verb determines whether the verb is singular or plural.

> The panda or the monkeys are my favorite attraction at the zoo.
> The monkeys or the panda is my favorite attraction at the zoo.

In the first sentence, the word *monkeys* is closest to the verb, so the verb is plural. In the second sentence, the word *panda* is closest to the verb, so the verb is singular.

Collective Nouns

Collective nouns, such as team, group, or committee, are considered a single unit and so take a singular verb, unless you are writing about the individual members within the group.

> The committee sets the rules.
> The committee have not reached an agreement.

In the first sentence above, we are writing about the committee as a unit, so the verb is singular: *sets* instead of *set*.

In the second sentence, we are writing about the individual members of the committee being unable to reach an agreement, so the subject is plural and takes a plural verb: *have* instead of *has*. One could always solve any confusion by adding the word *members* to this sentence:

> The committee members have not reached an agreement.

The key to subject-verb agreement is to find the subject and determine whether it's singular or plural. Remember to ignore any phrases that come between the subject and its verb.

Use Active Voice Not Passive Voice

Too often when we write, instead of using the dynamic active voice we slip into the cumbersome, vague passive voice. Learning the difference between active and passive voice, and employing active voice for the vast majority of your writing, will do more to improve your writing than almost anything else you can do.

Active Voice Moves Your Writing Forward

The active voice puts things in their natural order, the subject of the sentence does the action of the verb and transfers that action to the object of the sentence:

John [subject] *hit* [verb] the *ball* [object].

Passive voice puts things in reverse order, the object receives the action of the verb taken by the subject:

The *ball* [object] *was hit* [verb] by *John [subject]*.

Passive voice robs our writing of its life, energy, and authority. It saps the drama, the passion, and the immediacy. Take a look at what it does to the following fairly well-known phrases:

Active: Houston, we have a problem.
Passive: Houston, a problem is had by us.
Active: Don't give up the ship.
Passive: The ship should not be given up.

See how the active voice statement is authoritative, direct, dynamic, and dramatic? In contrast, the passive voice is wordy, awkward, and vague.

Active Voice Makes Your Writing Clear, Concise, and Interesting

Active voice in a manuscript improves readability, while passive voice makes your writing tedious and boring. Researchers have determined that passive voice takes longer to read because we have to mentally translate it. Passive voice is one of the hallmarks of bureaucratic writing. It's an indirect way of writing that creates an impersonal style.

Yet another problem with the passive voice is that it's possible to write a perfectly grammatical sentence in passive voice without including the subject. The writer may know who's taking the action, but the reader is left in the dark. "*The ball was hit*" is a perfectly grammatical sentence but leaves us in the dark as to by whom the action was taken.

Why Passive Voice Creeps into Our Writing

Why do we use the passive voice so much? Because back in Miss Strictgrammar's English class, we were taught to avoid using *I* or its plural, *we,* in our writing. Those of us who had to write term papers surely remember the admonition to site authoritative sources and to never include our own opinion. After all, we were students and not expected to know anything.

So, because we were taught to divorce ourselves from the proceedings, many of us write much differently than we speak. Unfortunately, some academic writing continues to be fraught with passive voice—and grandiose words—resulting in boring and virtually unreadable prose. Unless you're writing for the academic community, use the active voice. Using the active voice makes writing easier to understand, lessens the amount of words needed to convey the information, and makes it clear who is performing the action.

Recognize Passive Voice and Replace it with Active Voice

There are two ways to identify the passive voice: The first is to look for the "actor" or the "acted upon." When the subject is the actor, the verb is in the active voice. Someone does something. When the subject is acted upon, the verb is in passive voice.

The second way to identify the passive voice is to look for the characteristics of the passive voice. There are three characteristics of the passive voice:

1. A form of the verb *to be* (*is, am, are, was, were, be, been,* or *being*).
2. A past participle (a verb generally ending in -ed or -en, except for irregular verbs).
3. A prepositional phrase beginning with *by.*

So in our example: "*The ball was hit by John,*" we have all three characteristics:

A form of the verb *to be*: was.

An irregular past participle: *hit*.

A prepositional phrase beginning with by: *by John*.

Only use passive voice:

- When you don't know the actor: *The bank was held up.*
- When the actor is unimportant to the point you are making: *The delivery arrived on time.*
- When the emphasis is not on the actor but the acted upon: *The missing child was found.*
- When you don't want to identify the actor: *All leave is canceled until further notice.*
- When you want to vary your sentence structure to give your reader a change from the active voice.

As a rough rule of thumb, 75 percent to 80 percent of your writing should be in the active voice.

Vary the Length of Sentences and Paragraphs

Have you ever ridden in a car with a lead-footed driver who's constantly switching from flooring it to stomping on the brake? Stop and go, stop and go. That's how readers feel if you constantly use short sentences without a break.

On the other hand, constant use of long sentences can seem to the reader like a boat adrift, making the boat rider/reader tired and bored and eager to be back ashore.

Variety in the length of sentences and paragraphs will make your writing more readable and more interesting.

Get Help for Grammar Issues if You Need It

Don't let grammar and mechanics keep you from telling your stories. As I told Ernie about his great Russian novel: The hard part of writing is having something to say and saying it well, having a good ear for dialog, and a good feel for setting and characterization. Help for the rest is available.

Take a Class

If grammar continues to be a problem for you, consider taking a class in grammar or making use of some of the many resources available to writers, as described in Chapter 25. Also, you can join a writing group or sign-up for a writer's workshop to obtain feedback and help.

Hire a Professional Editor

If you simply can't make peace with good grammar, you can hire a freelance editor to help you fix your manuscript.

And, no, that's not cheating. Pros sometimes hire editors to help them improve their book proposals and manuscripts. Literary agencies and publishing houses have editors on staff, or they hire freelance editors to help their authors produce their best work.

For more about the types of editorial services available and how to locate and hire a reputable freelance editor, please see Chapter 23.

Part IV

Writing Techniques

Chapter 13

Constructing a Page Turner

Whether writing fiction or nonfiction, once you've attracted the reader to begin reading, you want to keep her interest all the way through to the end. Good reads don't just happen. They are constructed with care by the writer.

The Story

A story is the telling of fictitious or real events in a way that holds value for an audience. The value for the audience may be entertainment or education. What makes a story interesting, aside from any intrinsic interest the reader may have in a topic or situation, is in the way in which it is told by the writer.

Stories Must Hold the Reader's Interest

Let me tell you the story of Mary:

Mary grew up in a fine family in a beautiful suburb with everything she needed. She had terrific parents who gave her a wonderful childhood. She was a beautiful girl who made captain of the cheerleading squad in both middle school and high school. Her parents doted on her, made sure she got into the college of her choice, and paid for all of her expenses.

After graduating summa cum laude from college, she married her high school boyfriend Ron, an outgoing and good looking former captain of the football team who later became very successful in real estate. They made loads of money and lived in a beautiful home near the beach. They had three wonderful children, two boys and a girl, who never gave them a day's trouble. Other than the occasional cold or flu, Ron and Mary were healthy all their lives.

As they grew older, they were warmed by the thought that their lives had been blessed and fulfilled. They had saved much of their money, invested it wisely, and confidently looked forward to living a wonderful retirement and leaving a rich legacy, both spiritually and monetarily, for their children and grandchildren.

Does it sound to you like Mary lived a fairy tale existence?

Perhaps at first blush, but Mary's story could not be a fairy tale. It's far too tame and dull.

Fairy tales are interesting, exciting, and entertaining, filled with witches and monsters trying to thwart the hero or heroine; Mary's story is uninteresting, boring, and anything but entertaining.

Story Development—Conflict and Suspense

Techniques like revealing conflict and developing suspense enhance the reader's interest in the story and its outcome. As readers we want to sympathize, if not identify, with Mary and see how she deals with the conflicts in her life, while we imagine how we would deal with those same circumstances if we were in her place.

We all have obstacles we have to overcome to achieve our dreams. That's what makes life interesting. Sometimes you get the monster; sometimes the monster gets you—your reader wanting to know which it will be in the story you're telling is what holds her interest. Storytellers have known this and relied upon it in telling tales since the beginning of recorded time.

Conflict

A good story has a strong central conflict. Conflict can involve person versus person conflict, inner conflict, or conflict with the environment (either physical or social). Person versus person conflict can be as big as a larger-than-life hero like James Bond confronting a classic villain like Dr. No, with life as we know it hanging in the balance. Or it can be as small as a brother and sister quibbling over issues the rest of the world wouldn't consider even remotely important.

Inner conflict can range from a sniper with moral qualms about pulling the trigger to a shy middle school boy trying to work up the courage to speak with the girl who sits next to him in class.

Conflict with the environment can range from a ship running into an iceberg and sinking in the dead of winter, as in the movie *Titanic*, to a young girl desperate to be recognized by the in-crowd at her high school.

Without conflict your story will be flat and boring like Mary's. You should introduce the conflict as early in a story as possible, certainly within the first few paragraphs of a short story and the first few pages of a novel. Wondering how or even if the protagonist will resolve and overcome the conflicts and what will happen next creates suspense and keeps your reader turning pages.

Suspense

A good writer uses characters, setting, and conflict to unveil the story piece by piece carefully withholding details in a way that warrants the reader's continued interest, thus making her want to keep turning pages to find out what happens next. The desire created in the reader to find out what's next is called suspense.

A brief note here: I'm simply speaking of suspense in its generic sense of wondering what's going to happen. Don't confuse the term suspense as I'm using it here with the suspense/thriller genre of fiction where the protagonist is trying to keep something terrible from happening or is running from danger.

Your story doesn't have to be a life-or-death, action, and adventure tale. The stakes in a story can be something that, to an impartial observer, would seem to be relatively low. But if those stakes are high in relation to your protagonist's needs and desires, the obstacles and setbacks to your protagonist trying to achieve his goals will create the tension and suspense required to keep your reader reading.

Suspense in Nonfiction vs. Fiction

In nonfiction, if it's not immediately obvious—such as it is in *The Perfect Storm*, where failure meant death—reveal what your protagonist has at stake. Show how this is an important goal or need of your subject, for instance, a struggling dental school candidate whose mother has been financing his education out of her waitressing tips worries he'll fail her.

In fiction, construct your plot in such way that it's clear to the reader how much achieving her goal means to the protagonist. See Chapter 19 for an example of how to go about developing a plot where the stakes are relatively low, but very high from the character's point of view.

Story vs. Plot in Fiction

Story differs from plot in fiction

E. M. Forster, author of *A Room With A View* and *Where Angels Fear To Tread*, gave the perfect example of the difference between story and plot: "The King died. Then the Queen died."

That is a story. It's simply a statement of what happened, similar to what you might read in a newspaper.

"The King died. Then the Queen died of grief."

That is a plot. In a plot things happen for a reason. One thing leads to the next, and then to the next, and so on.

Coincidence

In fiction, unlike in life, there must be an internal logic and consistency to what takes place. Although in real life coincidences happen all the time, there is little room in fiction for coincidence, except perhaps to serve as the inciting incident—the incident that propels the protagonist into action. A love story might begin with the two characters both being assigned to the same airplane seat, or a thriller may begin with the protagonist coincidentally being at the place and time and dressed in a similar fashion as the hit man has been told to expect the intended victim to look.

But coincidence cannot be used to resolve a plot. Readers expect that the plot will be resolved by the protagonist making use of his or her primary strengths, skills, and abilities to bring the matter to resolution. A convenient coincidence will rob your readers of the pleasure of a satisfying ending. The plot needs to be made up of various causally related events that move the story forward to its climax and conclusion.

Plot Supersedes Real Life

"But it really happened that way" is never justification for scenes that don't ring true in a piece of fiction. Plot must advance through cause and effect relationships. Remember the concept of verisimilitude: This is not life, but a representation of life. Life can be random; fiction cannot.

Don't Allow Your Plot to Go Easy on Your Characters

One of the biggest mistakes new fiction writers make is not keeping the pressure on their characters, thus maintaining enough tension to keep the reader up all night turning pages to see what happens next. I'll show you how that's done later in this chapter.

Dramatic Structure

Classic dramatic structure is described in a compact and precise form in *How To Tell A Story: The Secrets of Writing Captivating Tales* by Peter Rubie and Gary Provost (the italics are as in the original):

> "Once upon a time, *something happened* to someone, and he decided that he would pursue a *goal*. So he devised a *plan of action*, and even though there were *forces trying to stop him*, he moved forward because there was *a lot at stake*. And just as things seemed *as bad as they could get*, he learned an *important lesson*, and when *offered the prize* he had sought so strenuously, he had to *decide whether or not to take it*, and in making that decision he *satisfied a need* that had been created by *something in his past*."

The authors further state that this "…is the plot for 90 percent of the stories you've ever read, 90 percent of the films you've ever seen—in fact, 90 percent of all stories ever told in all the world in all time. It's as true for narrative nonfiction as it is for fiction."

Rubie and Provost illustrate the veracity of this description of structure by demonstrating point by point how *The Firm* by John Grisham meets this criteria. The authors credit Aristotle with first defining this classic dramatic structure.

Have a Beginning, a Middle, and an End to Your Fictional Stories

Aristotle didn't insist on a three act structure as is standard in screenwriting, but he believed that plot should have a beginning, a middle, and an end. That's generally been interpreted by writers as: In the first act, you get your hero up a tree. In the second act, you throw rocks at him. In the third act, you get him down.

Developing Your Own Plots

Writers generally start plotting in one of two ways: They develop an interesting character or characters and put them together in interesting situations; or, they come up with an interesting situation and decide what kind of characters to put into that situation. Most of plot development begins with: What if?

What if there was a giant gorilla named King Kong who fell in love with a beautiful woman and as a result was captured, brought to New York City, and then escaped? (*King Kong*)

What if there was a young female rookie FBI agent who needed the help of the world's most dangerous serial killer to catch a new, possibly more dangerous, serial killer? (*The Silence of the Lambs*)

The lead character, also called the protagonist, must want or need something very badly—a situation he can't avoid either because of the makeup of his personality or because the circumstances are such that he can't simply walk away from the problem; he's forced to deal with it (after all, if he could walk away, why wouldn't he?). Think of the sheriff in *Jaws*. He hates and fears the water but feels duty bound to stop the shark from attacking anyone else.

As the story unfolds, there should be rising action and setbacks. That means that the obstacles (also called complications) become more difficult as the story progresses. And just when it seems that the character is making progress on overcoming an obstacle, the rug gets pulled out from under him and another bigger-yet complication confronts him. Plots don't have to be played out on a grand scale with Earth in the balance; but the stakes have to be high enough to motivate the protagonist and the person directly in opposition to the protagonist, called the antagonist (if there is one).

Theme and Story in Fiction

Theme refers to the underlying meaning of a literary work. You should be able to summarize the theme in just a few words. The theme is usually not directly stated. Readers understand theme from the way the characters interact and from the events taking place in the story. Some examples of themes include: love conquers all, the pen is mightier than the sword, life is futile, nice guys finish last, and nice guys finish first.

Don't confuse a theme with a moral. As James N. Frey says in his book *How To Write A Damn Good Novel II*, "Often, modern novels have an *immoral* moral, in the traditional way of seeing things, like don't tell the truth—it will wreck your marriage, or committing murder is a growth experience."

You don't need to know your theme when you begin a piece of fiction and you may never be conscious of it. However, when a story seems unfocused and not sure what it wants to be, it's often because the theme is muddled or in competition with a secondary theme.

How It all Comes Together in Fiction

Briefly said: In fiction, the story is what happens, what the tale is about. The plot consists of the steps that make the story unfold, and the theme is what the story means on a deeper level.

To illustrate these points it's useful to have an example, so I'm going to use the movie *Titanic*, which is the highest grossing film of all time, has been called by *Parade* magazine the most popular movie of all time, and is tied for most Academy Awards.

Titanic

In the movie *Titanic*, the story is a frame story about an elderly woman, Rose, who has traveled to the location where the sunken ship *Titanic* has been located. In a frame story the opening and the close of the present-time story frame a story-within-a-story, with most of the action taking place within the inner story, usually about past events which led up to the present events. (The popular 1969 film *Goodbye Mr. Chips,* which many prime-timers will remember for its pairing of Peter O'Toole with Petula Clark, is another example of a frame story.)

The time is 1996. Rose has seen a news story on television about recovery efforts at the site where the *Titanic* sunk in the North Atlantic in 1912. The news footage shows treasure hunters searching for the priceless Heart of the Ocean diamond, known to have been aboard the *Titanic* at the time of its sinking. However, when they recover a safe from the stateroom on the *Titanic*, where they believe the diamond to have been kept, it's empty but for a penciled drawing of a beautiful young woman reclining nude on a couch, wearing only a necklace upon which is hung the Heart of the Ocean diamond.

Rose contacts the treasure hunters and provides enough information to convince them that she is the girl in the picture. She travels by helicopter with her granddaughter to the salvage ship where she tells the story of the young artist who drew the picture, Jack, and of how they fell in love, and of what happened on board the *Titanic*. The rest of the film alternates between extended flashbacks of their time on the *Titanic* and present time in the movie where Rose is telling the story.

She has, as we later learn at the end of the film, when the story reframes, her own agenda. We find that the purpose of her visit was to leave something of value there, the necklace on which hangs the priceless diamond, which she has secretly held onto all these years. She drops it over the side of the boat into the Atlantic where Jack died.

Plot *in* Titanic

The story within the frame story is about how the two star-crossed young lovers meet and fall in love on the *Titanic*. Step-by-step we witness how their love grows and how Rose grows as a person as a result of this love, despite various, ever-increasing and ever-more-difficult obstacles in opposition to them. These specific events constitute the plot.

Theme *in* Titanic

The theme of the film is that despite all obstacles, including the ultimate obstacle, the death of one of the lovers, love goes on. The only place the theme is stated explicitly is in the film's theme song, *My Heart Will Go On.*

Conflict and Suspense in Titanic

As a writer, when you've put your character into a suspenseful situation, you must milk it for all it's worth. This is often called creating *dramatic tension*. Let me give you an example from the movie.

After the *Titanic* has hit the iceberg, Jack is framed for a theft he didn't commit by Rose's fiancé Cal, who has discovered their relationship. Cal's valet and bodyguard Lovejoy, a former Pinkerton detective, slips the necklace holding the Heart of the Ocean diamond into Jack's coat pocket to make it appear Jack has stolen it. Cal demands Jack's arrest. Jack is arrested by the crew and taken to a room deep in the bowels of the ship where he is handcuffed to a metal structure.

Most new writers would let it go at that. The boat's sinking, Jack is handcuffed to the boat, enough tension created.

But in the hands of writer, director, and coproducer James Cameron every drop of possible tension and suspense is wrung out of this dramatic situation. Watch as the story unfolds:

• Lovejoy sits at a table cleaning his pistol next to where Jack is handcuffed. Over and over he taunts Jack by placing a bullet on the table on its side which rolls back toward him. He shows and tells Jack that the ship is upending, and that Jack is doomed. The audience wonders if Lovejoy plans to use the gun on Jack.

• Lovejoy punches Jack, then leaves to save himself. Some tension is relieved because the audience knows Jack will not be shot. Relief is offset by increased tension caused by Jack being alone with no one to help him.

• Water gradually rises up over a porthole in Jack's direct field of vision. He sees that the ship's situation is becoming more dire. He struggles even harder to free himself.

• Water begins to come in under the door to the room in which Jack is imprisoned. Jack sees the water has now breached the ship while he struggles to free himself.

• Rose decides to risk her life to save Jack. She turns down the relative safety of a seat in one of the lifeboats. This reveals her growth as a character. She has learned from Jack to be more assertive about what she wants.

• Rose frantically searches for where Jack is imprisoned to free him. She comes across the ship's architect, whom she had befriended. He gives her complex directions. The audience wonders if she can find Jack.

• Water gets deeper in the room where Jack is confined and in the ship's passageways which Rose must traverse.

• Rose finds Jack. Tension is momentarily relieved until they discover after a search of the room that there is no key to the handcuffs.

• Rose must go back through the complicated passages to find the key to free Jack.

• Water gets so deep it's reaching the electric lights high up on the wall which causes sparking and danger of electrocution.

• Rose gets confused and again in danger of getting lost.

• Rose can't find anyone to help her.

• Water climbs higher around Jack.

• Rose finds a fire ax and makes her way back to where Jack is confined. Tension is partially relieved.

• She finds Jack standing on a desk to keep above the water.

• Rose must use the axe to cut the chain between the handcuffs to free Jack. The audience wonders if she can she hit so small a mark.

• Rose rears back to take a swing revealing the ax is too heavy for her. It's unlikely she can hit the mark.

• Jack stops her mid-swing and tells her to take a practice swing at a piece of furniture.

• Rose takes a wild swing. If she had been swinging at the handcuffs, Jack would have been hit.

• Jack tells her to take another practice swing and to try to hit the same mark as last time.

• She misses the mark by an even greater distance.

• Water continues to rise, time is running out, they have no choice, Jack tells Rose to swing for the cuffs.

• Rose swings the ax, and manages to cut the chain without hitting Jack. Tension relieved.

• Rose and Jack must now make it up to the deck but the water is almost to the ceiling and continuing to rise. This sets up the next series of plot events.

As you can see, Cameron has tightened, and tightened, and tightened the dramatic tension to where the viewers are on the edge of their seats wondering what will happen next. And this is just one sequence of plot events among many. That's suspense at its best, and that's what as a fiction writer you must do: Put your character in a tough situation and figure out ways to make it tougher. That's where half of the fun of writing fiction comes in—watching your characters figure out ways to use their strengths to overcome the seemingly insurmountable obstacles you've put in front of them.

Character-Driven vs. Plot-Driven Stories

From time to time you'll see the words "character driven" or "plot driven," usually in the context of literary fiction being character driven and popular fiction being plot driven. It's a false choice. Stories involve interesting characters in interesting situations.

Plot is influenced by character and vice versa. Some plots focus more on the interrelationships between characters, or the character's internal struggle, but nonetheless something is happening in the story and that something is plot.

Likewise, it's impossible to have a story that's nothing but action without characters performing the action or being impacted by it in some way. Interaction between characters, setting, events, and the choices made by characters all combine to shape the story. You cannot have one without the other.

There are of course books and movies where the events in the story overshadow character development and relationships, such as the James Bond series of books and movies. But the audience must nevertheless have sympathetic characters to root for because all of the explosions and car chases in the world are not in and of themselves interesting enough to keep us watching. Caring about what happens to the protagonist, and wondering how the protagonist will handle the obstacles, and thinking about how we would handle those obstacles if we were in the protagonist's place, will keep us glued to the page or to the screen.

It is also true that in many literary stories plot is secondary. Some are slice of life stories that focus heavily on atmosphere and characterization but don't have an inciting incident or a climax. In this type of story the quality of the writing is paramount. As a beginner, unless you read a lot of these stories yourself and really have a strong desire to write one, I suggest that you're better off writing a more conventional story that has, as Aristotle suggested in his *Poetics*, a plot with a beginning, a middle, and an end.

How It all Comes Together in Nonfiction

In nonfiction you must, of course, stick with the facts. You don't have the fiction writer's freedom to alter facts to make the best story, but how you present those facts makes all the difference. Creative nonfiction uses the tools of fiction to enhance the reader's interest and to look beyond simple fact-telling. You can and should tell the story in a way that is interesting, engaging, and has a rising arc that builds to a satisfying conclusion.

Think about how you tell your friends a story: You don't reveal the key information at once. You build up to the big conclusion. It's the same way when you tell a joke. The details build up to the punch line at the end. You should do the same in your nonfiction articles and books.

If you're writing a memoir, show us the protagonist overcoming the lousy hand he was dealt in life. In a history book, tell us how the battle was won, how the king managed to stay in power, or how difficult it was to convince the sides to come to a peace agreement.

Withhold Facts to Increase Drama and Interest

Don't reveal everything at once. Even though your reader presumes you know the entire story, she wants you to tell the story step-by-step in a way that makes her wonder about the outcome. Tease her with details, foreshadow things to come, make her vicariously suffer the defeats and exalt in the triumphs.

Make Us Care About the Characters and Their Struggles

Even though your readers may know the ultimate outcome, as fans of Civil War histories clearly know how the war will end, it's the individual details, the individual stories of the people involved, the desire to root for a character in the face of overwhelming obstacles, and the need to know what happened next that will keep your readers turning the pages.

Making It Real

Putting Your Words to Work

Take a few minutes to list ten stories that have become legend in your family, among your friends, or at your workplace. We all have familiar stories in our lives that are told over and over. Simply list them with a descriptive title like: When Uncle Fred Dropped the Bowling Ball, or The Time We Got Lost in Las Vegas.

Pick one of the stories and actually write the story the way it's usually told. Notice how the story begins, what details are provided and which are held back, how the story progresses, where the laugh-lines, if any, show up, and where the surprises are sprung. This will help develop your sense of how a story should be told to keep the reader interested.

Chapter 14

Developing Characters

Indiana Jones, Ebenezer Scrooge, Rocky Balboa, Winston Churchill, Fred Flintstone, Robin Hood, James Rockford, Wile E. Coyote, Monica Lewinsky, James Bond, and Dr. No: Fictional or real, each a unique character so colorfully drawn that the name alone instantly calls to mind a vivid impression. Characters populate your story whether you write fiction, nonfiction, poetry, or drama. Without characters there is no story.

Developing Fictional Characters

Protagonist

Most stories have one character at the center of the story called the protagonist, sometimes referred to as the main or lead character. This is the person the story is about, and in short stories, is usually, although not necessarily, the viewpoint character. The protagonist acts in response to an inciting incident. The inciting incident is the problem or event that moves the character to action thus putting the story into motion.

This is the point in the story when the protagonist encounters the problem that will change her life. For example, your character moves to a new neighborhood and is desperate to fit in. Or, in a detective story, a crime happens and the detective is assigned to the case. Something happens that moves our character to action. The protagonist possesses strengths and weaknesses which come to bear as she struggles with the complications in the story.

Antagonist

The antagonist is the character or force in opposition to the main character and the creator of obstacles to the protagonist reaching her goals. The antagonist does not create the obstacles simply to frustrate the protagonist; he creates them in furtherance of his own goals and needs. The actions of the antagonist may occur independently of the action taken by the protagonist, in direct opposition to the protagonist, or as a response to or result of the actions taken by the protagonist.

Round Characters and Flat Characters

Characters are said to be "round" or "flat." A round character is a character that is fully developed, possessing definite needs, emotions, beliefs, strengths, and weaknesses. They also have a back story, meaning they had lives before the events in the current story. A character's back story helps to define and explain the choices he makes in your story.

Your protagonist and your antagonist must be well-rounded characters. The protagonist should not be all good and the antagonist should not be all bad; otherwise what you have is a cartoon.

It is your job as the writer to show the reader the roundness of your characters. Let the reader gain insight into your character by showing the reader what the character chooses to say and what he chooses to withhold, whom he picks as friends, what he notices when walking down the street, how he spends his money, how he does his job.

Your supporting characters, a spouse or a sidekick for example, should also be well-rounded. However, the taxi driver who holds one piece of vital information, and who will appear only briefly, can be a flat character. That does not mean your flat characters should be uninteresting. Good writers make sure their flat characters are not simply a device to convey information but appear to have had a life before the scene and will continue to have one after.

Your taxi driver may be embroiled in an intermittent argument with her boyfriend on her cell phone, all the while profusely apologizing to your antagonist for the distraction.

Choose a Main Character

To choose the main character ask yourself: Whom is this story about? Who will achieve the goals that are the objective of the story. With whom will readers sympathize?

Know Your Characters by Knowing Their Back Story

To bring characters to life on the page you must know what motivates them; what traits they possess, both good and bad; what they look like; and how they will act in any given situation. This is where the character's earlier life, known as "back story," comes in.

Back story is what occurred before the actual story takes place. We want our readers to believe that our characters have a past and a future beyond the confines of the immediate story.

Like real people, characters do what they do today because of their past: Childhood events, education, culture, illnesses, traumas, dreams, successes, and failures all contribute to how characters will react. Some information in your back story will never be used in the present-time of the story. It's there only to help you understand how this character will react in different situations and what sorts of choices your character will make under pressure.

On the other hand, some information in the back story may directly influence your present-time story. For example, your main character may be a Vietnam war vet so the story or a subplot may involve the lingering affects of that war on the way he views the world.

Character Traits

If your main character does not have the requisite traits to bring your story to resolution, feel free to add or subtract traits to suit your needs. However, if the trait does not fit, if it does not seem appropriate for this character, if the character still refuses to perform in the manner you've chosen for her, you may have the wrong character in the story, or the wrong character as the lead.

Draw a Character Sketch

Many writers create elaborate character portraits of their characters that go into very great depth. Other writers create a character sketch that gives them some basics about the character. Some begin with a character in mind and build back story as they need it to explain why the character acts or reacts in certain ways. Others look for specific characteristics, needs, and drives and then their build characters around those.

I recommend using a combination of these. Write a character sketch that describes the character as you see her at the outset. Include the obvious things like name; physical description; age; educational background; family background; occupation; likes and dislikes in food, music, and movies; where she's from; significant events in her past life, both positive and negative; and any individual quirks or mannerisms that distinguish her from other characters.

Beyond that, describe her character traits in terms of primary and secondary traits. You should know your characters' strengths and flaws and how they came to possess both. Your character should have a dominant positive trait and dominant flaw along with other lesser traits. The character's traits may be in opposition with one another. For example, your character may be very enthusiastic but have trouble expressing that enthusiasm because she's very shy. That flaw may cause the character to come close to failing or to actually fail to achieve her goals in the story.

A partial list of positive and negative character traits to get you started in developing some of your characters appears below.

Positive Traits		*Negative Traits*	
Adventurous	Reliable	Boorish	Snobbish
Curious	Trustworthy	Argumentative	Self-centered
Brave	Loyal	Bossy	Rude
Calm	Humble	Cowardly	Demanding
Candid	Determined	Cruel	Shy
Fair	Adaptable	Disrespectful	Stubborn
Generous	Empathetic	Foolish	Violent
Logical	Ambitious	Greedy	Thoughtless
Charming	Easy-going	Gullible	Spoiled
Enthusiastic	Tolerant	Moody	Shiftless

Direct or Indirect Characterization

Characterization refers to how the characters are presented to the reader. Characterization can be either direct or indirect.

Direct characterization is stated outright. It has to do with the description of how the character looks, talks, and thinks.

Indirect characterization is conveyed to the reader by showing the character interacting with other characters and the environment.

Characters Based on Real People

Writers often use bits and pieces of different people they know in creating their characters. And probably all characters are to at least some degree autobiographical. That's fine. But when copying characters from life there are some hazards.

You may know the individual you're using as a character so well that you forget the reader doesn't know him as well. When writing you see and hear that character in your mind, but you must convey that to the page so that the reader can see and hear him as well. On the other hand, it's also possible to put too much of the person you know into the character and limit the character to the traits your friend possesses. When drawing from real life the best thing to do is mix and match so the character is an amalgam of several people and has the character's own combination of traits.

Motivate Your Characters

Make sure your characters, both protagonists and antagonists, have adequate motivation for their actions. Don't imitate those 1950s B-movies where, against all common sense and reason, the homemaker, all alone, climbs up into the attic to investigate suspicious noises.

In your fictive world, your readers must understand why your homicidal maniac does what he does, even if they must come to that understanding slowly over time. In fact, peeling the onion, layer by layer, revealing some, then a little more, and then more, keeps your reader interested, involved, and turning pages.

Take Note of Your Own Strong Emotions

When you experience strong emotions, write down:
- How you feel.
- What you're thinking.
- What you notice. Our minds often focus on odd things when we are experiencing strong emotions.
- What you say or what others say to you that either soothes the emotions or makes them worse.
- What crossover emotions emerge. Sometimes when we're sad we react by becoming angry.

When you experience these emotions, capture as much of the sensory details as you can. This is not as cold and clinical as it may sound. Obviously, wait until you're through the moment to begin writing, or taking notes, but try to take notes as close to the moment as possible so you don't lose any of the experience.

Having these emotions catalogued will serve you well when you transfer these feelings to your characters as they endure their own struggles. As a side benefit, I find that this process of analysis helps me understand myself better and helps me through whatever difficult situation I'm experiencing.

Some Tips on Writing Fictional Characters

- Use pictures cut from a magazine and post at your writing place if you have trouble visualizing your fictional characters.
- Whenever you add something new about a character in your narrative, add it to your character profile. Your character shouldn't be left-handed in Chapter 2, then fire a revolver with her right hand in Chapter 7.
- Keep a notepad by your computer to make notes to yourself of things that need to be done or followed up on. Cross them off after you've done it.

Nonfiction Characters

Although they are living, breathing people, the inhabitants of your nonfiction pieces are the characters in the story you're telling. To make them real for your reader look for the telling detail that reveals character. It may be related to their personality, to the way they enter a room, to how they dress, to how they dominate or shrink back from a conversation. Your goal is to make your character as true-to-life as possible, based on your research and observations.

Show the Nonfiction Character in Action

Portraying the way the people you are writing about carry themselves, react to adversity, suffer mistakes, treat subordinates, or react to questions all can provide external clues to the reader as to the person inside. As in fiction, look for the telling details in what he says and what he withholds and the other choices he makes. By capturing the details that convey your sense of the individual, you make the reader sense what you sense.

Making It Real
Putting Your Words To Work

To get a handle on character traits, list three people you know very well. This may be your spouse or significant other, your best friend, your boss, coworkers, or anyone else with whom you have a regular ongoing relationship.

Then list three people you see only occasionally. They may include the barista at your coffee shop, a cashier you see regularly at your supermarket, a coworker you don't know very well, or a neighbor down the street with whom you have a nodding acquaintance.

Next to each name describe the individual using only a single word. In other words, if you had to describe that person and could only use one word, what would that word be? It's not easy, so take your time.

Next, list two secondary or supporting words that describe each of the individuals.

Finally, describe in one word something you don't like or that annoys you about each of those individuals.

Now do the same exercise for the characters in your writing project. You should know your rounded characters as well as you know the first three people you identified. You should know your flat characters as well as you know the people in the second group. If you don't, spend some time developing the characters' back stories.

Chapter 15

Determining Point of View

Point of view refers to the viewpoint from which the story is told. Most stories are told from the point of view of the lead character, some by the lead character herself, others by a disembodied narrator.

Point of View Choices

First Person Point of View

In first person point of view the narrator is one of the characters in the narrative and tells the story. The reader experiences the story through the narrator's eyes.

First person point of view is often chosen by new writers because it seems natural to write from the "I" point of view. The downside of the first person point of view is that the reader can only observe that which this character observes. For example, you cannot go in and out of the minds of the other characters or know about events that are taking place away from this one character.

The character narrating the story does not have to be the lead character. The narrator may be an observer of the events in the story and may present the story truthfully and straightforwardly or the narrator may not be reliable and may present the story deceptively and colored by the character's own judgments and opinions.

A good example of the peripheral first person narrator is Nick Carraway in F. Scott Fitzgerald's *The Great Gatsby*.

A good example of an unreliable narrator is the barber in Ring Lardner's *The Haircut*.

Second Person Point of View

Second person point of view is rarely used because it is difficult to pull off successfully. In second person point of view the reader is treated like a character in the story. The reader is addressed directly. Here is an example:

> You've accepted the dare; it's too late to back out now. You enter the abandoned house. The lights are out. You flick the light switch, but nothing happens. The door shuts behind you with a loud click. Panicked, you grab the knob but the door refuses to open.
>
> Softly at first but getting louder you hear the sound of labored breathing. The echoes in the room make it impossible for you to tell where the sound is coming from, only that it's getting closer, ever closer. You shiver as cold sweat begins to trickle down your back. You raise your hands to ward off who knows what.

To read a successful novel written in second person point of view take a look at *Bright Lights, Big City* by Jay McInerney.

Third Person-Limited Point of View

Third person-limited point of view is often found in contemporary literature. In third person-limited point of view the narrator tells the story through the eyes of one character. It's similar to first person point of view because the story reports only what the viewpoint character sees, thinks, and feels. The reader participates with the character as the story unfolds.

Third Person-Omniscient Point of View

Third person-omniscient point of view can look through the eyes of all the characters. The narrator is not a character in the novel. Third person omniscient is sometimes called God's point of view. The omniscient narrator can enter any character's mind. The omniscient narrator can view the characters and events objectively. By that I mean not through the filter of a character's perspective.

Multiple Viewpoints Point of View

Multiple viewpoints refers to using more than one character's point of view. It is the most sophisticated and most flexible and is found frequently in contemporary literature, particularly in mystery and thriller novels to switch between the protagonist's and the antagonist's point of view.

Each character is limited to what they see, think, and feel, as in the first person or third person limited point of view, but the reader now sees the story unfold from various perspectives. Some novelists will switch viewpoints between chapters, using first person for the either the protagonist or the antagonist and third person-limited for the other to add interest and perspective.

Point of View in Action

The vignettes below show the same scene told using the viewpoints we've discussed except for second person point of view, since that point of view is so infrequently used.

First Person

I knew this would be a crappy night from the moment I signed in at the 37th. I was still nursing a hangover from yesterday's retirement party for the Chief of D's, and wouldn't you know it, of all nights, I catch the first call out of the gate.

Maybe it's the global warming. All week it's been monsoon season in New York. The whole way to the crime scene was like some pissed-off fireman was leveling his hose at my windshield. I get out of the unit and next thing I'm up to my ass in water. It was going to be a great night.

Third Person-Limited

Detective Donnie London slowed the NYPD squad car trying to get his bearings through the blowing sheets of rain. The noise of the rain drilling the roof ricocheted through his brain like machine-gun fire. His head felt like a bass drum with a whacked-out drummer banging it on both sides and he had a metallic taste in his mouth like he'd been sucking on pennies. The worst part was he had nobody to blame but himself. He knew better than to have tossed down tequila shooters at the Brass's retirement party.

Then, as if things weren't bad enough already, he stepped out of the car into at least six inches of cold water. This, most definitely, was not going to be a good night.

Third Person-Omniscient

There's never a good night for a homicide, but this was a particularly bad night. Already it had poured more than an inch and the weather people were predicting yet another inch overnight for New York City and vicinity. Detective Donnie London, his head pounding from a hangover, stepped out of his squad car and into a seven-inch-deep pool where a blocked sewer created a dam. The water went up over his ankle and into his shoe adding to his miseries.

Inside the brownstone, Sergeant Kate Flanagan sat at a Louis XIV desk, drumming her fingers, getting angrier by the minute, waiting for the homicide detective to arrive. At her feet lay the body of Sylvy Hoskit, a boning knife protruding from her side, a pool of blood surrounding her.

Multiple Point of View

(Combine the following paragraph with either the first person or third person paragraphs above to create multiple point of view.)

Inside the brownstone, Sergeant Kate Flanagan sat at an expensive looking desk, drumming her fingers, waiting for Homicide to arrive. She looked down at her feet where the body of Sylvy Hoskit lay in a pool of her own blood, a long skinny knife protruding from her side. Young, beautiful, rich—she was everything Kate wasn't. But that was okay, Kate also wasn't dead.

Damn homicide hotshots. NYPD was shot through with them. No problem for them—they didn't care how long they kept the uniforms waiting. She went to the window and looked out just in time to see that washed-up drunk Donnie London step into a puddle of water up to his ankle. Good. Serves the bastard right for taking his sweet time.

Point of View in Practice

In practice, short stories limit themselves to one point of view, because having more than one point of view is too confusing to the reader. In novels, point of view shifts often occur in alternating chapters. In contemporary novels multiple points of view may be present within a chapter, but usually the shifts only occur when the scenes shift.

Don't change point of view within a scene and generally don't change it within a short story. Inconsistent and needless point of view shifts are often the reason for failure of stories by inexperienced writers.

If your novel or short story isn't working, try changing the point of view from third person to first person or vice versa. Also, look at telling your story from a different character's point of view.

Chapter 16

Crafting Realistic Dialog

Well crafted dialog brings your writing to life for the reader. It is the essence of "show don't tell," the admonition every writer should heed, and makes your reader a direct observer of your lead character as he tries to resolve the obstacles to his goals. Dialog forms the basis of scenes in long and short fiction, and in creative nonfiction. It is fundamental to drama.

Benefits of Using Realistic Dialog

- Reveals character
- Propels the story forward
- Adds to the readers' interest and enjoyment by showing not telling
- Aids the reader in connecting with the characters
- Gives the reader a front row seat to the action

Verisimilitude

Verisimilitude is a term that refers to how real your writing seems, how closely it matches the reader's expectations of reality. It refers to the lifelike quality possessed by a story. Why lifelike? Because real-life has too many quiet periods when nothing of interest occurs. If you allow your story to become uninteresting, you will lose your readers.

Real-life conversations contain a lot of filler: a lot of hmms, and uhs, a lot of introductory words that simply mean hello, and a lot of repetition. Dialog must be lean, convey information, and move the story forward in some way, while giving the reader insight into the characters and their motivations. In dialog, the writer's job is to present a depiction of life that seems real to the reader while eliminating the boring parts.

Creating Realistic Dialog

Get to the Point

Effective dialog gets the reader right to the meat of the conversation without a lot of the "Hello, how are you?" that is heard in real life.

Start a New Paragraph for Every Speaker Change

Signal every change of speaker to the reader by creating a new paragraph, even if the speaker utters only a single word.

> "You want to go to the park?" asked Fred.
> "Where?"
> "To the park. Come on, we haven't been there for a while."

Use Speaker Tags

Use speaker tags occasionally so the reader doesn't get confused about who is speaking. Keep the tags simple such as "he said" or "she replied."

When you use speaker tags, unless the character is asking a question or making an exclamation, the speaker's words are enclosed within quotation marks and finished with a comma inside the quotes.

> "Okay, let's go," George replied.

If the character is asking a question or making an exclamation, instead of a comma the sentence is punctuated with a question mark or exclamation point, as appropriate. The question mark or exclamation point goes inside the quotation marks. If a tag follows the quotation marks, it is lower case. A name following the quotation marks is capitalized as usual.

> "Should we walk or should we drive?" asked Fred.
> "Should we walk or should we drive?" Fred asked.

When there is no speech tag, the character's comments end with the appropriate punctuation: a period, a question mark or an exclamation point.

"Are you ready to go now?"
"Sure! Let me get my jacket."

When a speech tag is inserted into what a character says, the structure of the dialog determines how it's punctuated. A tag interjected within the speaker's sentence is set off by commas while one placed between his sentences is set off by a period.

"Grab the Frisbee," George said, "we haven't thrown the Frisbee in a while."
"Nah, I don't think so," Fred said. "I'm feeling tired and stiff. Why don't we just take it easy today?"

Don't use words that describe body movements instead of speech in speech tags. You can't smile, frown, or grimace dialog, nor can you spit dialog.

Not: "I love you," he blushed.
But: "I love you," he said, his face blushing and perspiring.
Not: "I hate this place and everyone in it," he spat.
But: "I hate this place and everyone in it," he shouted (or yelled, or screamed).

Include Accompanying Action to Avoid Talking Head Syndrome

Good dialog is almost always accompanied by some kind of action. You don't want two people simply standing across from one another talking—it gets boring. Have your characters going about their business while they're speaking to one another. In this way, it's also possible to distinguish between speakers by what they're doing while they're talking. Such bits of action are sometimes called "beats" or "stage business."

George pulled his blue fleece from the closet. "You've been tired a lot lately. You okay?"

"Yeah." Fred stretched his arms over his head, arched his back, and half-stifled a yawn, "Just working a lot of overtime lately."

"I thought you wanted the overtime."

"Sure, but I don't want to be worked into the ground in the process." He grabbed his keys from the foyer table. "At this rate, I'll have plenty of money but be too tired or too dead to spend it."

Punctuating Lengthy Passages

If a character speaks for more than one paragraph do not close the quotation marks at the end of the first paragraph. Simply open the second paragraph with new opening quotation marks. Continue this format until the speaker is finished, then enter the closing quotation mark. Generally it's not a good idea to have a speaker go on at length for multiple paragraphs. Unless your goal is to show the character monopolizing the conversation, break up long dialog passages with bits of business and conversation with the other characters.

"My new boss is really driving me nuts," George said, sliding behind the wheel. "Seems like every time I stop to get a breath, she's found something else that should have been done yesterday. She's just incredible.

"Anyway, Fred, how about you? Everything going well in the lofty halls of academe?

"Oh, and how about that new blonde in the English department, she still giving you the eye in the faculty lounge?"

Fred sighed. "You don't want to know, George, everyday is a new adventure." He fidgeted with his sunglasses, "and no, I haven't seen her this week."

Avoid Ping Pong Dialog

Unless you're purposely introducing a staccato rhythm to convey a terse conversation, or tension between the characters, ping pong dialog makes the dialog choppy and less interesting to follow.

"You look great," he said.

"So do you," she replied.

"Want to get a drink?" he asked.

"Do you?" she inquired.

"Maybe later," he answered.

"OK, later," she said.

Don't Use Multiple Synonyms for Said

Try not to use multiple synonyms for *said* as I did in the prior example.

Some readers find the change distracting. The word *said*, on the other hand, goes unnoticed.

Use Strong Verbs that Don't Need the Support of Adverbs and Remember to Show Rather than Tell

It's much more effective and memorable to show the reader your characters' emotions than to tell them what the characters are feeling.

Not: "I've had it with this job," Tom said angrily.

But: Tom shouted, "I've had it with this job," tore the McDonald's ball cap from his head and threw it across the room where it skittered along the floor coming to rest at his manager's feet.

Be Subtle When Injecting Exposition into Dialog

It's perfectly fine and natural when one character informs another character of something he doesn't know, thus informing the character (and we the readers) of vital information. But don't dump in a big lump of exposition that would not be in normal everyday conversation. Let your reader discover the information over several exchanges of dialog, or if the information does not need to be dramatized, use narrative summary (just have the narrator summarize the information within the narrative) to get the information across.

Don't Have one Character Tell the other Something They Should Already Have Known

Dialog, included only for the sake of informing the reader, comes across as contrived and takes the reader out of the story long enough to wonder why something was said that should have been known.

For example:

"I think we need to have the ceiling painted before your mother arrives. You know how picky she is and how she complained the last time she was here, last August, about how dingy everything seemed, and what a poor housekeeper I am."

Here, the insertion of "last August" appears contrived since both the speaker and the listener should have known this.

Don't Overuse Character Names in Dialog

In normal conversation people don't use each other's names that frequently. For example:

"Hey Fred, how are you today?"
"I'm fine, Bill. How are you doing?"
"Good. Say Fred, have you seen that film Training put together for us?"
"No, Bill, I haven't, but Melinda did, and she said it was great."
"Good, glad to hear that after all the money we spent. Take care, Fred. See you next time."
"You too, Bill."

Each Character's Voice Should Be Unique

Each major character should be identifiable by the way he speaks. The words he chooses should be a reflection of his personality, his background, and the setting. In other words, your reader will expect language will be used differently in turn-of-the-century London than in 1860s Texas or today's New England. A demanding boss will use different word choices than the boss who needs to feel liked by his staff. We expect a college professor to speak differently than a rough-and-tumble private investigator.

Take a moment to think about the *Star Wars* movies. Assume you were reading the story rather than watching and hearing the different voices. Even without speech tags you wouldn't have much trouble distinguishing the voices in a conversation between the macho, devil-may-care Han Solo; the serious but plucky, can-do, and wants-to-learn Luke Skywalker; the slightly haughty Princess Lea; the refined, cautious, and solicitous C-3PO; and Yoda with his unique syntax.

Of course, you can make your character stand out by purposely switching expected speech patterns. This is what Robert B. Parker does with his macho but grammatically-correct, literary-quoting PI, Spenser. Just be sure your characters are consistent in this. You can't have them going from one pattern to another unless it is obvious they are doing it for effect, such as a street punk who uses the 'hood vernacular with his pals but switches to a proper Bostonian voice when courting the senator's daughter.

Avoid Strange Spellings

You don't have to phonetically spell words in a regional dialect to get your point across. If your character is a ranch hand with limited education, the statement, "He don't know nothing," gets the point across much better and smoother than, "He don' know nuthin." Your reader is perfectly capable of imagining the accent while she reads.

Chapter 17

Revealing Character Thoughts

In the real world we constantly carry on a dialog in our heads. Revealing this dialog to readers is one way that writers help readers to strongly identify with their characters.

Objective vs. Subjective Viewpoint

Most modern stories are told in the subjective rather than objective viewpoint.

Objective viewpoint keeps the reader at a distance from the characters. The reader is an observer watching the action as though she were viewing a drama; all she knows is what she can witness from the actions, the physical appearance, and the statements made by the actors. Here's an example:

> Harvey straightened his tie, adjusted his jacket, and quickly mopped the sweat from his forehead as he approached Janet's desk. She had her head down going over the time-sheets and didn't see him standing there. He began to turn away, but half way through he swung back to face her, squared himself, and cleared his throat. His face beginning to blush, he said in a voice almost too low for her to hear, "Hi, Janet. Interested in going to lunch?"

From this we get the idea that Harvey and Janet may work together and that Harvey is a little bit formal, definitely nervous about asking Janet to lunch, and probably not very experienced in dealing with the opposite sex. But we are watching from a distance, as though viewing a movie. We have to interpret the action from what is said and the descriptions provided by the narrator. We don't know what the characters are thinking or feeling.

Subjective viewpoint brings us much closer to the characters and invites the reader into the mind of the principal character so the reader can experience the character's thoughts and emotions. This technique helps the story and the character come alive because readers can vicariously experience the character's emotions as he encounters advances and setbacks as the story progresses. Here's the same scene but now we have a better view into Harvey's psyche:

> As he turned the corner, Harvey straightened his tie, adjusted his jacket, mopped the sweat from his forehead and breathed a sigh of relief. Good, she was at her desk, doing the time sheets. Now all he had to do was ask the question without screwing it up. But she seemed busy, her head down, making notations on the time sheets. Was she really busy or just trying not to see him? No, she was too sweet to be rude, she's just busy, maybe he shouldn't interrupt. He began to turn back, tomorrow would be another day. No, not again; now or never. He turned and approached her desk. He could feel the blood rising in his face, and cursed his traitorous voice as he barely squeaked out the words, "Hi, Janet. Interested in going to lunch?"

Techniques for Revealing a Character's Thoughts

Tell the Reader What the Character is Thinking

The easiest way to indicate that you're going inside your character's mind, is to let your reader in on what the character is thinking. Here's an example:

> During the drive home from the McCormac and Associates Christmas party, Melanie thought about what she should have said to Veronica. Who does that little tramp think she is making a play for my man? Wait till I get hold of her at the office. She'll wish she she'd never messed with me.

Note that in the example above we didn't say, Melanie thought to herself. While she can talk to herself, unless your story features telepaths, there's no one else to whom Melanie can think but herself.

Saying that the character thought something is appropriate when we're not going to spend a great deal of time inside the character's mind.

Use Quotation Marks

If you won't be going inside the character's mind frequently, you can let the reader know she's reading the character's thoughts by putting them in quotation marks.

> During the drive home, Melanie was still furious with Veronica. "Who does she think she is making a play for my man? That tramp. Wait until I get hold of her at the office. She'll wish she hadn't messed with my guy."

While the example above is perfectly fine, and works as illustrated, I recommend limited use of quotation marks because it has the most potential for confusing you and your readers. Your reader can mistake dialog for interior thoughts and vice versa and using quotes can make the writing more complicated. Let's imagine Melanie obsessing about the details of the conversation with Veronica, and thinking about the things Veronica said to her. In that case we'd have an interior quote, within the quotation marks.

> During the drive home, Melanie was still furious with Veronica. "Who does she think she is making a play for my man? That tramp, telling Craig, 'If you ever decide to go out with a real woman, I'm in the book.' Wait until I get hold of her at the office. She'll wish she hadn't messed with my guy."

Use Italics

Using italics is another way to cue your reader in that she's reading the character's thoughts. This has limited use because writing styles change, and today it's considered old fashioned to use italics for such things. Also, too many italic passages can burn the reader out and diminish the value of using italics. They should be reserved for special instances where you want to put particular emphasis on certain words, phrases, or sentences.

Save italics for special emphasis such as:

• *Thoughts the character is reluctant to speak.* To create emotional emphasis use italics for dialog the character thinks, but is reluctant to say.

> A slight breeze rustled the leaves and moonlight dappled the sidewalk as she felt around in her handbag for her key. An almost perfect end to a perfect evening. He seemed so nervous, like he didn't know what to do next. She said, "Yes, I had a great time with you tonight, too." *Aren't you going to at least try to kiss me? What are you waiting for? Don't make me have to ask.*

• *Says one thing but thinks another.* Italics are useful when the character thinks differently from what she says.

> "Yes, sir. I can see how reducing vacation time will enable us to increase productivity." *You miserable skinflint, you're going to increase productivity until you've driven all of our good people out and we go under. Then what?*

Merge the Character's Thoughts into the Narrative

The easiest way for your reader to understand when the character's thoughts are being revealed is to simply merge the character's thoughts in with the action.

> During the drive home, Melanie had trouble concentrating on her driving. She was still furious with Veronica. Who does she think she is making a play for my man? That tramp. Wait until I get hold of her at the office. She'll wish she hadn't messed with my guy. She began to shake so violently she had to pull off the road to regain control.

Sometimes italics can be used to put emphasis on a particularly important or emotionally laden thought, to highlight it within the merged thoughts.

> During the drive home, Melanie had trouble concentrating on her driving. She was still furious with Veronica. Who does she think she is making a play for my man? That tramp. Wait till I get hold of

her at the office. She'll wish she hadn't messed with my guy. She felt the car begin to shake violently. She grasped the wheel tightly then realized it wasn't the car shaking, it was her. She pulled to the side of the road. *Get a grip, girl! Remember what the doctor told you. Breathe. Take control. Don't let other people control you. Sleep on it. That's the best thing. Tomorrow's another day.* A few minutes later, no longer shaking, she checked the rear view mirror and pulled back onto the highway.

Chapter 18

Creating the Setting

Setting consists of the where and when of your story: Where does it take place and when does it happen? Is your story set in a jungle or the Antarctic, in New York City or in your own hometown? Is it set in the present, medieval times, or the future? Setting also includes weather conditions, characters' dress and customs, and the locations where characters meet and have dialog. It helps to define mood and tone. Is your piece a dark, twisted noir piece, or a sunny, light, and entertaining bit of froth?

Importance and Role of the Setting

Setting is more important in some stories than others. An historical novel, a story of survival such as Jon Krakauer's *Into Thin Air*, and a science-fiction story all depend heavily on setting.

In some stories the setting essentially becomes a character as in the movie *Titanic* or *The Call of the Wild* by Jack London. But in others, setting is less important. For example, most romances can as easily be set in the Middle Ages or as a Western without substantial modification to the story or the characters.

In much nonfiction, the setting is vital in terms of the times in which things happened and the location where they happened. What else is history, if not characters reacting within their setting? But, as in fiction, setting can take on more or less of a role depending on the individual story.

For example, much has been written about the Civil War. One cannot understand the civil war without considering the times, the geography, and the societal values of the day. A writer planning a book on the Civil War will have to do extensive research to convey very specific details of geography, weather, conditions on the battlefields, weaponry, and so on.

On the other hand, the story of the surrender at Appomattox is much more influenced by character than setting. While time of course is relevant, the story would be good and interesting no matter where the event had taken place.

In much nonfiction writing, setting is the reason for telling the story. No one, except the people who knew them personally would care much about the lives of admirals Peary and Byrd if not for their polar explorations. And, without the ocean, the boats, and the weather, there could be no *Perfect Storm*.

Setting and Dialog

What your characters say, and how they speak, must be consistent with the time of your story and the locale. The clever dialog in *The Great Gatsby* would seem totally out of place in a story about Elizabethan England.

The when and the where of your story also impacts your description of what the characters wear and what they do. Again using Elizabethan England as an example, the Emmy award-winning BBC television production *Upstairs Downstairs* uses dress, dialect, diction, education, and social standing to differentiate whether the character was an aristocrat living upstairs or a servant living downstairs, as was the case in Elizabethan England.

Setting and Plot

Setting substantially impacts plot as well as the type of story you can tell. For example, the pregnancy of an unmarried woman was enough to drive a plot through the 1950s; today, because times have changed, and with the times, social values, that plot would need substantial augmentation to make it plausible.

Likewise, the open living and lifestyle arrangements of today wouldn't fit into a story set in the United States in the 1950s or the early 1960s.

When Setting Is Inconsequential

When setting is inconsequential, it can be sketched in with a few telling details. For example, the rug in a hotel room can be stained or clean, plush or threadbare, soft or scratchy, depending on the scene you're trying to create and the point of view from which the story is being written. The narrator may simply describe the rug in a way that supports the atmosphere of the story at that point. If the story is being told through the point-of-view character, it may depend on his mood. If he's in an ebullient mood, the shape of the stain, resembling a cow, may strike him as funny. On the other hand, if the character is stressed and stretched to his limits, his disgust with the filthy carpet may be what finally pushes him over the edge.

When Setting Is Important

When setting is important you will want to include much more sensory detail but without overdoing it. The important thing is to give the reader enough detail so she can visualize the scene for herself, bringing to it her own inner vision, thus participating in the telling of the story.

Pulitzer Prize-winning poet Ted Kooser in his book *The Poetry Home Repair Manual* says, "I've talked about how you can trust your reader to supply a portion of every setting, based upon his or her experience. You may not need all the modifiers, all the explanations. For example, were you to write, 'I climbed very slowly into the strong branches of the tree and looked out over the green field of corn,' I would respond, 'Well, is it expected that someone might climb quickly into a tree? Climbing a tree is by its nature slow. And as to the tree itself, what do you climb into but its branches, and don't you choose the strong branches because they support your weight? And, is your first thought of a field of corn anything but of a field of green?'

"So the adequate sentence is shorter and more energetic, written with strong nouns and verbs, not sagging with modifiers: 'I climbed into the tree and looked out over the corn.' We readers supply all the other stuff."

Creating Realistic Settings

There are several methods you can use to collect the details to make your settings realistic.

Conduct Research

If your story is set in the past, unless you lived through that time and can rely on personal memories, research will provide the details to make the setting come alive for your reader. The research librarian at your local library can help you find information about the times, the dress, customs, housing, economics, or almost anything else you might need to provide realistic details of setting. And, of course, the Internet is the greatest research tool ever invented.

Likewise if your story is set in a place you've never been, research can provide the details you need.

Visit the Setting

If it's possible, there's no better way to learn the look and feel of a place than to pay a personal visit. During your visit remember to employ not only your sense of sight but your other senses as well, and to take notes.

Extrapolate Familiar Settings to other Settings

Extrapolate by taking a place you're familiar with and transport it to another locale. Frankly, with few exceptions, all seedy motels feel pretty much the same as do all luxurious hotels. The difference is in the specific contributing details.

Don't try to describe the Plaza Hotel in New York if you've never seen it. Call the hotel and ask to be sent a brochure. Check out the hotel's website. Search travel sites and travel articles to get firsthand accounts of people who have stayed there.

If it is the hotel's ballroom you wish to write about, if you've ever been in any fancy hotel ballroom, you know the feel of the place. Then all you need to do is to obtain a photo of the Plaza ballroom to give you the telling details.

Don't Go Beyond What Is Necessary to Set the Scene

If you spend a great deal of time describing an object, readers will expect that object to play an important role in your story. In a nonfiction story you may be fascinated by an unusually beautiful grandfather clock, and want to share those details. But, unless that clock plays a direct role, such as if you're writing an article about period furnishings, or has some symbolic importance, simply sketch it in. Don't over describe.

The same is also true in fiction. Keep in mind playwright Anton Chekhov's dictum: If you prominently feature a gun on the mantel in the first act, you better have fired it by the third act. If you go on about the beauty of California's Mono Lake and its migratory Eared Grebes, you need to show how this ties into your story. Perhaps your character is a botanist fighting commercial development on the lake's shores—or perhaps he's the developer.

Use Setting to Create Mood

Even when it's not a critical element, setting can be used to create mood. It can also be used to reinforce other story elements such as the theme, and as a contrast or complement to the character's emotional state.

Your viewpoint character's current emotion will have an impact on what he notices and what he perceives about the setting just as our own emotions affect our perceptions. When we're sad things like beautiful flowers that might otherwise cheer us up lose their power. When we're happy, things that usually annoy us don't seem so bad.

Your character's emotions help define the mood of the setting in the reader's mind. If you write about a character who's nervous and fearful because her son has been kidnapped, common elements in the setting will seem nerve-wracking and fearful to her. A colorful, noisy carnival or a quiet, incoming fog will be interpreted by the character— and your reader—as ominous.

In order to clarify this, think about what a kitchen looks like. We expect some counters, a refrigerator, a stove, a microwave, some appliances, and maybe a kitchen table with some chairs. My perception of a certain kitchen may be of a small, cramped, ugly space, but you may see the same kitchen as charming and efficient. If in our scene the kitchen is merely the location for a conversation which could have been held anywhere, then it's enough to simply say "in the kitchen," and let your readers provide in their mind's eye, their vision of a kitchen.

But, depending on the characters, the plot, the atmosphere, the overall mood you want to set, and how you want the character's mood to interpret the setting, you should provide specific details to plant your reader firmly in the room with the characters.

The following scenarios use a kitchen table to complement and enhance the emotional undertone of the story. We'll be looking in on Joe and Marley Harris as they sit across from one another at the breakfast table. Mr. Harris is the viewpoint character. The table never changes, but how it's viewed changes significantly depending on Mr. Harris' state of mind.

Mrs. Harris Has Just Discovered Mr. Harris is Having an Affair:

They sat across the kitchen table from one another as they had a thousand times before. The old oak table had always seemed a bridge between them. Now, from the way she sat with her arms against the table, rather than resting them on it as she always had, he could see she was making it into a barrier.

Mr. Harris Has Recently Begun an Affair with His Secretary, Twenty Years His Junior:

They sat across the table from one another as they had a thousand times before but now for the first time he noticed how worn the old oak had become. It had gone from something rich and beautiful and lustrous to something old and worn and utilitarian: something only of use until it can be replaced.

Mr. Harris Has Been Reassured of the Love of Mrs. Harris, which He Feared He'd Lost:

They sat across the table from one another as they had a thousand times before. His eyes drank in the natural oak table with its strong lines that showed so many shades of difference, and its worn but comfortable edges. It was still strong, still useful, something that could be relied on now and in the future. And somehow, through the years, as it took on the patina of time, it had become more beautiful.

A Passive-Aggressive Mr. Harris is Finally Moving Toward Taking Action Against His Domineering Wife:

They sat across the table from one another as they had a thousand times before. God how he hated that table—had always hated that table. But she had wanted it, had to have it, said it reminded her of home. Like this wasn't home, after twenty-three years in this house. And of course he'd gone along with it, as he always went along with whatever she wanted. But those days were over. For good. In fact, he'd go to the furniture store. Tonight. On the way home from work. And get this monstrosity out of his life.

Setting as Red Herring

Sometimes in mystery stories setting can be used as a sleight-of-hand device to mislead readers into a false set of assumptions.

Let's say one of our suspects has a wall lined with medieval weapons. Later we find a victim shot with the crossbow that was so prominently featured in the weapons display but which now is missing. Naturally, suspicion falls to the medieval weapons expert.

Moving Characters to Different Locations or Points in Time

As your story progresses characters will need to move to different locations and points in time to further the story or to dramatize past events that have importance to the present-time of the story.

Changing Location

Don't fall into the new writer trap of following your characters as they move from scene to scene unless it contributes to the story. We don't need to see your character take the bus home, check the answering machine, shower and shave, and then drive to the location of the next scene, unless those items are important components of the story. Usually they are not.

Instead, simply place your characters where you want them with a logical transition. Don't worry, your readers will follow.

Transitions

Transitions within and between settings should be handled smoothly and with minimal disruption to the reading experience.

Standard phrases, such as "later that evening" or "the next morning" make an easy way to move your character forward within the story and to a different scene and setting.

"Oh, come on Tom. You never come out with us on our Friday night rampage," Mary said as she slipped her time card into the factory punch-clock.

"I don't know, Mary. I'll see. Okay? If I'm there, I'm there."

Mary flashed him her usual exasperated look.

Later that evening, freshly shaved and smelling of talc, Tom stood outside Planet Action, his ears assaulted by the frantic music blaring into the night, trying to summon the courage to go inside.

"The hiatus" consists of simply skipping four lines between paragraphs and beginning the new scene. Some authors use a line with three asterisks centered on it, placing a blank line above and below that line.

Flashbacks and Flash Forwards

Good stories often begin *in medias res*, in the middle of the action. We don't want to bog down the opening of a story with a lot of background exposition. However, at some point a certain amount of background information may have to be conveyed to the reader so current events in the story can be put in perspective. In that case a flashback can be used.

Flashbacks should be used sparingly so you don't lose your readers by pulling them away from the forward progress of a story.

A flashback is a scene that occurs in a time previous to the present-time of the story, but which relates to present events. One of the best and most effective ways to integrate a flashback uses a sensory experience occurring in the present time of the story to ease the character into recalling the past event in a way that seems logical and natural in the context of the story. There are four elements to this type of flashback:

1. *The reflection phase*—The character in the present-time of the story sees, feels, tastes, hears, or smells something that triggers an association in his mind.

2. *The character remembers*—The sensory experience reminds the character of a significant event in his past which has relevance to the current story.

3. *The flashback unfolds*—The flashback scene is described as though it were happening in the current time of the story. The

flashback is closely focused on showing the reader only the information needed. Any digression or attempt to cover too much risks pulling the reader's attention away from the main story.

4. *The flashback closes*—The character's thoughts return to the present time of the story bringing the flashback to an end. A transitional phase or sentence cues the reader of the return to the present time. In the passage below, "The train lurched," serves this purpose.

In the following you can see first three of these elements at work:

Paul sat back and nestled his head into the cushion. The gentle rocking and the clickety-clack of the wheels against the rails brought some much needed rest to his troubled mind as the *City of New Orleans* made its way toward Memphis. It seemed like just yesterday he'd sat like this becoming one with the rhythm of the rails, but it had been almost three years now that he'd taken the *City* in the opposite direction toward Chicago.

What a shock that first taste of the windy city had been. As he carried his bags toward the escalator leading up from the platform in Chicago's Union Station that late summer morning, he couldn't help but notice a woman, two people in front of him. She was tall, but not overly so, with long hair the golden color of a ripe peach that seemed to bounce in rhythm with each step that she took. Her hair streamed halfway down a turquoise blouse tucked into a pair of jeans just tight enough to accentuate her assets, without seeming to advertise them. The jeans stove-piped over a pair of ostrich leather cowboy boots.

The rest of the flashback scene dramatizes Paul's introduction to the woman under unusual and slightly mysterious circumstances. At the conclusion, the fourth and final element of the flashback plays out, bringing Paul back to the present-time of the story. Note that the three months after their initial contact is merely summarized, because it's not relevant to the flashback or the overall story:

He looked at her and she at him, and he felt he should say something profound. "Welcome to Chicago," was what came out.

She seemed taken aback, but then she began to laugh, a deep rolling Julia Roberts kind of laugh, and then he began laughing, and in that strange, miserable, wonderful moment they connected. She took him home to her apartment in the Loop and three months later they were married.

He loved her with a ferocity that scared him. But now she was gone. A cryptic note saying she'd had to deal with a family emergency—she'd call when she got to Memphis. That had been two days ago. His calls to her cell phone and her mother's house went unanswered. His messages weren't returned. Something was wrong.

The train lurched. The conductor announced over the static filled public address system: "Now arriving Central Station, Memphis, Tennessee." He got up, retrieved his jacket and overnight bag from the luggage rack, and strode toward the door so he could be first off.

The Flash Forward—can be useful in both fiction and nonfiction, particularly in memoir, biography, true crime, and historical fiction to show the effect of current story events on future events, but instead of diverting from present-time to a scene from the character's past, we move to a scene from the character's future.

For example in the 1999 movie *Runaway Bride* about a woman renowned for leaving grooms at the altar, near the end we see that the main characters will indeed be married and live happily ever after through a series of flash forwards from the current time of the story.

A more often used technique is a variation that uses telling rather than dramatizing the flash forward in a full blown scene, as in the following:

Seven years from now, when he would face trial for treason, Paul would look back to this moment and say to himself that this is where it had all begun. But for now, he could think of nothing but the stacks of twenties in the open briefcase on his lap.

A well researched and realistically presented setting, and knowing how to move your characters through it in time and space, will add depth to your fiction, nonfiction, poetic, or dramatic writing and deepen your audience's appreciation and understanding of the story while making it more concise and readable.

Making It Real
Putting Your Words to Work

Take your pen and a notebook to a setting outside of your home. It could be to a park, a fast-food restaurant, a shopping mall, a city street, or anywhere else you choose. Spend about twenty minutes simply observing and taking it all in. Now write a description of the setting as though you were writing it for inclusion in your writing project. Make sure you use all of your five senses.

After you've written your description, go back and rewrite it through the eyes of someone who has just been betrayed by someone they loved. Notice how your perceptions of the setting change when viewed through the lens of emotion.

Part V

Forms of Writing

Chapter 19

Writing Fiction

Fiction is imaginary or real characters, interacting under pressure, within a setting, in an imaginary story where events are cause-and-effect related. A fictional story can be a complete fabrication with absolutely no basis in reality. Or it can be based on real events and real people but with the facts sufficiently reimagined that actual events and people are no longer recognizable.

Fiction is a contract between the writer and the reader wherein the reader agrees to suspend his disbelief in return for entertainment.

In return, the writer agrees to provide the reader with an entertaining work that is well written, well imagined, and that plays fair with the reader. By playing fair, I mean that there are no unbelievable coincidences within the plot or *deus ex machina* endings. Wikipedia, the free online encyclopedia (Wikipedia.org), an excellent resource for fiction writers, defines *deus ex machina* as a Latin phrase used to describe an unexpected, artificial, or improbable character, device, or event introduced suddenly in a work of fiction or drama to resolve a situation or untangle a plot (e.g., having the protagonist wake up and realize it was all a dream or an angel appear suddenly to deliver the denouement).

Size Defines the Form

The primary difference between a novel and a short story is…*ready, drum roll*…size. Short stories are short. Novels are long. In between the two are novellas. How short is short? Short stories generally run 12,000 words or less. Most short stories in magazines run anywhere from 2,500 words to 6,000 words. A very short story, called a short-short, runs 1,500 words or less. Before you submit your work to a publisher be sure to check its writer's guidelines which will tell you what type and size of stories the editors are looking for.

A work of fiction of 50,000 words or more is considered a novel. Most novels today range from 80,000 to 120,000 words.

The novella runs anywhere from 12,000 words to 50,000 words. Most magazines don't have the space for novellas so if you write novella, there are only a few markets open to publishing it. Usually novellas anchor a collection of short stories.

For our purposes here we'll limit our discussion to short stories and novels.

Novel vs. Short Story

Both short stories and novels employ plot, characters, setting, theme, and point of view but the similarity stops there. Generally a short story only has one plot line whereas a novel may have a main plot line and several subplots. A short story normally focuses on a small cast of characters. The novel can have an extensive cast of characters. In a short story the focus is most often from the viewpoint of a single character and employs a single point of view narrative. A novel can employ multiple points of view. A short story normally takes place within a limited time frame. A novel can cover both short and long time frames.

Genre/Category Fiction

Genre simply means a kind of literature dealing with a particular topic, setting, or issue. Genre is synonymous with category. Genre fiction is commercially successful because each genre has a dedicated audience. The various fiction genres include: mystery and crime; horror and occult; spy; romance; Westerns; action and thriller; science fiction and fantasy; mainstream fiction; and literary fiction. There are also subdivisions within a genre. Subgenres of science fiction include: hard science fiction, alien invasion, interstellar empire, interstellar war, space colonies, first contact, far future societies, mutants, post-holocaust, world disasters, utopias and dystopias, time travel, parallel worlds, alternate histories, and cyberpunk.

Some subgenres within mystery include private eye, police procedural, professional amateur, heists, capers, kidnappings, romantic suspense, tea cozies, and the locked room and other puzzles.

Genres and subgenres have their own rules, also called conventions, which the writer is expected to follow. For Westerns, cowboys and horses are common conventions; for mysteries, it's a murder or other crime and a professional or amateur detective.

It's okay to break some of the conventions, so long as you do it for a reason. However, doing so will likely make it more difficult for you to find a publisher. If publication is your goal, stick to the conventions until you have built a reputation with a publisher by establishing a readership. Had *Brokeback Mountain*, a short story which mixed the conventions of westerns, heterosexual love stories, and homosexual love stories, not been written by well-regarded writer Annie Proulx, it might never have seen mainstream publication nor been made into a movie.

Choosing a Genre

You should be well read in whatever genre you choose to write. It's important to know the key books, the premier writers, what's been done in the past, and what's being done in the genre now. This will save you from reinventing the wheel or plowing old ground. Also, it will enable you to spot what's missing, and where there is a need in the genre, a niche that you can fill. Some writers, like Isaac Asimov, have been successful writing in multiple genres, but they are the exceptions.

The Myth of Writing Only What You Know

In almost every writing book you open, or any writing class you take, sooner or later you'll see the phrase: Write what you know. This is generally good advice, but can be limiting to fiction writers.

To me, write what you know means know what you're writing about. That's not just a clever rephrasing. The difference may seem subtle, but it's not.

Traditionally, write what you know means write about those things with which you are personally familiar. If you are a nurse, writing about hospitals, working with doctors, and dealing with patients would be fair game. Likewise, any place you have personally spent some time is fair game for setting.

This is often too limiting and would mean that someone who has always lived in a city couldn't write convincingly about living in the country, or in the jungle, or the Arctic. Not true. That's what research is for.

Extrapolation also works. If you've ever experienced a culture clash, no matter how mundane, then you know something about all culture clashes. For example, let's say you join the PTA and you don't like the way the other parents run the organization and you say so. As a result they freeze you out of any meaningful involvement because they see you as the new troublemaker on the block.

Well, since you've been through this, you can extrapolate your experience to other situations. You can imagine, then, how it feels to be your lead character, the new pilot in the WWII bomber squadron, who clashes with the squadron crew about the way the airplanes are maintained. The emotion is real for you, it's only the setting that's different. The necessary details that will make your setting seem real, you can glean from reading about WWII maintenance of bombers.

Guidelines for Writing Fiction

Show More than Tell

Show, don't tell, in writing both fiction and nonfiction is another old adage you'll see and hear in writing books and classes. It's partially true. In fiction showing and telling both have their place, but showing should make up the preponderance of your short story or novel.

Showing means presenting the story in such way that the reader feels she is watching the story unfold. This is more interesting and entertaining for the reader and draws her actively into the story by allowing her to arrive at her own conclusions rather than simply being told what happened by the narrator.

Telling communicates information directly from the narrator to the reader. Telling keeps the story moving forward by providing information the reader needs to understand and enjoy the story but does not need to witness. Let's look at the difference by first showing and then telling about a brief encounter between Jenna and Jack.

Showing

As the bell sounded for break time, Jenna looked up and saw Jack standing in front of her desk.

"Come on, Jenna," Jack said, " I'll buy you an iced tea."

"Sure," Jenna said, hoping her face didn't betray her surprise. She couldn't remember Jack ever offering to pay for anything.

As they sat talking in a back corner booth of the cavernous cafeteria, Jenna had to suppress a smile when Jack smoothly slipped a couple of Splendas out of the little holder and into his shirt pocket, apparently for later.

Telling

Jack was the stingiest man in the factory, so Jenna couldn't believe it when Jack offered to buy her an iced tea.

In the "showing" version the reader observes in a brief vignette the interaction between Jenna and Jack and because Jenna is the viewpoint character, is privy to her thoughts. This enables the reader to conclude, without the narrator directly telling her, that one of the primary facets of Jack's character is frugality. Showing is best for revealing the character traits of major characters.

In the "telling" version the reader is simply told by the narrator that Jack is stingy and is told of Jenna's perception of his offer of an iced tea. Telling works best when used in scenes with minor characters or with peripheral information that is necessary to move the story along, but doesn't warrant a large investment of the reader's time.

Whether you show or tell depends on what purpose you are trying to achieve.

The essence of fiction writing is revealing the story to the reader in such way that the reader vicariously experiences the events along with the characters, including experiencing the emotions they experience. Showing works best when you want to convey these emotions to the reader. If the narrator simply tells the reader, "Jack nervously sat in the receptionist's office awaiting the interview," the reader understands what's happening on a conceptual level, and can empathize to the extent that we've all been in that position at one time or another. But look at the difference when we show the reader:

Jack shifted again in the big leather chair. He couldn't seem to get comfortable. He ran his fingers over this tie again to make sure it was straight. His eyes flicked again to the massive oak door to Mr. Johnson's office. He leaned forward, ready to jump up to greet him with a firm handshake, as the interview book had told him to. He rubbed his hands on his pants again to make sure they were dry. The receptionist had an annoying song playing on the radio on her desk just loud enough to distract him as he rehearsed again in his mind the five points he needed to make—you'd think she'd know better. It seemed stuffy in the room and Jack felt perspiration gathering on his forehead which he quickly toweled with his handkerchief. He looked to the door again. Was Johnson never going to get this going?

In watching Jack wait for his interview, the reader experiences Jack's nervousness right along with him and understands precisely what he's going through which will both enhance her reading experience and cause her to more closely identify with Jack and his struggle to achieve his goal.

Major story events and events that reveal character and emotion in the major players should be shown in scenes; minor events that simply provide information needed by the reader to follow the story and don't seek to impart emotion should be told in narration.

When Showing or Telling Use Concrete Nouns and Strong Verbs

Concrete nouns and strong verbs make your writing clear and unambiguous. Instead of using generic nouns like *room*, which could be any room, use concrete nouns like *bedroom* or *kitchen*, that leave no doubt in the reader's mind where the action is taking place and helps her visualize the story as she's reading.

- Not *flower* but *rose*.
- Not *house* but *split-level*.
- Not *drank a beer* but *slammed-down a Bud*.

When you tell, use strong, descriptive verbs. Look at the difference between "John went into the bedroom," and the following:

- John *entered* the bedroom.
- John *slipped* into the bedroom
- John *bounded* into bedroom.
- John *slithered* into the bedroom.
- John *crept* into the bedroom.
- John *erupted* into the bedroom.

Each has a different meaning and paints a different picture for your reader. This is enhanced with the use of concrete nouns: "John slithered into the bedroom," carries a different connotation from, "John slithered into the nursery."

Write in Scenes

Fictional stories are told in scenes connected and supplemented by narration. A scene is a self-contained unit that is a part of the story. A scene has a beginning, middle, and end. A scene should move the story forward in some way by advancing the plot, revealing character, or imparting important information. It should show the characters interacting with the setting and with one another in pursuit of their goals.

Narration may serve as a bridge between scenes and to summarize and relate less important but necessary events and information required to move the story forward.

In a well-written scene, readers will feel like they are witnessing the events of the story. This is the essence of show don't tell. Think of scenes in your writing the same way you view scenes in a film.

Look for Opportunities to Dramatize with Scenes

Reveal the significant events of your story via scenes with character interaction and dialog instead of simply telling the story via narration. The example below, which begins with narration and concludes with a scene, uses narration to summarize what has brought John to the point of possibly becoming a murderer and demonstrates how narration and scene work together.

In this case, it isn't necessary or practical to use scenes to lead up to the climax; narration works quicker to impart the information the reader needs. However, as John begins to act out his fantasies, his actions are best dramatized in a scene.

Narration—The thought of Mary remarrying had driven John nearly to the edge, but now he was back in control. They'd had so much together, so many good times. Tears filled his eyes as he thought about how often people remarked about the way they'd finish each other's sentences. They'd joke with one another about how they were soul-mates for life: salt and pepper, eggs and bacon, Adam and Eve, Bonnie and Clyde—John and Mary. He'd never felt that close to anyone before and knew he never would again.

Now he lived every day with a feeling in his gut like he'd swallowed shards of glass. If it hadn't been for her mother, the interfering bitch, they'd still be together. But that was okay. Now he was well on the way to fixing things. They'd be together forever, just as they'd always planned. He'd be the surprise guest at the wedding, but that wouldn't be the only surprise. Not by a long shot.

Scene—John crept through the rear door of the tiny chapel where Mary was already at the altar standing next to Ryan, that creep her mother had tricked her into marrying.

Good. All eyes were on the happy couple. No one seemed to take notice of him. He hurried to an empty folding chair near the aisle in the back of the crowded room.

Damn. Just as he was slipping into the chair, Mary's mother— Mother Grace as Mary called her, Mother-Effing-Grace, as John referred her when he wanted to stir Mary up—turned to speak to Mary's Aunt Joan sitting behind her. Her smile knotted into an angry slit when she caught sight of John.

Their eyes locked for a moment but John quickly averted his. He never could face her withering glare when he and Mary were married, and still couldn't. He felt his face flush and he began to perspire as the old anger welled up in him. He loosened his tie and unbuttoned his collar. *That's all right Bitch, I knew I'd be as welcome as a roach on a wedding cake. But don't you worry, Mother-Effing-Grace. After I give Mary and her new husband their presents, I've got one for you too. And maybe a little something left over for Aunt Joan as well.*

He slipped his right hand into the hip pocket of his brown corduroy jacket, the one Mary had said was her favorite because he looked so hot in it.

Now the fabric was worn at the cuffs, and an oily pizza stain on the lapel extended just beyond the white carnation with which he'd tried to cover it. But that, too, was okay. Mary would appreciate that he'd thought to wear it on her special day.

He slouched back in the chair, his legs crossed, ignoring the dirty look from a sixtyish woman he didn't know. She had a big nose and long skinny legs and was wearing a pink dress. A flamingo, that's what she was. A friggin′ flamingo.

Ryan was from Florida; this must be his Aunt Flamingo. He'd have something later for Aunt Flamingo, too. Meanwhile, he smiled and gave her a leering wink guaranteed to snap her eyes back to the altar. Bitch.

He wrapped his fingers around the Glock semiautomatic in his pocket and waited for the vows to be exchanged.

Read Your Scenes Out Loud

You should read your scenes out loud, listening to make sure you have developed dramatic tension and involved emotions and senses.

Remember, a good story is unveiled bit by bit by a careful release of details creating dramatic tension or suspense. Reread the section in Chapter 13 under the heading "Conflict and Suspense in *Titanic*" for a good example of this.

Revealing your character's emotions establishes motivation and gives us insight into your character. Providing sensory details creates depth and richness to your scenes.

Passages where dramatic tension, emotional involvement, or sensory experiences are called for but are missing will seem flat as you read the scene aloud. Mark these places for revision.

Use Symbolism

Don't be afraid to use symbolism in your stories. It is another way of showing without telling. A symbol is an image used in a story that carries multiple layers of meaning. Symbols are often an object used to reinforce the story or its theme. A crumbling house may decline in direct relation to the decline in the relationship of the couple living within.

In *The Picture of Dorian Gray* by Oscar Wilde, the entire novel is built on the portrait of Gray which grows uglier and older, reflecting Gray's ongoing debauchery while he maintains youth and good looks. The portrait serves as a reminder of the effect each foul act has on his soul.

Usually symbolism is more subtle. For example, in one of my short stories, the lead character, an elderly woman who is narrating the story, tells us about how, many years ago, she read the telegram notifying her of her husband's death in WWII while sitting on one of the roots of the giant oak tree under which she first met him, and where he later proposed to her. She says:

> "That spring, we had another drought, and the leaves come in all stunted and the branches had a bad case of droop. That was the saddest looking tree I ever seen. It took a very long time, but that's a strong tree with good roots, and little by little, season by season, it came back to its old self."

The tree's recovery is symbolic of her own recovery.

Beginnings, Middles, and Ends

There are very few hard and fast rules in writing, and all of them can be broken for good reason, such as using poor grammar in a character's dialog if that is the way the character would normally speak. While a piece of writing does not necessarily have to begin at the beginning and finish at the end, as a new writer trying to break into the commercial markets, you would do well until you get established to have beginnings, middles, and ends to your fiction writing projects.

Create a Narrative Hook—the Beginning

In fiction the objective of the narrative hook is to incite curiosity about what is going to happen in the story or pose a question that has to be answered. In a short story the main character, the problem the character has a need to resolve, the antagonist, and conflicts the character faces are introduced as early as possible. In a novel there is more leeway in time to introduce these elements, but it's a good idea to introduce them as early as possible until you get more experienced as a writer.

All writers must capture the audience's attention quickly or risk losing them. Don't waste time with a lot of lead-in material that sets up your beginning—what writers and editors refer to as "clearing your throat."

Begin in *medias res*, in the middle of the action. Take the reader to the interesting stuff, the question that the piece will answer, the hook that will keep the reader captivated. You can always flash back to the setup or provide the information through narrative and dialog if needed.

Introduce Complications to Create Tension—the Middle

The middle of a fiction story is largely taken up with the primary character's attempts to move toward his goal by overcoming increasingly difficult obstacles leading to the climax. As we discussed in Chapter 13, the protagonist overcomes an obstacle only to have the rug jerked out from under him, and then has to face another bigger obstacle.

Don't be afraid to set a clock ticking. A bomb set to go off, a deadline on a ransom demand, default on a loan if not paid by a certain time, a looming opening night for a theatrical performance are all techniques writers use to raise the stakes and increase the pressure on the protagonist and the suspense for the reader.

Make every word count in short stories. The middle of a short story is where things can begin to sag. Every word and every paragraph must move the story forward or contribute to character development. If you have a word, a paragraph, or an entire scene, that can be cut without it being missed, cut it, no matter how beautifully it may be written or how proud of it you may be.

Resolve Central Conflict—the Ending

At the end of the story the situation is resolved, one way or the other, and the loose ends are tied up. The protagonist either achieves his goals or he doesn't.

Tips to Make Fiction Writing Easier

- Use maps to be consistent when writing about locations within your narrative. Get maps of real places from Internet map sites

or chambers of commerce. For made-up locations draw a map yourself. This will help orient you within your fictional setting.
- Keep a pad next to you to make notes that occur to you while you're writing and to keep track of things like names of minor characters.
- Begin wherever it makes the most sense for you to begin. That can be at the end, at the middle, or at the beginning. Many novelists, and almost all mystery writers, begin at the end, so they know how the story will be resolved, and then go back and create the events leading up to that ending.
- If your novel or short story isn't working, try shifting the point of view from third person to first person or vice versa. Or consider telling your story from a different character's point of view.
- Remember to cluster or freewrite if you have difficulty with the beginning, the middle, or the end, character development, or any time you feel stuck.

Finding Story Ideas

Ideas for stories are everywhere if you know where to look. You can find ideas in news articles, in stories told by friends, or by simply being interested in an issue and wanting to explore it further in a fictional setting.

Asking "What if?" is a great way to develop stories. What if John Kennedy had not been assassinated? What if the director of the Drug Enforcement Agency became addicted to pain killers? What if I'm a psychologist who hates listening to his patients' constant whining? What if the space shuttle comes back with a stowaway virus on board? What if I'm a single parent who desperately needs a raise, but I'm too shy to ask?

Developing a Plot from Scratch

To illustrate story development, I'll explain how to develop a plot outline for a short story where the stakes would be low from an objective point of view, but high from the character's point of view.

In my clippings file, I have an article I'm saving as background for a story I plan to someday write about the carnies who work the rides and game booths at traveling carnivals. What catches my eye, though, is not the carnies but the mention in the article of a blue ribbon awarded to the winner of a pie baking contest.

So let's try to come up with a dramatic situation in which our protagonist has a strong need to win a blue ribbon in the pie baking contest.

For us to justify this as our protagonist's goal we have to ask: Why would someone need to win a pie baking contest? So our problem is: How can we raise the stakes so that winning the pie baking contest makes sense as a strong and understandable motivation for our lead character, and as a need with which our readers can sympathize?

Well, we would need to have a character for whom winning the baking contest would be a symbol or a key to meeting a deeper need. As I develop a cluster about the various possibilities, it strikes me that this is a good opportunity for a classic "fish out of water" story. This type of story involves a character thrust into a new setting and set of circumstances which is alien to her and to which she must adapt. Think of Mark Twain's *The Prince and the Pauper*, where a young prince switches clothes with a poor boy and they live each other's lives for a time; or maybe you're more familiar with the recycling of that plot into the Eddie Murphy comedy film *Trading Places*. Dorothy in *The Wizard of Oz* is a fish out of water story as well.

I'll add credibility by setting the story in the 1890s in a rural area, a time and place when competition in county fairs was taken very seriously.

For the back story let's say our lead character is Tracy Flynn, a woman whose dominant characteristic is her determination. Her dominant need is to be with and interact with other people. She can be headstrong, but she needs to be needed and loved. This contrasts with her dominant character flaw, which is that she's very shy.

Tracy was born and raised in Chicago and works at the commodities exchange there. Through her job she meets and falls in love with a cattle rancher from Texas; they subsequently marry. She gives up the life she has known to live with him at his ranch.

She finds the isolation intolerable, despite her shyness. In Chicago she had friends and coworkers. She finds she misses, even needs, the company of other women. She joins a local church, which has a women's group. Her need to be with others causes her to overcome her dominant flaw, her shyness, to attend a meeting of the group.

This is where our actual story begins. I'll sprinkle in the back story as necessary through narration or dialog as the story progresses, but rather than begin with a lot of back story, we want to begin at the inciting incident, *in medias res*, in the middle of things, which in this story can either be Tracy coming to her decision to join the group or the first time she attends a meeting. I'll choose the first meeting.

Waiting for the meeting to start, the members socialize and our heroine meets several nice people who find her big-city background and that she held a job outside of the home fascinating. However, this attention to Tracy seems to displease Mandy Detweiler, the chairman of the group, who in our story will play the role of the antagonist. Mandy's strongest need is for acceptance and acclamation; her most significant flaw is that she seeks that acceptance by bullying others. Mandy, not too subtly, puts the newcomer down. The others take their cue from Mandy and turn a cold shoulder to Tracy.

As the meeting progresses we learn that the club takes a great deal of pride in amassing more blue ribbons than the other ladies' clubs. People begin volunteering for different contests: flower arranging, spice growing, arts and crafts, and so on. Tracy, the city girl, not knowing anything about growing things, yet wanting to fit in, impulsively volunteers for the pie baking contest, thinking that because she's baked a birthday cake or two, how hard could a pie be? Thus, she takes action to overcome an obstacle, but in the process creates another, bigger obstacle. She does not know that winning the blue ribbon in pies has been Mandy's province for the past three years.

At first the other members are stunned and surprised, but weary of Mandy's domination, some of them encourage Tracy and she begins to feel acceptance. Mandy makes an argument that they should each compete in a different contest, but one woman says: "Come on, Mandy. Give the new girl a chance." Others murmur their agreement.

Sensing the way things are going, but not one to give in, Mandy suggests that they both submit pies and may the best person win. After some discussion, as usual, the others acquiesce to Mandy's domination.

This is another setback for Tracy because now she will have to compete for acceptance, and this contest with the group's leader will put her in the limelight she hates. Worse, she knows that if she loses to Mandy she'll always be the outsider. The only way to get what she most wants is to beat Mandy in the contest.

You get the idea. From here on we'll have a series of escalating obstacles as the plot rises toward the crisis which our readers know will be the inevitable face-to-face confrontation between Tracy and Mandy.

But on the way to that climax our lead character undergoes a series of escalating complications. First Tracy has no pan or rolling pin. How will she compete? The one store in town, Swensen's general store, is very limited and out of baking pans and rolling pins which, given the distances in 1890s Texas, won't be restocked until after the contest.

All seems lost until Mary, one of the women Tracy met at the meeting, who appeared to Tracy to sense the warmth beneath her shy exterior, and who used to be the pie champion until Mandy nudged her out of the competition, a grudge she still holds against Mandy, loans Tracy the equipment she needs along with her prize-winning recipe for peach pie.

Tracy practices and practices, using her husband, some of the ranch-hands and Mary as the guinea pigs, initially making a mess of things but getting better each try. Tracy can sense a friendship growing with the older woman as Mary mentors her in the kitchen.

A crisis occurs when Mary relates to Tracy that Mandy stopped by Mary's house, ostensibly on a friendly visit, but making it clear to Mary that if she allows her special recipe to be used, Mandy will see to it that her husband, who owns the bank, makes credit difficult for Mary's husband's livestock buy next year. Tracy is torn between her determination to win and her empathy for Mary and her husband. All seems lost and Tracy is about to give up when she and Mary come up with a plan to adapt Mary's recipe to an apricot pie, thus avoiding Mandy's threat. She and Mary head to town and buy up all the apricots on Mr. Swensen's shelf, eight jars. We make a note here to check the Internet to make sure there were jars of fruit available in stores at the time our story is set (there were).

Another minor crisis occurs when the first pie tastes terrible. But they experiment with the ingredients and by the Wednesday before Friday's contest, Tracy's confidence is at an all time high. Her practice has paid off. All agree Tracy's pies are so good she can't possibly lose.

Not willing to trust anything to chance, and determined as ever, Tracy and Mary go into town to get their supplies. Tracy is secretly relieved when she sees that there's plenty of everything she needs but distressed to run into Mandy who is there for her own supplies.

As Tracy is taking her basket of supplies out to the wagon, Mandy makes some humiliating comments. Tracy, being shy, can't think of an appropriate retort. She begins to cry and in her rush to leave the store drops the basket, causing more commotion, which makes her even more embarrassed. She leaves the basket where it fell with all of her supplies in it and gets into her wagon. She is ready to quit the contest and go home but Mary calms her down. She and Mary go for tea at the hotel where Tracy recovers. She is humiliated, but more determined than ever to win the contest.

When they return to the store, Mr. Swensen has Tracy's basket behind the counter for her, but the glass jar of apricots has broken and there are no more left because Mandy bought the remaining supply to sabotage her. This is the crisis moment. There's no way Tracy can win the contest now. But now Tracy is angry and determined not to go down without a fight. She buys the only fruit left—blueberries—and her determination drives her to spend the rest of the day and long into the night baking and testing.

On Friday, exhausted and depressed, but not defeated, Tracy brings her blueberry pie to the judging table. Mandy has a knowing grin on her face as the judges sample her apple pie and nod their heads. As the judges sample other pies, tension builds. They finally get to Tracy's pie and nod their heads in a similar way to the way they did when sampling Mandy's.

The grin has left Mandy's face. The judges go to the end of the table to confer, and it seems to Tracy an eternity until they make up their minds. They announce that the winner is:

Mandy.

Tracy's heart sinks; all is lost. Mary puts her arm around Tracy to console her.

Mandy, at the head of the table, smiling and blue ribbon in hand, awaits the congratulations of her club members. But none come to her. Instead they gather around Tracy and Mary, and they too console Tracy. It's clear that they all care about her. Tracy learns that after she left the store, some of the other women in the group had gone to Swensen's, and he told them what had happened. Tracy has lost the battle but won the war.

She looks across to where Mandy stands, stunned and weeping. Tracy, empathetic as always, feels her pain. She walks over and puts a consoling hand on Mandy's shoulder. The other women surround them both. End.

Plotting outline done.

(For insight into achieving success with fiction, see the interview with Richard Bausch in "Interviews with Professional Writers" at the back of this book.)

Making It Real
Putting Your Words to Work

Pick one part of the plot outline for the pie-baking story and write a scene to dramatize it. Use dialog and narration and make sure you involve as many of the five senses as possible.

If fiction is your primary writing interest, try your hand at putting flesh to the bones created above by writing the complete short story.

Chapter 20

Writing Nonfiction

In the old days traveling circuses pitched a gigantic tent, called the big top, under which the audience would watch all manner of acts performing: jugglers, high wire acts, trapezes, and clowns. Elephants seemingly as big as houses were brought under control and exhibited; wild lions and tigers bared their fangs and vastly outnumbered the lone lion tamer sharing their cage, yet yielded to his commands; bears danced, and dog and pony shows were performed. Impossible yet true feats were accomplished in full view of a live audience who were variously educated, thrilled, amused, scared, and most of all, entertained. Deception, trickery, and lies had no place there, and were banished to the side show, outside the big tent.

In writing, nonfiction is the big top. You'll find all manner of things to educate, thrill, amuse, scare, and entertain your readers: you'll find gossip on Britney Spears; a biography of Teddy Roosevelt; an exposé of the CIA; diatribes filled with hate; directions for launching your own tax-exempt church; a primer on finding true love; conflicting opinions voiced by politicians, pundits, and scholars; and the full scoop on how to build a birdhouse or keep your lawn green. A front row seat to sometimes amazing but true feats, all performed in full view of the audience under the big top of nonfiction.

And, like under the circus' big top, deception, trickery, and lies have no place here.

Types of Nonfiction

Nonfiction writing is designed to explain, argue, reference, or describe real events. In nonfiction, the events written about have to have happened in the real world. Conjecture and supposition must be labeled as such. Feature articles, memoirs, travel articles, essays, op-ed pieces, self-help, how-to, cookbooks, biographies, and reference books find their home here.

Essays

An essay is a brief piece of writing focusing on a particular subject. Essays may be narrative (tells a story), persuasive (attempts to move the reader to take an action or convince the reader to embrace a belief), expository (explains, shows, or informs about the topic), descriptive (imparts a sensory image of something), or some combination of these.

Essays range from affecting personal experience essays to op-ed and opinion pieces.

In choosing subject matter for an essay, you should think about topics you feel passionate about, or topics about which you have some expertise. Expertise does not necessarily need to come from formal training. If you've been a parent for a couple of years, you're expert enough to write a credible essay about parenting. No matter what type of essay you're writing, bring passion and emotion into it.

- When writing opinion pieces, it's useful to raise the arguments in opposition to your point to show why they don't measure up. Otherwise, your reader may be raising these same objections in her mind, but without the benefit of your insights. Also, when you are advocating a position, show the reader what it means to her if your recommendation is not adopted.
- When writing a personal essay, unless it's about intangible concepts like truth or justice, bring in the senses to make your reader feel, smell, and taste as well as visualize your subject matter.

- When writing essays to inform, it's important to put things in context. Tell readers why this is important. If you're writing for a particular group of insiders who would know the context, such as readers of a trade journal, you can make reference to the context, expecting they will know it. But, if you're writing for the general public, you must provide the necessary background, definition of terms, and context so readers understand the point you are trying to make.
- When writing essays about historical events, an unusual location or occupation, or anything else out of the ordinary, accurately rendering the setting is critically important. Bring the reader inside your topic. Let the reader vicariously understand what it was like to experience whatever it is that you're writing about by bringing the five senses to bear.

Articles

Articles include feature articles, personality profiles, self-help articles, and many other types of articles written for periodicals or websites. Articles can be on any topic. The length of the article usually determines the scope: The shorter the article, the narrower the scope. Many articles include interviews with authorities and individuals with a unique slant or particular knowledge of the topic, and may include illustrative anecdotes and case histories. Articles should include the answers to the reporter's questions: who, what, when, where, why, and how.

Articles are usually assigned by an editor to a writer with whose work the editor is familiar, or on the basis of a query letter from a writer proposing to do the article (See "Example of a Query Letter for an Article" at the back of this book). Often the editor will provide direction about the slant or angle to be taken and other aspects of the article.

The nut graph is a powerful technique borrowed from journalism that helps to center the reader and focus the writer. It answers the reader's WIIFM question (What's In It For Me?).

Were you to sum up the point of your article in a single line, that would be the nut graph. Nut graphs add context and significance. The nut graph is used when the lead is anecdotal or indirect.

Say the lead begins with a descriptive Amazon jungle scene, describing the overall setting in vivid detail then zeroing in on a small

Memoirs

A memoir is a story from the writer's past. It differs from autobiography in that a memoir deals with a slice of time, or a segment in a life, or an event, rather than an entire life. Usually written in first person, memoirs are most successful when they use individual personal circumstances and emotion to convey universal issues to which readers can relate.

Memoirs often chronicle the darker periods in a life. We can all relate to having dark periods, but, when we read about those of others, we realize that we're not alone in having problems and maybe our life isn't so bad after all. Memoirs also show how one person coped with major issues, helping readers to learn to cope with their own.

exotic plant found nowhere else on the planet but that particular part of the jungle. A following paragraph, the nut graph, would describe the significance of the scene: When harvested and ground up, the plant produces a lifesaving drug, but logging threatens that part of the forest unless readers take action now to help save it.

The use of a nut graph brings an eye-catching lead into context, lets the reader know where the article is going, and helps focus the writer to deliver on the inherent promise of the article. The nut graph gets its name because the paragraph gives the reader what the article is about "in a nutshell."

The central part of the article will serve up the examples, anecdotes, research, or interviews the writer has collected in support of the piece and consistent with the promise of the nut graph. We'll talk more about the structure of articles later in this chapter when we discuss beginnings, middles, and ends.

Books

Nonfiction books cover a wide variety of topics including memoir, biography, self-help, how-to, gardening, history, sports, child care, diet, cookbooks, true crime, and reference. Writing a book is a major commitment of time and energy. You'll be spending months, maybe years, researching and writing so, to sustain you through the days and nights ahead, choose a topic about which you are passionate.

Nonfiction Beginnings, Middles, and Endings

In writing any nonfiction, from article to book, you'll need:

- To engage your reader with a strong lead.
- Provide the information you, as the writer, wish to impart.
- Close in a way that brings the piece together and satisfies the reader's needs.

Create a Lead—the Beginning

The first part of a nonfiction piece is called the lead. The lead is similar to the hook in fiction. The objective is to get the reader's attention and to pique her interest sufficiently that she will continue reading.

You have only a few opening paragraphs to do this work.

Successful leads used in nonfiction include:

- *An unusual or shocking statistic.* The statistic must be eye-catching and relate directly to the subject. An article or a book focusing on a perceived breakdown in family values since the good old *Ozzie and Harriet* and *Leave It To Beaver* days of our childhood might begin with a statement that, in the 1950s, the percentage of births out of wedlock was less than 5 percent; today one in three children are born out of wedlock. The object is to surprise or shock the reader into reading more.
- *A promise.* Articles and books often begin by implying that, if the reader reads the work, she will learn how to do a something or how to solve a problem. Often a book or article's title will make this implied promise.
- *A compelling anecdote.* Like the statistical lead, the anecdote must link closely to the subject. A biographical article or book might begin with an anecdote that reveals the essence of the subject of the biography, and then go on to show how those characteristics were developed or came into play

in other situations. A self-help book on how to stop smoking might have an anecdote illustrating the consequences for not stopping or, conversely, illustrating the positive outcome for someone who had.

- *A quotation.* Like the statistical and anecdotal leads, an apt quotation, usually from an expert or famous person, works to grab the reader's attention. Some writers will also begin each chapter with a quotation to signal the intent and content of the chapter.
- *A question.* Opening with a pithy question can be a good way to engage the reader, particularly if the subject of the piece is weighty. A piece on protecting the reader's family in the post-9/11 world might begin with the question, "Would you know how to protect your family in the face of a 9/11-type attack in your city?"

Make the Case—the Middle

The middle of a nonfiction piece is where the beef is. It's where the information you are delivering to the reader is fortified, expanded upon and explained, using examples, research, anecdotes, and expert testimony. The middle delivers on the implied promise made to the reader in the lead or the title.

The length and what is included in this middle is greatly dependant on the nature and format of work you are writing. This is where your how-to will teach the reader how; your biography will reveal the subject's life; and, your cookbook will deliver dinner. Bon appétit!

Wrap it Up—the Ending

The end can be a call to action, a summary, a reflection on what has been said, a motivational pep talk, or anything else that satisfies the reader. Here are some ways to end your work:

- *Summarize.* Don't merely encapsulate what you've already said. Describe what it all means.
- *Quote.* Find a quotation that brings your topic together in the context of the bigger picture.

- *Circle back.* Bring your reader back to what you said in the beginning by finishing a thought for which you had laid the foundation and which helps to make your point. For example, in a self-help book about anger management, you may have begun with an anecdote about Jim who was sentenced to attend an anger management class because of a road rage incident. At the end, you'll refer back to Jim and complete the thought by saying something like: "Today when Jim is in heavy traffic, he does the relaxation exercise that Dr. Torres taught him. Now his biggest problem isn't the drivers around him, it's trying to stay awake, because he's so relaxed." This is a very effective technique.
- *Point the direction.* Use the evidence you've collected to point the reader in a particular direction or to show what the future holds if the trend you described continues. This is similar to the summary close.

Conducting Interviews

From time to time you'll need to conduct interviews with key witnesses or authorities in the field. This lends your piece an aura of current expertise you simply can't get from library books, the Internet, or other static resources. Further, it personalizes and enlivens your project by putting a human face on it.

Don't be afraid to make cold calls to experts or celebrities (or their PR representatives), who may have the information you need. People are amazingly helpful to writers, so never be shy about asking for the help you need.

Be Professional

If you are conducting an in-person interview, be on time and appropriately dressed. When asking someone to take the time to speak with you, you owe them the respect of not showing up for the interview in a sweat suit, with your grandchild in tow, or in any other way that is not professional. I mention these because I have been interviewed by members of the press exactly as just described.

Research Your Source

Do your research before the interview. If your source is an expert, find out from the Internet such things as the subject in which she holds her degree, what she may have written about your topic, and if she has taken a position on your topic.

Ask Information-Provoking Questions

Ask questions that require the source to respond with more than one-word answers. For instance, don't ask: "Do you think your MBA has given you an advantage over other entrepreneurs?" This gives your source the option of simply answering "Yes" or "No." Ask your question this way: "What advantages has your MBA given you over other entrepreneurs?" This type of question will get the person talking and yield much more information.

Recording the Interview: Pros and Cons

Recording is great if you're a poor note taker, or if there's any likelihood your source will deny saying what she said, lie about what she said, or claim to have said something different from what she said. But there are downsides. Some interviewees freeze and totally clam up when they see a recorder. Others perform for the recorder and begin speaking in ways and saying things they would not say were the recorder not present. Also, if the interview has gone on for any length, there's an amazing amount of listening you have to go through to pull out the useful nuggets of information.

It's usually easier to simply write down the important things as you go along. If your source speaks too quickly ask them to slow down or simply say, "Can you hold on for one second while I catch up?" Most sources will understand.

Wrapping Up the Interview

At the end of the interview ask your source if you missed anything that should have been included or if there's anyone else with whom you should speak on this topic. If so, ask if they are willing to introduce you to that individual. Alternatively, ask if you can use the source's name as a reference to help you get you foot in the door when you call.

Source Approval

When conducting an interview that will be quoted extensively, such as in a celebrity profile or the interviews at the back of this book, unless your name is Woodward or Bernstein, allow your source to read and correct what will go into the final piece.

Now I know some writers, particularly journalists, will think that's terrible advice, but unless you're trying to catch someone with their own words, what is there to lose?

In fact, there's a lot to be gained by putting an interviewee at ease by saying, "I want to assure you that you will have final approval of the language that goes into the article or book with regard to what you tell me."

Make sure you build in time for the source to review the material and get it back to you. Set a cutoff date so as not to jeopardize your own deadline.

Of course, you're not going to give your source prepublication approval if your book is an exposé or there's some other reason to believe that the source may renege on what they told you. But as a beginning writer, I don't think you'll find yourself in that position. And presumably by the time you find you're writing such serious nonfiction pieces, you'll have the experience to know how to handle it. When in doubt, check with your editor.

The 5B Method of Organizing Research Material

I developed the 5B method to keep control of the voluminous amounts of material I found myself collecting to use in writing books. The 5B method consists of taking five steps: boxing, browsing, batching, bundling, and building.

Boxing—Cut out articles or collect snippets of information from websites. Attach Post-It notes to remind yourself of why you are saving each item. Drop all of this into one small box labeled with the project's working title.

Browsing—As you're preparing to write, look through all of your notes to get an overall impression, to detect patterns, and to get a feel for what the layout and structure of your book should be.

Batching—When you're ready to write, go through the box of clippings and batch them into appropriate chapters and drop those into a labeled file—one for each chapter. Sometimes the batching process will reveal a new chapter that needs to be created. Add new material to the appropriate files as you come across it.

When it's time to write a chapter, read through the material you've collected for that chapter, thinking about how the material fits together Put the clippings away before you write to make sure that the writing comes out in your own words. After writing, go back to make sure you've gotten the facts right.

Store the file with the clippings you used so they will be available if you have to verify facts for the publisher's fact-checker. Put whatever you didn't use into a box for a potential new book, a box for potential articles, or dispose of it.

Bundling—As your writing progresses, bundle the chapters together in a loose-leaf notebook in chapter order. This makes it easy to read from beginning to end to see what's missing, what needs major revision, and if the organization and structure hold up. Now is the time to conduct additional research or interviews as needed to plug any holes you discover.

Building—Finally, build the book by adding the front matter (acknowledgments, dedication, table of contents, etc.) and back matter (bibliography, appendices, glossary, etc.).

For Additional Help

We've only had time to touch on the few types of nonfiction that are the most common. To find information and books about every conceivable type of nonfiction writing check out asja.org. This is the website of the American Society of Journalists and Authors. Founded in 1948, it is the nation's leading organization of independent nonfiction writers. It holds a wealth of information for writers of nonfiction including pay survey information and past copies of the ASJA monthly newsletter which is chock full of useful articles about nonfiction writing. You'll find additional resources in the back of this book.

(For insight into writing nonfiction see the interview with Donna Boetig in "Interviews with Professional Writers" at the back of this book.)

Making It Real
Putting Your Words to Work

Make a list of ten areas in which you have some expertise, do something well, or have a lot of experience with. The areas could range from parenting, to fishing, to shopping, to traveling, to pursuing a hobby, whatever. Pick the one you know the most about. Do some clustering or freewriting on that topic to explore your range of knowledge about it. Sometimes we can be surprised about how much we know without realizing it. Develop an outline for an article you can write to pass on some of your knowledge about this topic.

Chapter 21

Writing Poetry

After a great deal of thought I decided to include poetry because the techniques we've covered in this book for use in fiction and nonfiction prose are intrinsic to poetry and drama as well. The similarities outweigh the differences and writers of prose, poetry, and drama each have much to learn from exploring the methods and techniques, and the freedoms and constraints, of the other.

I don't consider myself a poet but I enjoy writing poetry from time to time and sometimes it fits what I'm trying to express in ways that other forms do not. Also, while I'm not at all fond of puzzles, least of all word puzzles, anagrams, crossword puzzles, and so on, I do enjoy trying to write structured forms of poetry because it's a challenge to express what I'm trying to say within the confines of a very specific structure. And while I can't prove it, I feel poetry gives me a more flexible approach to my other writing.

Poetry Examined

Poetry is one of the ancient arts. It was practiced by the ancient Greeks and Romans and can be found in many places in the Bible. The English poet Samuel Taylor Coleridge, who wrote *The Rime of the Ancient Mariner*, defined prose as "words in their best order" and poetry as "the best words in their best order." Nobel prize-winning poet T. S. Eliot said, "Poetry may make us from time to time a little more aware of the deeper, unnamed feelings to which we rarely penetrate."

Poetry Without Rules

We won't spend much time defining poetic terms. Poetry, because it can be so precise as to the words used, how they are placed on the page, how they sound, how they look, how many syllables they have, how a line ends, and so on, has its own extensive jargon.

Many people who might otherwise enjoy writing poetry are intimidated by what they perceive as the rules of poetry. But you can enjoy reading and writing poetry without becoming too involved with technicalities. This tendency toward intimidation primarily exists because the majority of poets we studied in high school were English poets from the 1700s and 1800s who used rhyme and verse to get their message across. As a result it's not unusual to see someone today trying to write a poem by using overly formal and archaic language based on what they learned in school. But this is not what poetry is all about. It's about communication, using today's language to communicate with today's readers.

Poetry is for expressing yourself, and if you feel you'd like to capitalize the first word in every line, as you did in school, go ahead. If not, then don't. If you want to work in a poetic form with rules, there are plenty to choose from—we'll talk about some later. If you'd prefer to work free-form, that's okay. Rhyme or don't rhyme, your choice.

Forms of Poetry

In poetry the emphasis is on how things are said as well as what is said. Poems may be formal and structured or informal and loosely structured; they may be rhymed or unrhymed. In poetry words are selected for their beauty and sound as well as their meaning. The words of a poem are usually sensory, intense, and emotion laden. Poetry uses concrete images and vivid phrases to evoke an emotional response in the reader.

Structured vs. Unstructured

Structured poetry follows a specific pattern. Examples of structured poems are sonnets, sestinas, and haiku. Unstructured poetry does not require a pattern. Prose poems and free verse are examples of unstructured poetry.

Rhymed vs. Unrhymed

Rhyme is the repetition of sounds. We are most familiar with what is called perfect rhymes. Perfect rhymes are different words that have an almost identical sound quality, for example, *cat* and *hat, house* and *mouse*. There are several other types of rhymes, but for our purposes all we need to know is that unless we are writing a formal type of poetry, like a sonnet, it doesn't matter if there's rhyme in a poem at all. In fact most modern poetry is free verse which does not rhyme.

Formal, Structured Poetry

All formal, structured poetry, both rhymed and unrhymed, contains the following:

Stanza—a stanza is a unit of poetic lines. A stanza consisting of two lines is called a couplet; a stanza with three lines is called a tercet; one with four lines is a quatrain. A six line stanza is a sestet.

Syllable—a unit of pronunciation forming all or part of a word. For example, the word *beneath* has two syllables, *be* and *neath*. The word *microcosm* has three syllables, divided as follows: mi/cro/cosm.

Scansion—reading a line of poetry to determine the patterns of syllables.

Let's take a look at some poetry, just to see if you'd like to try it. Most of the examples are my own. They are not set forth as examples of good poetry; only as examples of the type of poetry I'm describing, and to show you that anyone can write poetry, formal or not, using modern themes and subjects.

Haiku

Haiku is a Japanese poem. It has seventeen syllables arranged in three lines. There are five syllables in the first and third lines and seven in the middle. Traditional haiku has some indication of the season. Haiku generally uses plain everyday language and doesn't worry about rhyming. Here's an example:

> Her scent on a breeze,
> Stirs memories of lost love.
> Gusts blow dreams away.

Do you see how scansion works? Let's identify the syllables in this poem. Count them.

> Her/ scent/ on/ a/ breeze,
> Stirs/ mem/ or/ ies/ of /lost /love.
> Gusts/ blow/ dreams/ a/ way.

As you can see there are five syllables in the first line, seven syllables in the second line, and five syllables in the third line.

Sonnet

Let's try something more formal, with rhymes—a Shakespearean sonnet. I'm sure you remember those from school. The sonnet is a fourteen-line poem, consisting of three quatrains (three four-line stanzas) and a concluding couplet (one two-line stanza) with a set rhyme and a set syllable scheme called *iambic pentameter*. Iambic pentameter is much easier to understand than it sounds. An iamb is simply a two-syllable set with the stress on the second syllable, so it sounds like: ta DAH. Pentameter, without getting into the definition of meters, simply means there are five of those iambs on each line so it sounds like: ta DAH, ta DAH, ta DAH, ta DAH, ta DAH.

The rhyme scheme for a Shakespearean sonnet is *abab cdcd efef gg*. That means the first line rhymes with the third, the second line rhymes with the fourth, the fifth with the seventh, the sixth with the eighth and so on.

Let me give you an example that will make things clear. Here's a Shakespearean sonnet, *Sonnet 130*, which you probably didn't read in school. It shows that Shakespeare had a sense of humor, yet managed to stay within the bounds and requirements of the sonnet form. In fact he's poking fun at love poetry here.

> My mistress' eyes are nothing like the sun;
> Coral is far more red than her lips' red:
> If snow be white, why then her breasts are dun;
> If hairs be wires, black wires grow on her head.
> I have seen roses damask'd, red and white,
> But no such roses see I in her cheeks;

And in some perfumes is there more delight
Than in the breath that from my mistress reeks.
I love to hear her speak, yet well I know
That music hath a far more pleasing sound;
I grant I never saw a goddess go;
My mistress, when she walks, treads on the ground:
And yet by heaven, I think my love as rare
As any she belied with false compare.

As you can see Shakespeare is writing a love poem, but poking fun at the false comparisons sometimes made in the poetry of his day.

If you examine the structure you'll see that there are fourteen lines, each consisting of five iambic syllable sets. The last word in the first line, *sun* rhymes with the last word in the third line, *dun*. The last word in the second line, *red* rhymes with the last word in the fourth line, *head*.

Now let's take a look at a modern sonnet. As you can see there's no stilted words, no archaic vocabulary, and it uses contractions. It fits the requirements for a sonnet with regard to the number of lines, iambic pentameter, and rhyme scheme. Sometime when you have some time try writing a sonnet of your own.

A Sonnet on Writing and Jogging

I often wonder why I want to write.
The pay's bad and writing's never easy.
Sometimes I have to stay up half the night,
Then spend the whole next day feeling queasy.
It reminds me of how it feels to jog.
When I'm running it always seems so hard:
I pound the pavement panting like a dog,
Then struggle back to collapse in my yard.
Still I struggle to do both every day,
Because the experts all seem to agree,
To succeed in these, the course you must stay,
And it's practice makes perfect is the key.
Seems whether you want to write or to run,
It's not so great to do, as to have done.

Sestina

Okay. Are you ready for a really big challenge? It's not for the timid. But, it is a good exercise in making words work the way you want them to. It's called a *sestina*. We'll take a look at the sestina and I promise after that we'll go to the much less structured, and much less difficult-to-write poetry of today: free verse and prose poetry.

A stanza of six lines is called a sestet, hence the name of the form: sestina. A sestina consists of six sestets, with a concluding tercet (stanza of three lines). No rhymes are required. The sestina form is thought to have originated with troubadours and later was popularized by the Italian poet Dante Alighieri. Now here's the tricky part—each stanza repeats the same six end words in the following sequence: $1 \rightarrow 2 \rightarrow 4 \rightarrow 5 \rightarrow 3 \rightarrow 6 \rightarrow 1$.

What that means is that the end word of line one of any stanza becomes the end word of line two of the following stanza. The end word of line two becomes the end word of line four of the following stanza, and so on. The choice of end words is yours to make. Again, it's easier understood by an example. In the sestina that follows, the six end words we'll be using are in this order in the first stanza:

1. travel
2. friends
3. love
4. studying
5. far
6. home

So the end word in line one, *travel* will become the end word in line two of the next stanza; the end word in line two of the first stanza, *friends* will become the end word in line four of the next stanza, and so on. It's okay to vary the end words slightly so travel can be traveling, studying can be study, and so on.

Travels with Charlotte

Charlotte always dreamed she'd someday travel
Throughout the world making new friends,

And, who knows, maybe find love,
In some exotic location, while studying
The flora and the fauna of some far
Distant land. The whole world would be her home.

National Geographics filled every corner of her home
As relentlessly she searched out the places she might travel,
On a bio teacher's salary, hoping to find a tour group far
Better than the rest: not too expensive and with a chance to
make new friends.
One night reading in her study,
A pile of brochures in her lap, she found the trip she knew that
she would love.

A safari in Rwanda, where, according to the brochure, people
who loved
To see wild animals, could visit Mighty Simba in his home.
And get up close to study
Herds of wildebeests, antelopes, and gazelles, then travel
Across the savanna to see other animal friends:
Monkeys, ostriches, and giraffes roaming near and far.

She cried at the airport. Her teacher friends had chipped-in for
binoculars far
Too expensive. Then she journeyed in an airplane, a boat, and a
car that she loved
The adventure of as it bounced on rutted roads. She made friends
With her fellow travelers, who told her about their homes,
And how far they'd had to travel,
And how much it had been worth it to have so many wild animals
to study.
One night as Charlotte sat by the campfire, studying
the itinerary, she heard a noise, at first far
Away but coming closer, the sound of footsteps traveling
In the dark. Suddenly, a band of soldiers who looked as if
they'd love

Nothing more than to slice her end to end, erupted from the forest and homed
Right in on Charlotte. It was clear they had no intention to be friends.

The guide stepped up and shouted "Don't hurt us, we come here as friends."
But the soldiers just ignored him. Charlotte noticed their leader studying
The pair of Zeiss binoculars hanging on her belt—the one from her friends at home.
She offered them to him and said, "With these you can see quite far."
He raised the glasses to his eyes and clearly loved
What he saw. He signed to the guide, who to his party said: "Time for us to travel."

Today Charlotte rarely ventures far from home.
She's happy reading in her study or going out with friends,
And talking of how there once was a time when she thought she'd love to travel.

There's no doubt about it: sestinas are a difficult form, but also fun to do and rewarding. I hope you'll take the time to try one.

Free Verse

Free verse is poetry of any line length, any stanza length, no meter (no counting syllables or concern for how they're stressed), and no rhyme, unless you choose to put rhyme into your poem.

I sometimes use free verse when I want to tell a story that's small and infused with emotion but which I feel is not of sufficient size to make a prose short story. I believe the compactness of poetry can make for a better result. Take a look at the following free verse poetry which has a narrative story and includes dialog, characterization, and many of the other techniques we've discussed in prose writing.

Semper Fi, Dad

Shauna, the three-year-old, came running today,
Carrying a prize so valuable

It took a moment to catch my breath.
"Whose ring, Mommy?" she said.

My voice almost cracked, I couldn't believe it.
"Honey, this is Grandpa's magic ring,
the one he lost last year when he was living here with us.
Remember?"
I could see my excitement reflected in her deep green eyes,
So like my Dad's.

"Where did you find it?"
No detective looking for clues,
Had ever spent more time,
Than had I looking for that ring.
"Inna toy chest," she said,
as if, of course, I should have known.

It must have fallen off Dad's finger,
He'd been losing so much weight.

"Magic?" she said.

For a moment her eyes were my Dad's,
All curiosity, wonder, and excitement.

"Yes, honey. Magic."
I told her how, when I was her age,
Grandpa would slip off this thick gold ring
With the red stone,
Upon which sat an eagle on a globe,
from his stubby farmer's finger,
And place it on my thumb,
where it was still too big,
And would roll around on my finger
Until we'd begin our game.
He'd always remind me this was

Not just any ring, but his magic

MARINE CORPS RING,

Uttering the words as if a sorcerer's incantation.
"If you wish on it," he would say,
"It can take you far, far away."

Then he'd remind me of how,
When he was living in the jungle,
He would blow on his ring and make his wish,
And it would bring him back to my Mom and me.

We'd sit on the floor,
Just he and I,
Facing each other.
I'd hold up my thumb,
and we'd both wish and blow,
And then be whisked to wherever we wanted to go.

We played in deserts fighting sheiks,
And battled pirates on deserted islands,
And even flew to the Land of Oz
Where we had tea with Dorothy
And the wizard.
"Can we do it, Mommy? Can we," my baby-girl said.
"Sure Baby, where should we go?"
"The jungle, the jungle," she screamed.

So we placed the ring upon her thumb,
And with all our might,
We wished and blew.

In our minds, to the jungle we flew.
And, I knew we'd see my Dad there too.

As you can see, free verse is very flexible and can accommodate almost anything you might want to write.

Prose Poetry

Prose poetry straddles the line between prose and poetry. Prose poetry has no formal line arrangements and appears like loose paragraphs.

After he graduated college, my oldest son, Brian, was moving his stuff out of our home to begin his new grown-up life and it became a surprisingly emotional moment for me. Surprising because even though our lives lead up to this moment, having prepared our children to go on their own and begin making a life, when the moment finally arrives, we can't accept not continuing to protect our adult child.

Later that night, after Brian had gone, I walked my dog Rusty before going to bed. That's when I noticed a cardboard box next to the trash can containing Brian's old soccer trophies from elementary and middle school. Obviously, he'd grown beyond them; I hadn't.

I simply couldn't let them all go, so I took one, and fearing to appear a sentimental fool, in the eyes of my wife, and Brian, and my younger son, Craig, I hid it in the basement.

When Rusty and I went back upstairs I knew that this had been a special moment, one that I wasn't quite ready to let go of. As a writer, the natural thing for me to do was to try to capture the moment and the strong feelings. A journal entry didn't seem enough and there wasn't enough material to make it into a short story or an essay. A prose poem seemed just right.

It allowed me to capture everything about the experience and the emotion that I wanted to retain, in a way that felt pleasing and satisfying to me and one of these days I'll finish it.

Prose poetry is also perfect when you just want to explore a theme. I liken it to a visual artist using a sketchbook to experiment with color or shadow, or to capture a scene that may or may not fit into a larger piece later. It's also good for capturing a vignette that by itself does not make a complete story, or to experiment with a mood, a tone, or a sensory impression.

The following prose poem uses short paragraphs loosely wrapped into a chronology to tell a story through a representation of various colors.

Colors in a Life

Brightest gold of glowing sun, ripened verdant hope of endless tomorrows, the day she came into my life.

Multicolored quilt of brightest blues, ruby reds, and honeysuckle greens, warmed the days of our courtship.

Love's deepest red infused the flowers of her wedding bouquet. Flashing neon and marquee lights illuminated our path so bright with promise.

Blue serenity channeled the flow of our twenty-three years— sometimes white-caps tipped dark green waves, but most often a placid lake with endless vistas to far horizons.

Jagged smear of muddy brown intruded, laden with harsh diagnosis. Blackest-black the threatening cancer—pale and empty my promise to protect her.

Sharp-edged stainless steel and sterile blue, the hospital— softened only by a pastel rainbow of stuffed bunnies, bears, and gorillas; expressions of our grandson's love.

White, the snow we pierced to place her in her final rest, while naked trees and transparent icicles bore silent witness, my soul the color and the texture of diamonds sunken in ice-water.

But years pass, and blessed time and seasons' turn yield serene green, underlain with flecks of gold, looking back along the path we shared.

And, glorious anticipation of brilliant white light sustains me until we meet again.

I continue to find poetry amazing in its ability to capture moments, impressions, and feelings so compactly, so economically, and yet so tellingly. That's why I so strongly recommend that you try it. I don't think you'll be disappointed.

Making It Real
Putting Your Words to Work

Okay, now you try it. Take some time to try laying out a few lines of haiku. Remember, poetry, especially haiku, can also be humorous or playful.

Then pick one other of the forms above and create a poem that combines elements of where you've been in life and where you're headed. Relax and have fun with it.

Chapter 22

Writing Drama

I'm using the word *drama* in its broadest definition to include writing for stage, screen, and television.

Drama by its very nature is a collaborative process. The writer is but one of a number of professionals who by working together will produce the finished artistic experience for the audience.

When you're writing a novel or short story, an essay, or a nonfiction book, unless you have a writing partner, it's your creation. You may receive feedback from a writers' group, an agent, or an editor, but they are essentially supporting you in producing your artistic product. You have a lot of control over the end product.

In live theater the writer is a key and continuing player in the process, even in some cases having veto power over the choice of director and actors. But the writer is part of a team. The actors, the director, the set designer, the costume designer, and the lighting designer will bring their artistic talents to bear on the production. If rewrites are necessary, the playwright will do the rewrite.

In film and television, the writer has much less control over the end product. The writer is one participant among many, and often not the key participant. The director, the actors, the producers, the cinematographer, and the film editor will bring their artistic talents and judgment to bear on the product.

In the film industry is not unknown for a studio to send a creative premise to several writers to write a film around that premise, just to see what kind of ideas come out of it. Then, if the potential producers are able to acquire the funding, and the movie is going to be made, it may be assigned to yet another writer to complete the final, or shooting script. Even then, big-name actors and directors may make changes to the script and unless the writer is uniquely powerful, those changes will stand.

In Hollywood the financial rewards are great, but the stakes are very high, and the psychological rewards can be nonexistent. Some writers make a very good living from writing films that are never produced or which get produced, but are only credited to the writer of the shooting script.

Writing for Print vs. Performance

The techniques of fiction and nonfiction writing that I've discussed in other chapters including plot, conflict, characterization, point of view, and so on apply to drama. But there are substantial differences between writing for printed matter and writing for performance. The following are some of those differences:

- In drama, plot and characterization are primarily conveyed through dialog and visual activities observed by the audience. The writer describes the characters and setting in broad strokes to provide general guidance to the actors, director, and set designers who will bring the writer's concepts to life.
- In drama the writer must use soliloquy or voice-over to directly reveal the characters' thinking. Most often the audience can only surmise what may be in a character's mind by observing the external clues provided by the actors' performance and by what the characters say.
- In drama the audience can see the setting, so less description needs to be conveyed.

Script Format

Scripts for plays don't look the way you may remember from school with the character's name at the left margin, followed by a colon and then the dialog. What you read then was published play format. A working script looks like the one laid out below.

This is the opening of a full-length play I wrote for a competition called *A Story to Remember*. A full-length play runs anywhere from 90 to 120 pages. As a rule of thumb, one page equals approximately one minute of performance time.

As you review the format, note that the act number is written in Roman numerals while the scene number is in ordinary numbers.

It's important to set the stage so that the set designer has a good idea of the visual concept and the atmosphere you're trying to evoke with the setting. Instructions are provided within brackets and in capital letters to distinguish them from dialog.

This particular play was written with the idea that it would be staged and performed by college students and townspeople. If this was written for the professional stage, less detail would have been provided in expectation that the set designer would bring her professional expertise to bear.

The characters' names are in capital letters and centered, while their dialog is set flush left in upper and lower case beneath the name of the person speaking.

You'll notice that unlike in a prose piece, the characters' physical action is only sketched in. The director and the actors will determine exactly how the scene will be played. The writer need only give them a general idea of what his intention is. The actors and the director will come up with the stage business. Stage business means actions like getting up, crossing the actor's legs, taking a sip of a drink, etc. Unlike a novel or short story, the writer need not be concerned about these.

To situate the actors and props on the stage, the term upstage refers to the back of the stage, farthest away from the audience. Downstage is the front of the stage closest to the audience. Stage left and stage right refer to the actor's left and right, assuming the actor is facing the audience.

ACT I - SCENE 1

[THE TIME IS TODAY. THE PLAY OPENS IN THE PARLOR OF LIDDY MOORE'S GROVE CITY HOME. IT IS A COMFORTABLE ROOM WITH PLENTY OF FRESH FLOWERS. THE STAGE IS SET UPSTAGE CENTER. THINGS ARE OLD FASHIONED BUT NOT WORN OUT. BEGINNING AT STAGE RIGHT THERE IS A COMFORTABLE ARM CHAIR FACING DOWNSTAGE LEFT, A TABLE WITH A LAMP THAT GIVES THE ROOM A VICTORIAN

FEEL, AND A MATCHING COUCH FACING THE AUDIENCE. THE BACKS OF THE ARMS OF THE CHAIR AND COUCH HAVE DOILIES ON THEM. IN FRONT OF THE COUCH IS A COFFEE TABLE WITH A SILVER COFFEE SERVICE LAID OUT ON IT. IN FRONT OF THAT IS A BRAIDED OVAL RUG THAT BRINGS THE PIECES TOGETHER. THE BACK WALL IS DONE IN VICTORIAN WALL PAPER AND CHAIR RAIL. THERE IS A MIRROR AND SOME CANDLE HOLDERS. THE WALL GOES FROM USR TO USC WHERE IT JAGS FORWARD ABOUT 3 FEET TO ALLOW FOR THE MAIN ENTRANCE TO LIDDY'S HOUSE. THE AUDIENCE CAN SEE THE DOOR, BUT NOT BEYOND IT. THE WALL THEN CONTINUES TO USL WHERE IT IS COVERED WITH PLAQUES AND LETTERS OF COMMENDATION FROM LIDDY'S MANY YEARS OF PUBLIC SERVICE. THERE ARE ALSO FAMILY PHOTOGRAPHS AND AWARDS LIDDY'S DAUGHTER WON AS A YOUNG GIRL. LIDDY IS AN ATTRACTIVE WOMAN OF ABOUT 75 YEARS OLD. SHE IS DRESSED IN A HIGH-NECKED PRAIRIE STYLE DRESS - NOT AN OLD DRESS, TODAY'S FASHION. AS THE PLAY OPENS DR. JAKE BARRETT, ABOUT THE SAME AGE, AND SOMETHING OF A DANDY IN HIS DRESS, IS PUTTING ON HIS COAT GETTING READY TO LEAVE]

DOCTOR BARRETT

Well Liddy, I think that's as good a lunch as I've had in all my days. If folks only knew, they'd quit eating at the Grove City Diner and line up right outside your door.

LIDDY

Good. Glad you liked it. You can take it off those outlandish bills you've been charging me.

DOCTOR BARRETT

Now Liddy. You know I haven't sent you a bill for at least 10 years now. Since you qualified for Medicare, I've been sticking it to your Uncle Sam.

LIDDY
[OBVIOUSLY ENJOYING THIS]

Then take it off the government's tab. I know you're cheating someone on the bill, you good-for-nothing quack.

DOCTOR BARRETT
[FLIRTING]

You keep up like that, and I'm going to have to stop asking you to marry me.

LIDDY

God, if I'd known that was all it would take to stop you, I'd have called you a quack twenty years ago.

You get the idea. If a character's dialog goes on to the next page, it's indicated by writing the character's name and *cont'd*, like this:

LIDDY (cont'd).

Format is Critical.

While the rules are not quite as rigid in play writing, there are expectations within the industry of what a working script should look like. For screen and television writing, the format is rigid. Your screenplay or teleplay will not be read if it is not rendered in the required format.

If you're seriously interested in writing drama, my advice to you is to make it easy on yourself by investing in script formatting software like *Final Draft* or *Movie Magic Screenwriter*. They run a little over $200 but are well worth it. You'll save five times that amount just in the aggravation of trying to format your script in a regular word processor.

The Difference Between Writing for the Stage, Screen, and Television

Stage

- The limits of stage sometimes require imaginative settings. Obviously a real locomotive won't fit on the stage, even if you could get one there.
- Performance is mutable. It varies from night to night. The actors will sometimes play the lines differently, or try a different bit of business to get a better handle on the character; or, in a play they've done many times, they'll vary it to keep themselves interested.
- The play, as an artistic dramatic expression, exists only during the duration of the performance. Once the show is over the performance no longer exists, unlike a book or a movie.
- The primary shapers of the audience experience are the director and the actors, not the writer.
- There are no seconds takes, no do-overs. The actors must get everything right the first time and every time.
- No close-ups. The actors must project out to the audience. As a writer, you cannot rely on a subtle movement like a wink or a grimace to play a critical role as you can in a movie where a close-up of the actor's face is possible.
- The performance is sequential. The play must be performed in sequence from beginning to end. The audience cannot skip forward as they can in a book or film media.
- The playwright makes the play affordable to produce by limiting scene changes and number of characters.

Film

- Film relies much less on the audience's imagination than written media or stage productions. The filmmaker can go anywhere and do anything, including creating special effects. The filmmaker doesn't have to give the audience the impression of a locomotive; the filmmaker can use a real locomotive.

- The performance is fixed. The performance always looks the same unless the film is recut. Once you shoot the movie and edit it, the movie is committed to permanent media so that every audience will experience, without variation, the same performance.
- The primary shapers of the audience's experience are the actors, the director, and the film editor.
- There is room for error in creating a movie. Multiple takes can be done of each scene until the performance is successful.
- The camera can take close-ups of the actors, so the actors can draw the audience in with small gestures.
- The writer will include general camera directions to give the cinematographer an idea of what the image should look like. The director and the cinematographer will make the final call.
- The performance can be shot in any order and then assembled into the finished piece.
- Budgets for professionally produced movies are generally very large.

Television

- Television is much like shooting a movie with the exception that time must be very strictly observed so that the television show, including commercials, will fit within the allocated time.
- Most TV shows are serials, so the writers must make use of continuing characters and assure that each has a role to play in every show.

(For insight into making a successful career writing drama, see the interview with James Manos, Jr. in "Interviews with Professional Writers" at the back of this book.)

If you decide you want to write drama, I recommend that you check out The Writers Bookstore at writersstore.com. They have an excellent collection of books and videos about writing drama as well as prose, and a terrific e-mail magazine that costs nothing and regularly provides excellent tips from practicing writers in the field of drama.

You'll also find there software for writers, including the two formatting software programs I previously mentioned. They provide Internet classes as well as traditional classes if you happen to be in the Los Angeles area.

Another good source for books about writing drama is the Writer's Digest Bookstore at writersdigest.com.

Two good websites to check out are playwriting101.com and screenwriting.info, both of which provide excellent information for beginners and are sponsored by The Writers Store and the people who produce *Final Draft* formatting software.

And, of course, don't overlook quilldriverbooks.com, the website of the publisher of this book and other great books for writers.

Part VI

Publishing, Freelancing, and Going on from Here

Chapter 23

Publishing Your Work

Once you commit yourself to your writing, you must decide whether you're writing only for yourself or writing for others. If you're writing for others, beyond your immediate family, that will entail publication either commercially or through self-publication.

Commercial Publishing

If you plan to submit your work for commercial publication you must understand that:

1. You are moving from the world of Art into the world of Commerce. Commercial publishing is a business.

2. To be successful you must, as you would in any other business, follow the established conventions and take a businesslike approach to marketing your work.

Submitting Your Work

Every submission you make to a publisher or agent must include a cover letter, which will vary depending on the nature of the submission (more on that later), must include a stamped, self-addressed envelope (SASE) with enough postage either for return of your manuscript if that is what you desire, or to receive notification of its disposition, and must follow generally accepted manuscript format.

Manuscript Format

Always check the submission guidelines for the publication to which you're submitting your work and follow those guidelines. In the absence of specific guidelines, you can use the guidelines below.

For fiction and nonfiction pieces of less than book length:

- Use standard 20-lb. white paper
- Use a standard business font like Times New Roman, double spaced. No script or fancy fonts, and no smaller than twelve-point.
- On the first page, list your identifying information in the upper left corner including your real name, address, telephone number, and e-mail address.
- Put the approximate word count (within fifty words) in the upper right hand corner.
- About one-third down the page, centered, type the title. On the next line type the word "by" and then your name or your pen name if you're using one.
- Drop down a couple of lines and begin.
- Subsequent pages should not repeat your identifying information or word count, but should have, in the upper right hand corner, your last name and a key word from the title.
- Number the pages consecutively in the upper right hand corner, next to your last name and key word.
- Do not staple or bind the pages together.

For book length works, use the same format as above but instead of beginning the text under the title, the title page is a separate page. Begin your text on the next page, under the chapter title, with the chapter number and title approximately one third down the page, and the last name, key word, and page number in the upper right corner as described above. Each additional chapter should be formatted the same way. (See "Standard Manuscript Format" in the Resources section of this book.)

Agents

Unless you're writing a book, you need not concern yourself with trying to engage an agent. As payment for their services, agents receive a percentage of your earnings. There is too little money in writing short pieces for agents to be interested.

On the other hand, once you have established yourself with book-length fiction or nonfiction and obtained an agent, she may be willing to help you sell short stories or essays. For book-length fiction and nonfiction, while an having an agent is not necessary to achieve publication with small to midsize independent publishers, acquiring an agent is a requisite to opening the door to publication with the major publishing houses.

Most, if not all, large commercial publishing houses will look only at work submitted by agents because they trust agents to provide them with publishable manuscripts. An agent who routinely submits a poor product will, over time, be ignored.

Agents will in most cases be able to get you the best possible deal both for money and favorable contract terms. The more money an agent gets for their client, the more the agent makes, too.

The author/agent relationship is a business relationship, not a friend-ship. For it to work, both parties must bring value to the table: the writer, a saleable manuscript; the agent, a sale resulting in the best deal pos-sible. If your agent is not actively promoting your manuscript, it's time to find a new agent.

Beware the agent who solicits you and wants to charge a reading fee to look at your work. These are scam artists. Agents who are mem-bers of the Association of Authors' Representatives agree to abide by a canon of ethics. For more information about agents, what they do, and how to find one check out the AAR's website at aar-online.org.

Editors

There are various types of editors. The big publishing houses will have several types of editors but an important one in the world of book publishing is the acquisitions editor who has the responsibility of find-ing prospective book projects. In larger publishing houses, when the acquisitions editor finds a project he likes, it goes on to an editorial meeting. Once there, it is evaluated and discussed by other editors, the publisher, and the marketing and sales staff who all have input to the final decision on whether to make an offer to acquire it or not, and, if so, for how much money.

Having your book picked up by a publisher should be the beginning of a long and beautiful friendship. Your editor is your voice within a publishing house. An editor, like an agent, is as successful as the books he or she publishes. A good editor works with and nurtures talent. So, listen to what your editor has to say. Remember that editors are pros who make their living turning out publishable works.

If you decide to self-publish your book, hire a freelance editor. With the consolidation of the publishing industry, there are many editors who have been squeezed out of jobs. Many fine quality editors have turned to freelancing part time or full time.

One good source of information about freelance editors and what they charge for various services is the Editorial Freelancers Association, the-efa.org.

Another source is the ads you'll find in the back of writer's magazines. Always check the references of freelance editors and "book doctors." While most are reputable, as in any profession, there are scam artists who will take advantage of new writers.

Marketing Short Pieces for Magazines and Newspapers

Fiction

Send the completed manuscript with a brief cover letter that:

• States the name of the story
• Cites how it will fit in with this magazine
• Shows any publishing credits or training you've received

The cover letter should not try to sell the piece. It's simply a transmittal document, but it should be neat, clean, and with no typographical errors. Make sure it addresses the editor by name. If you're not sure of the editor's name call the magazine and ask the receptionist to spell it for you.

Nonfiction

If very short (less than 1,000 words), such as the recurring columns (sometimes called departments) you find in the front of most magazines, submit the completed manuscript with a cover letter as above.

If you are interested in writing a longer article, send a one- or two-page query to the editor. Take your time writing this letter. Make your query stand out. Use a narrative hook to catch the editor's attention. There's nothing wrong with using the same hook you plan to use in the article. Briefly describe:

- the key points you plan to cover
- the people you will interview, if any
- the angle you plan to take
- why you are qualified to write the article

Treat this as an audition. Put the time and effort into this that it deserves. Your query letter should demonstrate to the editor that you can write this article.

Poetry

Follow the guidelines for the market to which you are submitting. If there are no specific guidelines, use the following as a general guide:

- Send three to five poems
- Single-space the poems, one poem to a page or set of pages
- Type your name and other identifying information in the upper left-hand corner of single-page poems and on the first page of multiple-page poems and include your last name, a key word from the title, and the page number on the upper right of all subsequent pages
- Make sure your cover letter mentions any previous publications
- Include a SASE

Novels

Do not try to sell any book-length fiction until it's written. Until you establish a successful track record, you must write the entire book before you can try to sell it.

- Send only a letter query providing a brief summary of the book and inviting the agent or publisher to read the manuscript. There are several good books on this subject listed in the annotated bibliography at the end of this book.
- Don't be modest; the query letter is a sales letter. The letter should be single-spaced and addressed to a specific editor or agent and be no more than two pages long. Open with a good hook, give the title of the book, and a few lines describing what the book is about. Follow the opening with short paragraphs that show why you are the best person to write this book, describe the target audience for the book, and explain why you think it will sell. End with a call to action: Ask the agent or publisher to review your proposal or manuscript as appropriate. Include a SASE.

If you have previously published a novel that met with some success, depending on the agent or publisher, you probably can get by with offering a detailed proposal which should include:

- The novel's title and a short synopsis (one or two pages)
- A chapter-by-chapter outline. Each chapter should be described in one double-spaced page
- A marketing statement describing the potential audience and ideas for how to sell the book
- Endorsements from other authors, celebrities, or anyone else whose endorsements will help to sell the book
- A brief description of your literary background including what else you've published and why you're qualified to write this particular book
- One or two sample chapters or the entire manuscript
- A SASE

Nonfiction Books

With nonfiction, in most instances, you can sell the book before you write it, based on a detailed proposal. This is because it's easier for the acquisitions editor to make a judgment of your ability to handle your subject based on your sample chapters than it is with fiction which also relies on the story as well as your ability to tell it.

- Send a query letter to the publisher or agent inviting them to read the full proposal for your book. Either include the full proposal with the query or have it written and ready to go should you get a "yes."

- Don't be modest. As with fiction, the nonfiction query letter is a sales letter. Address the single-spaced letter to a specific editor or agent and be brief: no more than two pages long. Open with a good hook that will engage the editor or agent.

- Give the title and subtitle, and a few lines describing the high concept of the book. The high concept is a succinct one- or two-line statement that gives the essence of your book in a nutshell. The high concept for this book was: "*Time To Write* is a quick-start, how-to book to equip readers who have dreamed of becoming an author to realize their dreams...authoritative, but written in an informal style with a touch of light humor. It can be described as *The Joy of Writing* meets *USA Today*: all of the key information but none of the frills."

- Tell the editor or agent why you have selected her. Usually you've selected an editor because your research showed her company has published similar books. You will want to contact agents who have represented authors whose book is in the same genre as yours or whose information in the published guides states they handle this kind of material. If another author you know recommended this editor or agent say so.

- In the query, include a four- or five-paragraph synopsis of your book that explains what it will cover and in how great a depth; into which publishing category it fits; why the book is needed; whether it's beginner level or advanced; who the potential market is; if there's a time element involved, such as if it's tied in to the anniversary of a major event or some such; how the book fits in with what's already on the market on this topic and why it will compete favorably.

- Have a paragraph that shows your qualifications, why you are the best person to write this book, and what you are willing to

do to help market it, such as presenting seminars, attending book signings, writing articles, or funding a book tour. Include any other special ability you may have to promote the book, such as if you host a well attended blog or Web page, or are an officer in an organization related to your book's subject.
- End with a call to action: ask the publisher or agent to review your proposal.

The nonfiction proposal will include all of the information in your query letter but in greater depth and detail. In addition it will include:

- An expanded synopsis which explains in detail all of the information described in the query as well as in what style your book will be written; any charts or art that will be included; any sidebars or special features; how long it will take to write (the expectation is twelve months or less); an anticipated word count (take the average word count of the three sample chapters you'll be submitting and multiply by the number of chapters—don't worry, this is just an estimate); a comparison with four or five competing books, showing (without knocking the others) why your book is better or different; and, promotion and publicity ideas and, in detail, what steps you'll take to market the book.
- A table of contents.
- A chapter-by-chapter outline. Include the chapter title and a one or two paragraph narrative description, in bold strokes, describing the contents of each chapter.
- Three sample chapters. If you've already written the book, pick the three that are most interesting and which you feel are well done. They don't have to be consecutive chapters. If you're taking an unusual approach, you'll probably want to include the first chapter where that approach is described.
- Any supporting material such as clips, articles about you, or anything you believe will help to convince the publisher or agent to go forward with your book.

A final note: Do not take this lightly. Take your time with the query and the proposal and get them right. Nothing short of whether your book sees publication or not is riding on it. This is your vehicle for getting your book published.

I strongly suggest you read not just one of the books I've recommended on this subject in the bibliography at the back of this book, but all of them. Each has good examples of query letters and proposals that succeeded. You can get them from the library and then buy the one you like best to keep for quick reference while writing your query and proposal.

Book Advances and Royalties

Advance

An advance is a payment you receive up front from the publisher that will be earned back from the royalties from the sale of your book. You won't see another penny more than the advance until the publisher recoups the advance.

Generally, advances are paid in two or three payments. One on signing the contract, another on submission of the manuscript, and in a three-payment agreement, a third on the publication date. Expect that your advance will be modest for the first book. The success of your first book will influence the size of the advance for your next book, and so on.

Royalties

Royalties are usually calculated based on a percentage of the publisher's recommended retail price or net price (what the publisher receives after discounts to wholesalers and retailers).

The royalty percentage can vary, and can be anything from 4 percent to 15 percent of the cover price. In some cases an "escalator" is built in so that the percentage increases after a certain number of copies have been sold. Once the advance has been "earned out" the publisher will make periodic, usually every six months, payments to the author. This is spelled out in the contract. If your book does not earn back the advance, you do not have to repay the advance.

If you have an agent, the agent is responsible for tracking and collecting your royalties. The agent will deduct her percentage and send you the remainder.

How to Find Publishers for Your Work

Look for books similar to yours. The publishers of those books are likely to be the right ones to approach. Also, there are several annual market guides that will help you find publishers for your work listed in the bibliography at the back of this book.

Multiple Submissions

The market listings and writer's guidelines for many publishers and agents indicate that they do not accept multiple submissions. Multiple submissions means submitting your work to more than one publisher or agent at a time.

With average turnaround times as slow as they are in the publishing industry, submitting to one publisher or agent at a time might mean that your literary property would be off the market for months until the editor or agent to whom you submitted it could get around to responding. This is totally unfair to the writer. Ignore that prohibition and submit to five or ten publishers at a time, but keep careful track.

If a publisher or agent makes an offer that you accept, immediately notify the others that your manuscript is no longer on the market. You don't have to go into detail or say that someone else wants it; simply write a brief memo that says, "Thank you for considering my manuscript (insert title). I'm hereby withdrawing it from the market." That's all you have to say.

Self-Publishing

Self-publishing cuts out the middleman and puts you in control of your book project with all of the profits going in your pocket. Some people have self-published with great success and occasionally self-publishing can lead to acceptance by a legitimate publishing house. However, many self-published writers end up with a garage full of books for which there is no demand.

If you self-publish, understand that you are going into the book production and selling business and now must be responsible for, in addition to writing the book, designing the book cover, designing the page layout and selecting the type of paper, getting it printed, marketing the book, storing and shipping inventory, fulfilling book orders, accounting for and collecting sales taxes, obtaining a merchant account to enable you to accept credit card charges, dealing with returns and requests for refunds, and a host of other business activities.

Self-publishing works best when there is a niche market for the book, i.e. a market that's too narrow, too hard to penetrate, or too limited for a commercial publisher to reach profitably. Self-publishing can be a good option for you, if you regularly make presentations to groups on a particular subject and can engage in what is called back-of-the-room sales.

The most difficult books to market are those without a strong focus, such as novels and nonfiction works of a general nature. Think seriously about the difficulties in addressing the general market before investing significant time, energy, and money into what is at best a risky venture.

One benefit of self-publishing is that an author may keep the book in print longer than a traditional publisher.

If your goal is simply to distribute the book to family and friends or within your company, or to your business customers, then self-publishing makes a great deal of sense.

Types of Self-Publishing:

- *Vanity Presses*—make their money from the writer, whether or not the book sells. Vanity publishing is characterized by high cost, low value, and high risk.
- *Print on Demand (POD)*—can be a good way to publish to a tightly defined market or for personal and family use. Print on demand can be characterized as moderate cost, high value, and low risk. This is a constantly shifting and developing business so if you're thinking about POD, make sure you research the market carefully to find the best combination of services and price for your project. Some leading POD publishers include Trafford Publishing (trafford.com); iUniverse which is owned by Barnes & Noble (iUniverse.com); and Xlibris, which is affiliated with Random House (Xlibris.com). Newer POD publishers with different business models worth looking into include LuLu.com and blurb.com.

- *Publish it yourself*—the overall most cost-effective way to produce books, but one which is more costly at the front end, and comes with no guarantee you won't be stuck with crates full of books you can't sell, is publishing books yourself using a standard book printer. Publishing it yourself can be characterized as high cost, high value, and high-risk.
- *Hand make your book*—This is sometimes done by poets with chapbooks that are expected to have a relatively small distribution and by individuals producing books to give to family members. Depending on your publication budget you may want to consider POD publishing as an alternative.

See the bibliography at the back of this book for resources for writers considering self-publishing.

Be Persistent

The keys to achieving publication are knowledge, having a good product, and persistence.

Research your markets carefully. Try to read copies of magazines to which you plan to submit your work. Read the publisher's guidelines and the market guides. You wouldn't submit your homemade apple pies to the auto parts store to sell, yet that's what happens every day in the publishing industry. Publishers receive hundreds of submissions every month that are totally out of sync with and inappropriate for their publications.

Be persistent. If your work is rejected, send it right out again. If you believe in it, and it's well written, it will find a publisher.

Chapter 24

Freelance Writing as a Business

At prime time many of us are not ready to give up the world of work or are financially unable to, but we are ready for a change to something we'd find more pleasing or psychologically rewarding. Some of us are ready to become our own boss and wish to open a small business. There are ways other than writing books or articles to put your writing skills to work if you want to combine your desire to write with your desire to keep working.

Many small to midsize businesses outsource their writing chores to freelance writers. Some freelance writers do quite well providing writing services, but a word of caution: It takes as much time and effort to launch a writing services business as it does any other home-based business, so take that into consideration before you quit your day job.

Providing Writing Services

Freelance writers offering writing services to businesses work as independent contractors. If writing for businesses appeals to you, depending on your skills, interests, and background, you can provide services such as writing annual business reports, feature articles, books and booklets, business plans, case histories, instruction manuals, technical manuals, press releases, in-house newsletters, proposals, responses to proposals, and advertisement copy writing.

Embrace a Businesslike Attitude

Once you begin selling your services, congratulations, you are now the owner of a small business.

As in any business, you must approach providing writing services in a professional manner if you hope to win customers and the all-important repeat business. Sure it's great to write at home in your pajamas or your sweats but don't let that creep into your business demeanor.

In the corporate world, when making phone calls to potential clients, I kept a small mirror by my desk so that I would remember to smile. Smiling as you speak lifts your voice in a pleasant way, and the person on the other end of the phone can hear it. In your home office, when you make a business call, no matter what you're wearing, sit up straight in the chair as though wearing business attire.

It's a simple but important concept: Business people expect the people with whom they do business to be businesslike and professional.

Tools

In addition to your computer, your printer, your reference books, and a high-speed Internet account, you'll need a separate telephone line for your business, a fax machine or Internet fax account, and an e-mail address. You'll also want a website.

You'll need to set up a checking account for your business to receive payments, pay business expenses, issue refunds, and so on. If you're operating under the name of your business as well as under your own name you may need to file a certificate at your county or municipal courthouse showing the name of your business. In the Virginia county in which I live, it's called an Assumed Name Certificate. You'll need to show this to the bank in order to open a checking account in your business' name. Check at your courthouse; they can tell you what you need.

While you're at the courthouse check to see if you need a license or permit to run a business out of your home. Most places do not require a license unless you have employees working for you, but check to be sure. Some localities draw a distinction between a writer simply submitting work for publication and someone providing what the locality considers to be business or professional services.

In Virginia, for a business home office you need what's called a Home Occupation Certificate.

Don't let this discourage you. It's all easier than it may sound.

How to Get a Domain Name and a Website

You can find someone in the Yellow Pages or on the Internet to obtain a domain name and build a website for you. But if you have minimal computer skills and can use the Internet, it's just as easy to do it yourself.

To obtain a domain name, go to Google.com and enter "buy domain name." That will yield an extensive list of domain sellers from which to choose. I use two providers: GoDaddy.com and 1and1.com. Both are inexpensive, easy to use, and provide hosting services for your website. All you have to do is type in the domain name you want and if that name is available the domain name provider will register it on your behalf. Simply provide the information requested on the screens. It costs less than $10.00 a year and the name is yours to use as long as you continue to pay the fee.

Getting Your Website Up

Most domain hosting services have very easy to use software, usually available for a low price, that will enable you to create a site, even if you've never created one before and know absolutely nothing about programming. Most freelance writers' websites are not complex: a few samples of your work, some links to other sites, some information about your publications, and links to places to buy them are usually what writers are looking for in a website. For a simple starter website like this expect to pay less than $10 per month to a provider for hosting your site.

Other Things You'll Need

To get your business going you'll need business cards, stationery, and a clips file or portfolio to show potential customers what you have done.

I find that the templates available in Microsoft Word are sufficient for me to create my own business letters, invoices, and proposals. The only thing I have professionally printed are my business cards.

On your business card placing the word "Writer" after or under your name is considered the mark of an amateur. Most put "Writing Consultant" or some such or simply their name and contact information. On my card, under my name it says "Writing Services, Training, and Consulting."

How to Get a Clips File Started

You'll need to show prospective clients samples of what you can do. But, when you first start out, you'll hit the typical Catch 22: Clients will want to see examples of the services you provide, but no one will hire you to provide services until you can show examples of the services you provide.

Here are some suggestions for how to get a portfolio of clips started when you don't have professional experience:

- Query your local newspaper. Local publications are often interested in freelance articles. If you show them you can do good professional work on time, they may begin making assignments to you. Don't expect much pay.
- Write an article about something of local interest and send it unsolicited to your local newspaper. If they use it, it gives you a clip. If not, chalk it up to experience.
- Write an article for your company's in-house publication, if you're still employed. This is often an easy and a good way to develop a clip.
- Write an article for an association to which you belong. Larger associations have their own public affairs staff and sometimes their own magazine staff. Telephone the public affairs office or the editor to see if they're interested in having a member article appear.
- Write an article for your church's publication. Church newsletters are always looking for input.
- Write an article for a nonprofit organization. Nonprofit organizations are notoriously underfunded and often willing to take a chance on a writer who can get their story out to the public.

Use your nonpaying clips to garner paying jobs, and over time, replace your nonpaid clips with your paid clips.

Under Promise and Over Deliver

Remember to under-promise and over-deliver. If a client says to you, "Can you have this by Friday?" and you happen to be pretty sure you can get the job out much sooner, don't do what many writers new to the business world do: In an excess of appreciation and desire to please the customer they'll say, "Sure, I can have it for you by Wednesday."

Instead, simply give the client exactly what he wants. Say, "Sure, I can have it for you by Friday." You'll make the customer happy simply by meeting his needs.

If you are able to get the work done by Wednesday, call the customer to tell him you thought he'd appreciate having the job in his hands before promised. You will make the client happy and it's likely he'll use you again.

On the other hand, if you promised Wednesday, and couldn't provide it until Thursday, even though you were one day ahead of what the customer originally requested, in the customer's mind you did not keep your promise and that's a mark against you. Try to make the calendar work for you, not against you.

Marketing and Selling Are Critical to Your Success

To get business and customers you must network, network, network. I was once associated with an outplacement firm for senior executives. Their motto was: "You can network or not work. The choice is up to you."

Tell everyone you know that you have opened a writing business. You never know when you may be at a neighborhood cookout and find someone whose company needs your services. Please don't misunderstand, I'm not telling you to use every social occasion to be a bore and push your services. Most people ask one another what they do for a living. Be prepared to say that you're a freelance writer or that you own a business that specializes in providing writing services.

Join Business Associations

Join your local chamber of commerce or board of trade. Take part in the frequent "meet and greet" get-togethers these organizations sponsor for business people to get to know one another. Make sure you have a supply of business cards to give to possible contacts.

Find a Niche

What are your interests, hobbies, or special areas of knowledge? What kind of articles do you like to read?

Was there a need for a written publication where you formally worked that was not being met? What sorts of writing did your company outsource? Are you technically competent to write those items?

Bottom line: Look for business in areas where you already have expertise.

Specialist or Generalist?

When getting started as freelancers, most people like to keep their options open, but soon realize that referrals, knowledge of the subject, and introductions by past clients to potential clients require one to focus in a particular specialty area. Over time and with experience, most find that as they learn more about a particular subject, and make contacts in that area, they tend to focus on that area. Choose an area in which you have a passionate interest and specialize in it from the beginning.

Find a Golden Goose

The goose who lays the golden egg for any business is the recurring customer. Recurring customers provide a continuing and relatively predictable source of revenue. Steady revenue is what pays the bills and allows you to stay in business. Once you find this creature you must treat it right, nurture it, and keep it from wandering off. If you are dependant on a reliable source of income, I recommend that you work your business part time and do not give up your day job until you have a reliable goose or two in your barnyard.

How Much to Charge

You can charge by the hour, by the day, by the week, by the word, by the page, by the project or any other way that seems to make sense to you and the client. When setting your price, just remember to think about how much time it will take you in addition to the writing itself. This includes research, travel, conducting interviews, and so on. A dollar a word for a 1,500 word project may sound terrific. It may actually be terrific if it will only take you ten hours from beginning to end; $150 an hour is good money in anybody's book.

But if it takes you a full week including research and writing, now you're down to $37.50 an hour, not bad but not terrific either. If it takes you two weeks, that will halve the rate to $18.75 an hour. If you're new to freelance writing, and you need the clips and the experience, then $1,500 for two weeks' work may not be a bad assignment for you. However, if you've been freelancing for some time, and you have plenty of work on your desk, this amount may not be enough to attract you.

You have to look at your own financial situation. If you're a prime-timer who's retired with a pension, medical benefits, and life insurance you may not need to charge as much as someone who has to include those costs in her fees.

Setting Your Rates

You can base your rates on what you need to make to pay your bills, the national average for the service you're providing, the local standard for the service you're providing, or whatever the market will bear. You may decide to provide high end services to a limited well-heeled clientele or cut-rate services to attract volume. To set an effective rate, you'll need to have an idea of the price point of the services you plan to provide.

To get a feel for national pay rates the annual *The Writer's Market: Where and How to Sell What You Write*, published by Writer's Digest Books, contains a section called "How Much Should I Charge?" which includes average pay rates for a broad variety of writing jobs. It provides individual rates for various assignments such as writing annual reports, writing brochures and flyers, writing business and sales letters, editing newsletters, and so on. The National Writers Union (nwu.org) also takes a survey every year and publishes the going rates for its members.

Writing on Spec

You may have a potential customer ask you to write a piece for them on speculation or "on spec." What that means is that the potential customer is asking you to write the article as an audition, with no commitment from him to buy it. You may spend hours researching and producing the article only to find that the customer decides not to buy it.

Until you have some clips to offer, you may want to do some spec work as a way to break in. However, if you already have legitimate clips, I don't recommend it.

There are several good books for additional information about freelance writing listed in the bibliography at the end of this book. Additional sources for good information include the National Writers Union, NWU.org and the American Society of Journalists and Authors, ASJA.org.

Chapter 25

Going on from Here

There has never been a time when there were more resources available to new writers eager to learn more. The resources available include everything from books to writers' groups. Let's take a look at them.

Writer's References

Every conceivable aspect of writing has a book or books dedicated to it. There are general books, like this one, about various aspects of writing; books about writing in each genre; books about all of the forms of writing; books about overcoming writer's block; books about writing as an aid to solving medical and psychological problems; books about plot development and character development, and almost any conceivable writing related subject you can imagine. And new books about writing are coming out every day.

Finding the Best Reference Works

The trick is to find the books that are most useful to you without getting swept up in reading so much about writing that it interferes with your writing. Below, I've listed a few good sources for obtaining writing books.

Writer's Digest Book Club

Writer's Digest Book Club (writersdigestbookclub.com) functions like most book clubs: You receive a flyer in the mail periodically with a primary choice and several secondary choices. If you do nothing, the primary choice is sent to you automatically. The book club is pretty easy to work with, they produce a lot of good books, and they have a website to make declining or ordering the books fairly easy.

Book Stores

Most book stores, whether small or large, selling used books or new, have a writing reference section. Whenever I'm in a new town and find a new bookstore I'll explore that section first.

Used Book Stores

Used book stores can be a great source for building your library of reference books. I also like to peruse old writing books to see what advice has changed and what has stayed the same.

The Internet

In addition to new books, Amazon.com carries listings of used books and out-of-print books for sale via their affiliates. Another good Internet resource to check is bookfinder.com.

Your Local Library.

Most libraries have fairly good collections of books for writers.

Writer's Magazines

Reading writer's magazines is a great way to keep up with what's happening in the writing community. These usually include a variety of articles that cover craft, marketing, markets for your work, writers' conferences, and other matters of general interest to writers. The four magazines below are available at bookstores throughout the country as well as by subscription.

- *The Writer* (writermag.com)
- *Writer's Digest* (writersdigest.com)
- *Poets & Writers* Magazine (pw.com)
- *The Writers Journal* (writersjournal.com)

Book Reviews

Most large newspapers have a weekly or monthly book review section. Also, some of the large city newspapers, like the *New York Times* and the *Washington Post*, have separate book review sections in their Sunday newspapers to which you can subscribe without subscribing to the entire newspaper.

In the book review section you'll find reviews of new books, authors doing readings and signings in your area, and sometimes how-to articles about writing.

Publishers Weekly, which you can probably find at the library, has prepublication reviews and articles on authors and publishers, as well as gossip about the publishing scene.

Industry Source

Publisher's Lunch is a subscription newsletter available at publishersmarketplace.com/lunch/subscribe.html to which most people in the publishing business subscribe. It has industry news as well as a marketplace component where freelance writers can advertise.

Audio Books

Audio books are a great resource while driving or doing those mindless tasks around the house like painting walls or cleaning out the garage that don't require a great deal of concentration. You can get audio books about writing, or audio books that fall within the genres in which you want to write.

Software

Software is available for every conceivable task, including word processing, organizing, outlining, clustering, researching, keeping track of your notes, and providing assistance and guidance in the writing process. Most of the latter category is available for trial use via the Internet. Definitely try them before you buy them.

Classes

There are any number of classes for aspiring writers ranging from Internet classes to formal degree programs.

Correspondence Schools

At one time mail-based correspondence courses were a common way for new writers to study craft. Courses such as the Famous Writers Course, and the Writer's Digest Correspondence Course were well known to neophyte writers. However, the advent of the Internet has put most of these correspondence courses out of business. In 2004, the Writer's Digest Correspondence Course was abandoned in favor of the Writer's Digest Online workshops.

Internet

Learning via the Internet is terrific if you can't commit to taking a writing class in a physical classroom either because of your schedule or because classroom courses are not geographically feasible. Schools listed below offer a variety of classes with good instructors, lots of feedback, and interaction with fellow students.

- Gotham Writers School (writingclasses.com)
- Writer's Digest (writersonlineworkshops.com)
- Ed2Go (ed2go.com)

Traditional Attendance Classes

If you are in a position to commit to classroom training there's a wide variety of choices ranging from one or two hour classes to degree programs.

Adult/Continuing Education Noncredit Courses

There are many noncredit writing classes available from a variety of private and public sources. You'll have to check for local availability. Ask at your library, bookstore, or coffee shop. Some may even be advertised in the newspaper.

College Credit Courses

For-credit writing courses are available at most community and four-year colleges. Likewise many universities and colleges offer degree programs in writing ranging from bachelor's degrees to a master of fine arts degree.

The MFA degree has traditionally been viewed as the terminal degree in writing, meaning the highest degree available in the field; however, more and more Ph.D. programs in writing are springing up at universities around the United States. Again you have to check for local availability.

A good resource if you're interested in taking a degree in writing is the Association of Writers & Writing Programs (awpwriter.org). The most convenient way to find all of the options available to you is to purchase a copy of *The AWP Official Guide to Writing Programs*, which contains information on 300 graduate programs, 400 undergraduate programs, and 250 writer's conferences, festivals, and centers.

Writers' Groups

Writers' groups present another opportunity for continuing learning. There are a number of professional and amateur writing groups that are willing to share materials with new writers. A site with good links to various of these groups is writerswrite.net.

(For insight into writing as a national journalist, writing fiction and nonfiction concurrently, as well as overseeing graduate level writing instruction, see the interview with David Everett at the back of this book.)

Chapter 26

A Final Note

If, like me, you're a member of the prime time generation, you surely remember *The Carol Burnett Show*, the last of the great TV comedy variety shows.

At the end of the show, Carol would sing her closing theme that ended like this:

> Seems we just got started and before we knew it
> Came the time we had to say, 'So long.'

I've had fun writing this book for you; I hope you've enjoyed reading it and have found it useful. Writing is a fun, rewarding, stimulating, occasionally frustrating, but always fascinating way to spend your time and it keeps the mind sharp. At the end of a day of writing, you'll also have something to show for your efforts: something that's worthwhile, and a unique expression of yourself, that only you could have created. And what you create is a little piece of yourself, in your own voice, that not only has purpose today, but tomorrow, because you can leave that little piece of yourself behind to those about whom you really care.

I wish you every success as you grow as a writer.

I'd love to know how useful you found this book, and I'm interested in any suggestions you may have for improvements. I'd also very much like to hear of your writing successes. If you get a chance, please drop me a line at Frank@writingafter50.com to let me know how things are going with your writing.

In closing, I think Pulitzer Prize-winning poet and Poet Laureate of the United States Ted Kooser said it best in his *The Poetry Home Repair Manual*. What he wrote there applies to all writing:

> I urge you to write from your soul no matter what form you choose because that's what really matters. You want to write poems that connect with others, that can show your readers new ways of seeing, understanding, and enjoying the world. Again, you can define those readers however you wish. But whether you are hoping to reach one very special reader or a broad general audience, write from the heart and let your poems find their shapes (forms) as you proceed, then perfect what you've written through careful revision.

Amen.

Interviews with
Professional Writers

Robin Hathaway

Robin Hathaway is the author of the Dr. Andrew Fenimore mystery series. Her first novel, *The Doctor Digs a Grave,* won the *St. Martins Press/Malice Domestic Award* for Best First Traditional Mystery in 1997 and the 1998 *Agatha Award* for Best First Novel. Other books in the series include *The Doctor Makes a Dollhouse Call* (2000), *The Doctor and the Dead Man's Chest* (2001), *The Doctor Dines in Prague* (2003), and her latest in this series *The Doctor Rocks The Boat* (2006). Her Jo Banks mystery series include *Scarecrow* (2003) and *Satan's Pony* (2004). Her mystery fiction has appeared in *Ellery Queen Mystery Magazine* and *Alfred Hitchcock Mystery Magazine.*

Tell me the story of how you got started writing.

At ten years old I had rheumatic fever and was in bed for almost a year. I really felt fine most of the time, but the doctor said I shouldn't get up. Listening to the radio and reading books were my only entertainment. Then, one day, I found I could get police calls on my radio by jiggling the dial. I would listen in about burglaries and on a good day, homicides.

My mother gave me lots of things to read, particularly Agatha Christie novels. One day, when my mother got fed up with me, she gave me a pad and told me to write a story of my own. In college, I took every writing course I could.

I didn't start writing seriously until later in life. At the age of 50 I remembered that writing was what I had always wanted to do. My husband suggested that I start. It really was a kind of therapy for me. I was going through some tough times. My parents were elderly and I was spending a lot of time in nursing homes and hospitals.

I was amazed when I started writing because it was as if the characters had been trapped in my head for all those years. Dr. Fenimore, and nurse Doyle, this teenage kid named RAT were fully formed in my mind.

Is it enough to write for yourself or does writing have to be published to be worthwhile?

In writing, you have to have an audience. It's a communication between you and the reader. You need to write for publication to feel you've completed your work; otherwise, you'll never know if you can really do it.

The best thing that happened to me was when I got out of my garret and went to meet working writers and talked to them and to real editors and agents. It does wonders to get out into the real world of writing.

I think you have to have people read and react to your stuff. Stephen King talks about having a "favorite reader." Every writer needs a favorite reader, someone to whom they can show their writing and get useful feedback.

Do you have any regrets about waiting until age 50 to become serious about your writing?

No. By the time I started really writing I didn't have other responsibilities: my children were grown and out of the house and I had enough life experience to have gotten over the angst.

Are there any particular advantages or disadvantages to starting writing at mid-life?

We live longer now so there's so much more we can choose to do in life. And we've gathered so much material over the years that we have at our fingertips if we start writing later in life. It's amazing how things you thought you'd forgotten come right back to you.

How do you define success as a writer?

If you have fans you can depend on, that look for your next book, then I think you're successful. If people want to reread your work, then I think you are really successful. I regularly reread my favorite authors—people such as Dorothy Sayers, Raymond Chandler, and Josephine Tey, even though I know the plot, I enjoy being with their characters.

Can writers earn enough to live on from their writing?

Only those writers at the top of the heap can really make a living from it. Writing can provide a nice side income, but as I said, for the vast majority of writers, not enough on which to support yourself. You don't want to go into writing for the money.

What about freelance work?

I know a lot of writers who work as publicists or in some other aspect of freelancing to support themselves while they pursue what they want to write during their off-time.

How has becoming a successful writer changed your life?

So many doors opened that wouldn't have opened otherwise. In addition to teaching at the Gotham Writers' Workshop, I now edit for some small presses. I also do some editing work privately for individual writers. It changed my life completely.

You told an interviewer in 1999 that you had written a lot of literary short stories that you were unable to get published. Why did mystery click for you but not literary stories?

I took myself too seriously when I was trying to write literature with a capital L. What I produced was very uptight. I relaxed a little more writing mysteries so I think they came out better, which is not to belittle the mystery genre. There's some amazing writing going on in mystery today.

Why did you write your first three novels from a male viewpoint?

I didn't sit down to purposely write a cross-gender story. It just came out that way.

Recently, in my new series I've been writing in the first person. The first person viewpoint brings a lot of freedom because you're closer to the character. But it also limits you because everything has to be seen through the eyes of the viewpoint character. You can't get in and out of just anybody's head, only the lead character.

A Kirkus reviewer described your Doctor Fenimore novel The Doctor Dines In Prague *as more of a thriller than a traditional cozy. Is this a new direction you're moving in?*

That reviewer said something about it being a runaway cozy that wants to be a thriller. I don't think it's a new direction. I think you need to keep trying new things and seeing what you're capable of. My second series will definitely be darker than my first. I like to think of myself as a suspense novelist. Suspense is not so much what happens as the expectation of what could happen.

Do you have a preference for writing short stories or novels?

I love short stories. When I finish a novel, I'll write a short story as a break. The problem with short stories is that from a practical viewpoint there aren't that many markets for them. I really enjoy doing both.

Did your degree in English help or hurt you as a creative writer?

It probably delayed my succeeding somewhat. Trying too hard to be "literary." On the other hand, it kept me writing. I made a point of taking a writing course every year in college because it kept me writing. But there are so many things going on. Women especially have to do things in stages.

Have you ever considered writing anything other than fiction?

Yes, I wrote some nonfiction articles, mostly about Philadelphia and the Society Hill area that I'm very familiar with. I also did some photography.

During the in-between years, before I started writing fiction again, I did some nonfiction and sold some stories with photos to the *Philadelphia Inquirer*, etc.

Your big break came from a writing contest. Would you recommend them for new writers?

Sure. What can you lose? St.Martin's is one of the few publishers who go out of their way to help new writers with their yearly contest. And they often publish submissions that don't win the prize. Many writers don't realize that both agents and publishers are desperate for good, new writers. Right now I'm judging for the Edgar's. It's amazing how the really good stories jump right out at you.

What is your writing routine?

I write on a yellow pad with a ballpoint pen all the way through the whole first draft. Then I put it into the computer. I edit it as it's going into the computer.

How much of the plot do you know when you begin a story or novel?

I write intuitively. I don't have an outline. I let the characters lead me. I often have a general idea of the ending, but just as often the ending changes by the time I get there.

Right now, I'm finishing the second novel in the second series, *Satan's Pony*. I have a male character and I can't decide whether he should hit the love of his life or stop just before he does. I feel I'm in this position because I don't understand this character well enough. I'm leaning toward not being violent, because he's not a violent person.

How extensive a back story do you develop on them?

I don't do the back story stuff. I think if you do too much of that you can run out of steam before you do the book.

What percentage of your students at the Gotham Writers' Work-shop are in midlife or later, and do you find any noticeable difference between them and your younger students?

Teaching writing at the Gotham workshops is wonderful! I have students of every age. It's an amazing mix of people in different careers who also want to write. Their enthusiasm is amazing. And the great thing is that, unlike traditional classes, everyone wants to be there. Nobody's being forced to take a writing course that they don't want to take.

If I see any difference between the age groups it's that the older students are more careful in their writing; the younger ones are fresher and more original. The older ones tend to worry about mechanics and craft more than the younger ones.

Do you recommend joining a local writers' group or workshop?

In the beginning it helps to take courses and to belong to a group of writers. But after a while you can depend on them and listen to them too much, and wind up making changes in your work that were not necessarily good changes, but changes to satisfy the group. You have to develop your own confidence as a writer and learn to accept the good and filter out the bad advice.

What advice do you have for midlife writers?

Join an organization like Mystery Writers of America and Sisters in Crime. Use them to get known in the business and to get your name out.

MWA has a great mentor program. A published writer will critique your work. I was very fortunate in getting a really good critic who said, "Start your action sooner." That was the best advice I ever received. My critic told me she wanted to see the body in the first chapter. I learned to get right to the murder or critical event, and that has made all the difference.

When you're an unknown writer you have to grab the reader in the first chapter, get to the action immediately. After you've become known, then you can take your time, because people who enjoy your writing trust you and will be willing to wait a little longer.

Don't worry about beginning at midlife. It's the quality of your writing that counts, not your age.

Also, when you're writing, read your stuff out loud religiously. When I started doing this I noticed that my sentences were a little reserved and staid. My husband was a great help to me in overcoming that tendency by pointing out where I could use two short sentences instead of one long one and make the same point.

Another thing is not to expect to be published overnight. While it does happen, it's very rare. You have to learn your craft. It took me almost ten years from the time I started writing at age fifty to publication when I was age sixty. A lot of people say that your third novel is the one that makes it. That was certainly true in my case. *The Doctor Digs A Grave* was my third novel. Once you break through to publication, you can go back and try to get the early stuff published.

It always amazes me that, unlike beginners in other arts, for some reason people seem to expect writing success to come right away. You have to do a lot of writing to learn your craft. In my first Gotham workshop, the students didn't like it when I told them they had to do exercises in class. But they quickly learned that the exercises got them going — got them writing.

And be sure you read a lot, especially the kinds of books you want to write.

The most important advice is just to start. Begin writing and keep going. Get in touch with the writing world and get to know the mechanics, the business, and the craft. Gather the essentials in the craft of writing, then the rest is up to you. Like anything, if you have the tools and know the basics, then you can take-off without having to worry about that part of it and let your imagination, your talent, and your creativity guide you.

Richard Bausch

Richard Bausch is the author of ten novels and six short story collections. He is the recipient of numerous fellowships and awards, including the O Henry, Pushcart, and PEN/Malamud. He is the editor of *The Norton Anthology of Short Fiction* (2005). His most recent novel is *Thanksgiving Night*. He is currently at the University of Memphis Creative Writing Program and holds the Lillian and Morrie A. Moss Chair of Excellence.

Do you decide at the outset to write a novel or short story, or do you let it take its course?

Usually I have a pretty good sense what I've got. But I never keep myself to any of it if things turn in a way I hadn't anticipated.

How much outlining do you do?

Only a little, for the next few days' work when composing a novel. Very much less than that with short stories.

How much do you know about plot before you begin?

The trouble part of it—what the trouble is. Not much else.

How much do you know about your characters before you begin?

I know instinctively, under the flow of thinking, more than I'm quite able to express. The writing of the story is how I find that expression.

Are there any particular advantages or disadvantages to beginning writing at midlife?

None. I know the temptation is to think about Time as the limitation or disadvantage for someone in mid-life, but how many years did John Keats have, starting out as he did, at nineteen years old? He had six little years and he got out several of the greatest Odes in the English or any other language. He was twenty-five when he died.

How do you define success as a writer?

You hope to write something with emotional truth in it, that will move anyone who happens upon it, whenever that takes place—now or a long time from now. You hope to do that, to write that well. And you live in the plain knowledge that most or all of what you do will disappear forever with you when your time comes. Other than these rather sober concerns, the activity provides a measure of happiness.

Is becoming a successful and critically acclaimed writer all that you hoped it would be?

It's very hard to imagine what my life would've been if I hadn't written the books. The acclaim you speak of, though, is not something you hear, or even particularly notice. Celebrity changes people, I suppose, but I am a writer and not a celebrity and I like that just fine. I like having my privacy and also being able to make something of a living with my work.

What's the downside to becoming a writer?

There is no downside. It's a good and healthy thing whenever and wherever it happens, if for no other reason than the fact that you can't pick up a gun and fire it while you're scribbling.

What is your writing routine?

A couple of hours a day, every day, whenever I can get those hours in.

Do you recommend new writers joining a local writers' group or workshop?

One time, or two, tops. After that, you should be on your own. Unless you have ambition to teach.

I read an interview you did recently for Our Stories: A Unique Literary Journal. *I loved your description of your perfect writing night. Would you recount it here?*

You don't know the night has passed. You are so gone in the work that you do not hear a thunderstorm come and go, and when the light comes you see the rain on the leaves out the window, and you have that feeling of using your talent well and virtuously. And then maybe you have one small shot glass of whiskey so you can sleep. Or you take a friend's book to bed and read slow, until the drift starts—that psychic snow shutting you down. I think I like working at night better than at any other time, though I am lucky in that I can write at any hour, if there's something to write. So far, there has always been something to write.

What advice do you have for writers who are just getting started at midlife?

Remember what I said about Keats, and get your ass to work.

Donna Boetig

Donna Boetig is a freelance journalist who began as a staff writer for *The Baltimore Sun,* then moved on to writing magazine cover stories and feature articles—especially real life dramas—for publications such as *Reader's Digest*, *McCall's*, *Family Circle*, *Woman's Day*, *Brides*, and *Smithsonian*. She has led writing seminars with thousands of writers, editors, and publications' practitioners throughout the United States and Canada, and to groups as diverse as the editorial staffs of *USA Today* and Doubleday Book Club, AT&T, and World Vision Canada. She has also taught in the Writing Program at Johns Hopkins University. She was the coordinator of The Writing Center at University of Maryland, Baltimore. Her book on writing women's stories, *Feminine Wiles: Creative Techniques for Writing Stories that Sell,* is a Writers' Digest Book Club feature selection. She holds a Master of Arts in Writing from Johns Hopkins University.

Are there any particular advantages or disadvantages to beginning writing at midlife?

There are a lot of advantages to beginning writing at midlife. For one thing, you have perspective. You're not simply writing about something that's happening to you at that moment; you've experienced some of life. For example, let's say you're doing an article for *Brides* magazine on some aspect of what it's like to have a new daughter-in-law. Well, someone in their twenties trying to write a story like that really doesn't have perspective on the issues.

Another thing, at midlife you've had to know how to pull the strings to make things happen for you. If you're freelancing, you know how to contact people, how to use organizations to do research, and to get what you need to write the article. You also have so many skills and strategies you can put to use. At midlife you have the intelligence, the background, and the chutzpah to know how to do things. At that age you're also more willing to take risks. You've won some and lost some and survived it all and it makes you a little more daring.

By midlife you're more open-minded, and that makes you a better interviewer. It makes you much more empathetic and that's a quality you need if you're going to be a successful freelance writer.

Finally, you realize that time is finite and with that realization comes a sense of urgency, tomorrow was yesterday. This is the impetus to put pen to paper: If we're going to write that essay, article, or book—we better do it now.

How do you define success?

Waking up and being really excited about what you're doing. Success is having the fire and passion and feeling really alive. When I'm working on a project, I have this dynamic feeling that makes me want to leave no stone unturned. I get really excited about digging for the story.

The journey itself has to be fun, not just the fact of being published. I'm never more awake, more aware, and paying more attention to everything than when I'm in the middle of the story. It makes me want to never let an opportunity go unexplored.

I also think being successful as a writer means that it widens your life both in terms of the challenges you encounter every day and in terms of the things you learn and the people you meet.

Is becoming a successful writer all that you hoped it would be?

Yes, in many ways—but not from the money. People interested in money would be much better off sticking to their day jobs.

Being a successful writer is great for opportunities. For example, I recently spent five years as coordinator of the writing program at the University of Maryland. Normally a position like that would require a Ph.D., while I hold a master's. But, because of the clips I've earned over the years, my experience as a writer was taken as the equivalent. I had a ball doing that job.

Also, as a freelancer I've gotten to go to places and seen things and meet people I never would have otherwise. I've crisscrossed the country and the Atlantic and Pacific oceans on others' dimes, teaching, writing, meeting the famous, the infamous, and the ordinary who have accomplished extraordinary feats.

What's the downside?

The downside is that there are some things beyond your control. For example, I did a story for *Life* magazine. I originated the idea, I pitched it, the story was accepted, and we were even to the point of doing the layout for a specific issue. However, the photos that were to accompany the article, taken by the magazine, didn't rise to the level that they were looking for and so the story got killed.

Sometimes an editor will leave the publication and a story that was accepted winds up being shelved. You can do everything right and things just don't work out. Sometimes it depends on plain luck. That's another reason I believe people beginning writing at midlife have an advantage: they've lived long enough to have experienced disappointment that can come through no fault your own. They know how to live with it and move on.

What is your writing routine?

Well, that's changing because the market is changing so much. I find that the articles being run by the women's slicks like *Women's Day*, *Family Circle*, and others are getting shorter. They're doing more with breakouts and fragments and less of in-depth stories. There seems to be less interest in the life drama type of article than there used to be.

So now I'm looking at writing books. I think I was moving in this direction any way. This way I can concentrate on writing more of what tickles me. Also, when you're writing for magazines, sometimes you have to stifle your own voice because they're looking for a more homogenized voice. At this point in my life I'm going to focus more on what I want to do in the way I want to do it, than on exploiting opportunities as they come along, as you do in magazine writing.

Do you recommend joining a local writers' group or workshop?

Yes and no. Writers' groups and workshops are great for making friends in the business and it's nice having writing friends, but it can become too much fun, and easier to talk about writing than to do it. Writing groups are fun because it's nice to have conversations with other people who are interested in writing and seeing what they're up to. But for feedback you ultimately have to be the final deciding factor in whether your work is good or not. It's not a group decision.

I think you're much better off, if you're looking for good feedback, to find yourself a good editor. Send your stuff off and see what real editors think about it.

Is it difficult to break into the major women's magazines market?

Yes. There's lots of competition. Pay rates haven't changed all that much in the past twenty years, about $2,500-$3,000 for an article. The national magazines typically pay $1.50 a word; the top writers get more. While it's hard to break in, that shouldn't discourage anyone from trying. If you don't have a long writing pedigree then you need a great idea or a great voice and ideally both. Show the publisher that you can provide something new and fresh, something different that they can't get from their existing stable of writers.

Be creative and a little bit daring in your query. I always tell new writers to read columnists to get a feel for the conversational yet distinctive voice employed in their column. That's what you want to get into your query. Don't be afraid to stand out. Take an unusual approach to a conventional story and that will make you stand out in the editor's mind.

What's the difference between the women's slicks and other magazine markets?

Women's slicks are definitely geared to their readership. You'll find very big differences between *Redbook* and *Good Housekeeping*. Look at the ads in both magazines. Most of the ads in *Redbook* would never find a home in *Good Housekeeping*. Women love to learn, and if that information is cloaked in anecdotes women readers can relate to, all the better.

What advice would you offer for starting to freelance at midlife?

Do a lot of marketing and find an editor. Send your work to the very best magazines, but in the meantime find local editors at regional and local magazines that you can approach to allow you to do a story.

Ask them if they've got a story sitting in their files that their other writers have shunned. Almost every editor has a pet story they'd like to see done but which no one wants to do. Be the one to do it. Break in that way and get good editing.

Having a good editor is much more valuable than having a group critique your writing. But it has to be a good editor, not one from a publication in which you wouldn't be proud to see your article published.

Gather clips and write a marketing plan. Send out queries; if they get rejected, then move on to the next. Don't sit around worrying. Keep moving forward. And read as much as you can. Read the good writers, the kind you'd like to become.

With the proliferation of 24/7 news, coming up with a novel idea and keeping it virgin until publication is tougher than ever. Therefore, it helps to look inward, to probe yourself for ideas, and your perspective on others' ideas. Your angle, your presentation of it, and your distinctive voice will set you apart. Just go for it. There are a lot of rewards to freelancing other than the monetary. Be open to new experiences. You can meet a lot of people and do a lot of things you wouldn't do otherwise.

James Manos, Jr.

James Manos, Jr., is an award winning writer and producer. He won the 1999 Emmy Award for Outstanding Writing for a Drama Series for *The Sopranos*, "College." He won the 1994 CableACE award for Best Producer of a Movie or Miniseries for *The Positively True Adventures of the Alleged Texas Cheerleader-Murdering Mom*. He has been associated as a writer and/or producer of several critically acclaimed and award winning series or movies including *The Shield* and *Apollo 11*. His novel, *Little Ellie Claus*, was published in 2000. Most recently he created, executive produced, and wrote the pilot for the critically acclaimed and edgy Show time series *Dexter*, about an incredibly likeable forensics expert for the Miami Police Department who moonlights as a serial killer, trained by his adoptive father, also a cop, to kill other serial killers who have escaped justice.

Are there any particular advantages or disadvantages to beginning writing at midlife?

In my case I was definitely better off starting to write at midlife. My feeling is that my life's experiences leading up to when I started writing professionally in my mid-thirties have contributed to my writing. You have to be relatively self-effacing, and hopefully that comes with age, but I also I believe that one's best work is relatively autobiographical and without life experiences what's there to write about?

I've read that ageism is an issue in Hollywood and wonder if you've seen much of that?

Some. In most cases, younger writers have a greater advantage in the half hour comedy arena. Why, I don't know. But it makes no sense because the older you get the more competent you get at your craft. Hollywood can be shortsighted.

How do you define success?

Wow, there are so many things going through my mind for that one.
I think you're successful when no one is messing with your work. I'm very proud that I created and wrote the pilot for the new *Dexter* series on Showtime. What makes me so proud of it is that what you saw on the screen was exactly what I wrote. Nobody—not the actors, not the director, not the other producers, or the execs—changed it.

I think another measure of success is avoiding the "payday" jobs. Everyone needs to make a living, and in Hollywood you can make a really good living, but when starting out, every writer has to write something they're not particularly interested in—they have no choice—they need the money, but it's nice when you finally don't have to do that because, and this is the important point, because when that becomes the norm, writing becomes nothing more than a job and that just saps whatever artistic aspirations one may have had.

Is becoming a successful writer all that you hoped it would be?

No, not exactly. This is a tough racket with a lot of pressure. It goes back to a Hollywood tradition which is you're only as good as your last success. "Love your latest," they used to say and they still say it.

To many not in the business, there's a perception that Hollywood is a very laid back, casual, easy going place—lounging by the pool, drinks in hand, coming up with stories, but that is most certainly not the case. It's hard work. Everyone I know in Hollywood works twelve to fourteen hours a day. The problem is, there's so much energy is wasted. What I mean is that it's not unusual to work for months on a story, fight for weeks to protect your vision, then a star gets hired who "suggests" a few changes and suddenly everything you did is thrown out the window to service that star—the story now takes on a completely different direction and everything you expended so much energy fighting for is no longer an issue.

What is your writing routine?

I tend to write in spurts. You go into a new project with trepidation and it may take you twenty or thirty pages before you find that one line, that one moment in a scene between two people before it all clicks, when it all makes sense, and when that happens, it can be magical. It's hard to describe that feeling—knowing—being absolute that what you're writing about is going to work, has a meaning, confident that your characters will tell the story that you want to say. There's nothing better.

Do you recommend joining a local writers' group or workshop?

I'm not a big fan—frankly I'm suspicious of any formal educational program claiming they can teach anyone to be an artist. I suspect it works for some, but I bet those who benefit already had what it takes and they would succeed with or without the degree. I'm probably biased, because I had no formal education in writing. I just read a lot and kept writing.

If you have the choice—traveling the world is a far better education. Take any job you can because at the end of the day, it will all add up and make you a better writer.

Do you think being an English major helped you or hurt you as a writer?

Definitely helped. All of the reading I did in college contributed. I only wish I had read more history and religion in addition to all the fiction.

What do you think of beginning writers who have difficulty writing creatively because they can't let go of the grammar rules?

You can't let grammar hang you up. You have to trust your ear, and really learn to listen to how people talk, how they communicate, and if you do that, then you'll be more truthful and honest about how your characters express themselves. Nailing that is in some ways a primary difference between the novelist and the screenwriter.

What's the difference between writing a TV show and writing a TV movie?

Basically and most obvious is the length. A two-hour movie is finite—there's a beginning and an end. To get a series up, you first have to write a pilot and in the pilot you have to do, what I call "laying in the DNA" for all of the characters. Establish the character's likes and dislikes, their idiosyncrasies, their fears and goals, the nuances that make us all special, and present them either through dialogue or behavior with such conviction that anyone watching will be intrigued, and that alone should be enough to provide the necessary engine to keep a series going. So if you're lucky enough to get a pilot produced then the network executives making the decision will see what the possibilities are, what the series potential is.

When I created and wrote the pilot for *Dexter*, I really concentrated on laying in all that DNA, and fortunately I did it well enough because after producing the pilot, the show was picked up for twelve episodes and, even better, Showtime recently committed to a second year.

How did you decide to go with writing dramas for TV instead of writing novels?

Actually I started writing for the theater. I wrote plays, I acted, and I was a director for eight years before making a living as a writer in television and film. But my theatrical background, rooted in the three-act structure, was the best training I could get. I won the CableACE award for best picture after producing *The Positively True Adventures of the Alleged Texas Cheerleader-Murdering Mom* for HBO and the movie won three Emmys. That success gave me the right to play in the sandbox—to play in Hollywood, but one can never forget that they can always kick you out of the sandbox.

How much of the plot do you know when you begin a story or novel?

I can only speak for myself but one of the great ironies in Hollywood is how so many studio executives preach the importance of character but all they really care about is plot, which is why, as far as I'm concerned, outlines have become a necessary and an almost unavoidable evil. But I'm in the minority, because most writers I know not only embrace the concept but value the process—which as far as I'm concerned, stifles the creative process. Outlines are predetermined, a cold and calculating detailed blue print, defining the beginning, middle and end of a story, which everyone expects to be faithfully followed without deviation. When I'm writing I know the beginning, middle and end of the story but the fun of it all is getting to those points and I don't want to be beholden to a process that negates spontaneity and experimentation.

How much do you know about your characters before you begin?

Everything. I know their histories, habits, likes and dislikes, how they speak and how they behave. I know their agendas. Knowing this and being true to the characters informs the plot. Everything begins with that.

I tend to see the scenes visually and that's critical to success in this business because it's a visual medium. All of us, all writers have access to the same words, and it really has nothing to do with the words we choose. What separates the good from the pedestrian is *how* one sees the world and the good writers see what others don't. Finding the right words to express that is almost academic. It's that simple.

Do you outline, even when it's not required?

Depending on the story, absolutely—but it's a private matter. I did it for myself and not for the studio. I recently wrote a movie called *Four Corners* which is all about the illegal world of gunrunning. It's a massive epic, with hundreds of characters operating in every part of the world. The enormity of it demanded an outline, a structure, because without it, I would have been lost. It's like the famed Russian director Stanislavsky said, "Anything is the enemy of art."

Do you agree that most of the really good writing going on in Hollywood is taking place on the cable TV networks rather than in the traditional film studios?

Maybe—certainly HBO and Showtime in particular have produced magnificent shows; but, then again, there's always been a beautiful moment in every theatrical film I've ever seen.

The nice thing about writing for a series is that the episodes are written quickly. A big screen movie can be a ten-year process from pitch to production. For cable movies, it runs about seven years. That's a long time. That's why a lot of writers like writing for series television: you don't have that tremendously long development time.

Must you live on either coast to be successful in movies and television?

You're better off living on either coast. You need to make the personal connections and you need to get an agent. Agents can't read all the scripts they get from their signed clients, never mind reading an unsolicited script from somebody in Iowa.

David Everett

As senior associate chair of the Master of Arts in the writing program at Johns Hopkins University, David Everett is the academic director of the program. He has taught writing, journalism, and editing at the university and professional level since 1986. As a journalist, he spent two decades traveling across the nation and around the world writing about economics, social change, the environment, politics, and other topics. His reporting and writing have won many awards, including the highest honor for Washington correspondence from the Society of Professional Journalists; investigative awards from the University of Missouri, the Associated Press, and various other organizations, Washington reporting honors from the National Press Club; foreign correspondence awards from the Overseas Press Club, and various business and economics honors, including the John Hancock Business Writing Award. He twice earned the nation's top two awards for writing about the automotive industry. His freelance journalism continues to appear nationally and internationally, and he has published fiction and creative nonfiction in several literary journals. He is the contributing author of three nonfiction books.

You were a successful nonfiction writer when you came to Hopkins, yet you majored in fiction writing there. How difficult was that transition?

At first it was very difficult. I think the difficult thing for anyone who tries to make the transition from nonfiction to fiction, at least initially, is that you try to over-explain everything. Fiction is less fact based. I was an investigative reporter so it became natural for me to always try to develop facts. It becomes instinctive.

I found I could solve part of this problem by getting up early in the morning and writing from five to seven or six to seven, before I went to work as a reporter. Anyone who tries to make this transition has to find ways to break their journalistic voice. I also found it difficult to write fiction while I was traveling as a journalist because you have to be so focused on assignment and you wind up spending most of your time on the assignment.

One thing that worked for me and still does is to read poetry before doing creative work. Poetry gets me into a different frame of mind from the fact-based frame of mind.

At midlife, you also have to balance your everyday job with your creative writing, whether you write for a living as a journalist or do something else that involves a written product. This is a very individual thing. For me, it is doing my creative writing before my regular workday gets started. Another option is to do some activity not involving writing—to make the break between work-related writing and creative writing.

I still struggle with it. I do both fiction and nonfiction now, and I have a very different voice in fiction. Some days I have trouble grabbing onto that voice. What I'm writing now is nonlinear, nontraditional, almost experimental fiction. But my nonfiction generally can be a fairly linear, standard, straightforward reporting of facts. The transition can be difficult for me day to day. It's a luxury for me now to be able to spend time on the sort of fiction that I want to write.

Is it better to specialize in one area of writing?

I've seen people here at the Writing Program sign up for one type of writing but then be drawn to another. You have to see what satisfies you and not be afraid to try it.

One of the great benefits of writing nonfiction is that you can take lifelong obsessions and write about them. I have a friend who's an accomplished writer and an accomplished runner. He's combining the two by writing about running and he's never been happier.

What impact have the scandals like the Frey/Oprah one and others had on creative nonfiction?

I think the scandal in that case had less impact on readers than on writers. But every scandal in the nonfiction community hurts the credibility of the profession.

People want to pick up a nonfiction book and know that what's in it is true. Nonfiction writers have to stick with the facts and those who make up things have forgotten that the reader matters.

Also, there are too many definitions of nonfiction or creative nonfiction out there. Anything called nonfiction carries the assumption by the reader that it's true.

To me, the key is that you don't try to fool the reader, to try to pass off something as fact when you know it's not. You can be creative with factual writing as long you let the reader know what you're doing. They drum it into you in journalism school: the three most important things about journalism and nonfiction are accuracy, accuracy, and accuracy. If you want to make up things, even only a few things among lots of facts, that's still fiction.

Isn't part of that problem that the bigger bookstores want everything to fit into a pigeonhole sales category that they've defined?

Megastores have their shelving process and many books don't fit into a particular category. Narrative nonfiction books like *Into Thin Air* and *The Perfect Storm* tell stories in a narrative form and so to a degree defy the classification system that the bookstores use. Are they history or biography or memoir or what?

For serious writers and readers, "literary journalism" is a more reflective term and a more useful term than nonfiction. In literary journalism the emphasis is on the form and how it's told more than the news aspect of the story. I would love to see a shelf called Literary Journalism.

Would disclaimers keep narrative nonfiction writers from getting in trouble?

Disclaimers like Sebastian Junger's in *The Perfect Storm* are good. I think everyone realizes that Frank McCourt wasn't taking notes as a child, so readers understand that the conversations he relates from his childhood in *Angela's Ashes* are not direct reportage. The poet Mary Karr, who started the current popularity of memoirs with her book *The Liars' Club,* discloses that she remembers things happening a particular way but that her sister does not remember them happening that way. There was no attempt to try to fool the reader, and that's the key.

Writers also can fit qualifiers and disclaimers within the text itself, such as, "I can't know what occurred in someone else's mind but it might have been something like this:...." Another method is to incorporate dialogue without quotation marks, or with a qualifier that could say: "The conversation that took place likely sounded like this." Again, the key is never try to fool the reader.

Roughly, what percentage of your graduate students are over fifty years of age?

Probably about twenty-five percent. That's held constant for a few years now.

Are there any particular advantages or disadvantages to beginning writing at midlife?

Older students have more life experience; they have something to write about. They've had good and bad experiences with family and have lived a life. They've been in the military or had another career. They take a more mature approach and are more realistic about living life.

One disadvantage is that older students are often anxious about being back in the classroom and very concerned about grades, but their anxiety usually evaporates after the first class. The joke in the Writing Program is that we tell older students they are required to have their children sign their report card.

Another problem with older students who are or have been in a writing-related profession: They have to learn how to break the formulas they used and relied upon in their professional lives. That's especially true of lawyers and government employees who tend to write in legalese and governmentese.

For example, one writer in the program kept trying to write about AIDS, which was something that she also did as a government editor and writer. She kept slipping into government-speak. I finally suggested that she avoid writing about AIDS in the program, at least at first. When she began writing about anything except AIDS, she did fine. Later she even discovered that what she really wanted to write about with regard to AIDS was the personal and human costs of the illness, and she did that very well when she was able to apply her new creative writing skills to her favorite work topic.

How do you keep your energy up for the long haul when writing a book?

I have a writing routine. My target is to produce a page a day. If I'm sick or traveling or tired and miss a day, I have to make it up. A lot of people have done novels on a page-a-day basis. But don't let the target stop you: When you get in your cocoon of writing—that's what I like to call it, you're so thoroughly involved you don't see or hear anything else—go for as long as you can. With an hour a day you may hit your stride in the last ten minutes and have to break off to make the kids breakfast or go to work. Other writers plan a day each week to write. Whatever your approach, it's easier if you establish a routine.

I get up an hour or two early in the morning and write then, before the kids get up, and before I have to go to work. I admit I don't always meet that goal. I'm in midlife myself, and children are exhausting.

I also approach books by chapters. I don't think about the whole book, because that can make you feel overwhelmed. I do longer projects piecemeal to keep my energy up. When I get a chapter done, I celebrate. Then I plan and outline the next chapter. Planning is important. On the novel I'm working on, I got about sixty percent done and found out it wasn't structured right. A minor character needed to become a major character. I restarted it from the beginning.

How do you define success as a writer?

My first career as a journalist put me on a course to see things and do things I could never have done otherwise. I traveled across and around the country many times, and I was able to travel to foreign countries as a reporter. As a reporter you get to approach people on a very human level. It motivates you and it helps you to grow intellectually. You get a broader view of the world, and the United States' role in the world. Being a reporter also gives you a pass to do and say things most people never get to say and do. For example, I've interviewed the president in the Oval Office and I have interviewed people who lost their kids to war. As a result of my investigative reports, people were sent to jail. The press plays an important watchdog role in society, and I was proud to be part of that. I would never have been able to do all of those things had I not been a journalist.

Now, in the second part of my writing life, I get a lot out of teaching and working in the classroom and building a graduate program. And with fiction, I feel enormous personal satisfaction. When I get a short story published, it touches me deeply inside. I hope to publish a novel, too.

I find fiction to be a way of figuring out the world. As a news journalist I was looking at how things work; now I'm trying to figure out deeper things—things about character or emotion. My novel is about love, and parental love in particular, and the writing helps me to figure things out. I find news journalism is primarily external, while fiction is primarily internal.

As a national journalist I had complete confidence in my ability to get the job done and felt I could compete with anyone on that playing field. But with creative writing I feel much more challenged, and much more that I'm working in an art form. I sometimes wonder if I can ever write the kind of novel that I want to. I feel myself struggling with the goal of writing something important, something that has staying power in the world of fiction. I had no idea I'd find it so challenging.

What's the downside?

The downside to most creative writing is that it's solitary. In news journalism there was a group process: a lot of input from others as well as interaction with others. People who are naturally gregarious have to learn to put the brakes on that aspect of their personality.

The creative writing process also can leave you emotionally drained. Sure, I felt drained as a news journalist, and sometimes emotionally, but mostly mentally and physically. I find the fatigue for fiction is different. Time stops when you're in the writing cocoon. You look up and find that hours have passed. Maybe it's because the stakes are different. In the end, one of the biggest reasons I left news journalism is that it is so temporary. I think one of the reasons for writing fiction or serious nonfiction is that you're trying to leave something behind, something more permanent and something that's more important than you are. That's quite hard work.

How much outlining do you do?

I'm absolutely an outliner, even when my structure isn't traditional or linear, but I'm not bound by it. When I'm in the cocoon and stuff comes up that wasn't in the outline, I have to go with it. One of the traits that defines a good writer is the ability to leave your outline and your previous ideas behind when you need to—to follow the muse. But yes, I outline the book first, and then individual chapters, and even scenes. I will even outline stuff after finishing it, to see if the structure still makes sense. The outline or scene or chapter or book may be intentionally chaotic rather than orderly; that's okay. But the structure always needs to make sense and to be able to be followed by a reader, however disorderly.

What advice do you have for writers who are just getting started at midlife?

First, I recommend they get help through a writers' group or class. It doesn't have to be a graduate or college writing class. But find a mentor or guide by taking a noncredit course or a community college course or joining a writing group. Going off to learn it by yourself may take you ten years to learn to write that way. A good guide can save you a few years, or even most of those years. Also you'll get exposed to more varied things. Most of our students read and study things in the Writing Program that they likely would have never read on their own.

I also suggest that new writers look to their passions and hobbies from their lives. It doesn't have to be the same topic from your professional career. If you have had a lifelong passion for golf or cooking, for instance, maybe you should write about that.

Developing writers also need to understand that it's different to read as a writer than as a reader. Learn how to read properly, as a craftsman. Be able to tear apart someone's writing to see what works and what does not. A cabinetmaker looks at a cabinet differently from someone who simply stores things in a cabinet. It's an acquired skill, but once you learn to read like a writer, that skill can serve you for the rest of your writing life. You can learn from that analysis and not need to take so many classes. It's similar to how visual artists learn: A painter looks at paintings in a different way than someone who simply enjoys looking at pictures.

Finally, the medical profession is now telling us that if we use and stretch our minds, our lives will be longer and healthier. I assure you that something as rigorous as writing will keep you sharp and keep you challenged and excited and spirited. It will keep your mind vibrant and healthy. Look at writing as something to keep your brain exercised. Retirement shouldn't mean backing off from doing something new and different in the second half of life.

Resources
Redundant Phrases

Common Redundancy	Preferred Short Form
absolute necessity	necessary
absolutely complete	complete
absolutely essential	essential
active consideration	consideration
advance reservation	reservation
advance warning	warning
advise and inform	advise; inform
after the time of	after
aid and abet	aid; abet
amount of $10	$10
any and all	any; all
appreciate in value	appreciate
at a time when	when
attached please find	attached is
baffling enigma	enigma
both alike	alike
both of them	both
brief in duration	brief
brief minute	minute; moment
bright and shiny	bright; shiny
cancel out	cancel
Capitol building	Capitol
city of New York	New York
close proximity	proximity; near
collect together	collect
color of yellow	yellow
combine together	combine
compare and contrast	compare; contrast
complete monopoly	monopoly
completely unanimous	unanimous
component parts	components; parts
conclusive proof	proof
consensus of opinion	consensus
continue on	continue
cooperate and work together	cooperate; work together

cooperate together	cooperate
deeds and actions	deeds; actions
demand and insist	demand; insist
depreciated in value	depreciated
different kinds of	different
distance of five feet	five feet
doctorate degree	doctorate
during the course of	during; while; when
during the time that	during; while; when
each and every	each; every
eliminate completely	eliminate
enclosed herein	enclosed is
enclosed herewith is	enclosed is; here is
enclosed please find	enclosed is; here is
end result	result; conclusion
equal halves	halves; in half
estimated at about	estimated
exact same	same
face up to	face
fair and equitable	fair; equitable
fear and nervousness	fear; nervous
few and far between	seldom
few in number	few
filled to capacity	filled
final conclusion	conclusion; end
final outcome	outcome
first and foremost	first; foremost
first began	began
follow after	follow
for the purpose of	for; to
for the reason that	since; because
free gift	gift
future plans	plans
future prospect	prospect
great many	many
he is the man that	he

help and assist	help; assist
hopes and aspirations	hopes; aspirations
hour of 5 P.M.	5 P.M.
hurry up	hurry
if and when	if
immediately and at once	immediately; at once
individual person	individual; person
intents and purposes	intent; purpose
irregardless	regardless
join together	join
large in number	many
large in size	large
made out of	made of
make a statement saying	say
many in number	many
meeting held in	meeting in
mental attitude	attitude
merge together	merge
might possibly	might; possibly
month of May	May
more superior	superior
mutual compromise	compromise
mutual cooperation	cooperation
mutually agreeable	agreeable
my own	my
my personal opinion	my opinion
new and innovative	new; innovative
new innovation	innovation
new recruit	recruit
null and void	null; void
obligation and responsibility	obligation; responsibility
old adage	adage
one and only	one; only
one or another reason	some reason
past history	history
penetrate into	penetrate

peace and quiet	peace; quiet
period of five days	five days
period of time	period; time
personal opinion	opinion
pick and choose	pick; choose
plain and simple	plain; simple
plan in advance	plan
point in time	then; point; time
positive growth	growth
positive identification	identification
present time	present; now
price of $59.99	$59.99
prompt and speedy	prompt; quick; speedy
proposed plan	plan
question as to whether	whether
renovate like new	renovate
repeat again	repeat
result and effect	result; effect
resultant effect	result; effect
right and proper	right; proper
rules and regulations	rules; regulations
self-confessed	admitted; confessed
she is a woman who	she
sick and tired	sick; tired
sign your name	sign
sincere good wishes	sincere wishes; good wishes
single unit	unit
small in number	few
small in size	small
smile on his face	smile
solid facts	facts
some reason or another	some reason
someone or other	someone
spell out in detail	spell out; detail
square in shape	square
successful triumph	success; triumph

sum of $10	$10
surrounding circumstances	circumstances
temporary reprieve	reprieve
temporary loan	loan
this day and age	now; today
three weeks' time	three weeks
tire and fatigue	tire; fatigue
true facts	facts
unjust and unfair	unjust; unfair
unless and until	unless
unrelentless	relentless
unsubstantiated rumor	rumor
until such time as	until; when
usual custom	custom
various and sundry	various; sundry
variously different	different
visible to the eye	visible
visit with	visit
way, shape, or form	way
weather conditions	weather
wet precipitation	precipitation
widow woman	widow
year of 2009	2009
7 P.M. in the evening	7 P.M.

Wordy Phrases

Wordy Phrase	Preferred Short Form
a great deal of	much
a large number of	many; several
a limited number of	one, etc.
a majority of	most
a number of	several
a significant proportion of	some
a sizable percentage of	many
accounted for by	due to; caused by
accounted for by the fact that	because
acknowledge receipt of	have received
add the point that	add that
after very careful consideration	after considering
ahead of schedule	early
all of the	all
along the lines of	like; about; similar to
an example of this is the fact that	for example
an overwhelming majority	most
another aspect to be considered is	concerning; regarding; in addition
are engaged in	are; are in
are in a position to	can
are in receipt of	received
are in the process of	are
are not in a position to	cannot
arrange to send	send
as far as we are concerned	DELETE
as a matter of fact	DELETE
as a result	therefore
as a result of	because
as of this date	now
as regards	for; about
as related to	for; about
as such	DELETE

as to	about
at a later date	later
at all times	always
at an early date	soon; at once; today; immediately; tomorrow
at that time	then
at which time	when; during
at your convenience	soon; today; tomorrow
be cognizant of	know
be in possession of	have
be in receipt of	receive
be of the opinion that	believe
because of the fact that	because
both together	both; together
by means of	by; via
by means of this	by this
by virtue of the fact that	because
certain person	person
come in contact with	meet
come to a decision as to	decide
concerning the nature of	about; concerning
conditions that exist in	conditions in
conduct an investigation	investigate
date of the policy	policy date
destroyed by fire	burned
despite the fact that	despite the; although
draw to your attention	show, point out
due to the fact that	because
during the course of	during; while
during the time that	while
except in a small number of cases	usually
exhibit a tendency to	tend to
first of all	first
for the sake of	DELETE
from the point of view of	for; to

give consideration to	consider
give rise to	cause
goes to show	shows, proves
had occasion to be	was
have an input into	contribute to
have the ability to	be able to
have the need for	need
if at all possible	if possible
if it is at all possible	if possible
in a satisfactory manner	satisfactorily
in a timely fashion	timely; promptly
in accordance with your request	as requested
in advance of	before
in any case	anyway
in case	if
in case of	if
in compliance with your request	as requested
in connection with	about; concerning
in due course	soon; today; tomorrow
in due time	soon; today; tomorrow
in excess of	exceed(s)
in favor of	for; to
in light of the fact that	because
in many cases	often; frequently
in many instances	often
in most cases	usually
in order that	so that; for
in order to	to
in rare cases	rarely
in reference to	about; regarding
in regard to	regarding; about
in relation to	about; concerning
in some cases	sometimes
in spite of the fact that	although; though; despite

in terms of	in; for
in the case of	regarding; concerning
in the case that	if; when
in the course of	during
in the early part of	early
in the event that	if; in case
in the field of	in
in the final analysis	finally
in the first place	first
in the majority of instances	usually
in the matter of	about
in the nature of	like
in the near future	soon; today; tomorrow
in the neighborhood of	about
in the normal course of events	normally
in the not-too-distant future	soon
in the vicinity of	near
in view of the fact that	therefore; because
inasmuch as	because
inquire as to	ask about
inside of	inside
involves the necessity of	requires
is at this time	is
is at variance with	differs from
is defined as	is
is dependent on	depends on
is indicative of	indicates
is of the opinion that	believes; thinks that
it is clear that	therefore; clearly
it is imperative that you	you should
it is observed that	DELETE
it is often the case that	often; frequently
it is our conclusion in light of investigation	we conclude that; in conclusion
it should be noted that the	please note

it stands to reason	DELETE
it was noted that if	if
it would not be unreasonable to assume	I assume
leaving out of consideration	disregarding
made the announcement that	announced that
make an examination of	examine
make inquiry regarding	ask about; inquire about
make mention of	mention
make use of	use
may possibly	may
needless to say	DELETE
not in a position to	unable to, cannot
not of a high order of accuracy	inaccurate
notwithstanding the fact that	although
of considerable magnitude	important
of minor importance	unimportant
of such difficulty	so difficult
on a few occasions	occasionally
on a regular basis	regularly
on a theoretical level	in theory; theoretically
on account of the conditions described	because of the conditions
on account of the fact that	because
on the average	on average
on the grounds that	because
on the occasion of	when; during
on the order of	about
on two separate occasions	twice
outside of	outside
over the long term	ultimately
owing to the fact that	because; since
perform an analysis	analyze

perhaps it may be that you	perhaps; it may be that; you may
placed under arrest	arrested
please don't hesitate to	please
previous to	before
prior to	before
proceed to investigate	investigate
pursuant to our agreement	as agreed
put in an appearance	appear; appeared
reach a conclusion as to	decide; concluded
reach the conclusion	conclude
refer to as	call
relative to this	about this
seldom ever	seldom
subsequent to	after
take into consideration	consider
take this opportunity	DELETE
that is	AVOID
that kind of thing	that
the bulk of	most
the data show that we can	we can
the fullest possible	most; fully
the information in our files	our information
the majority of	most
the only difference being that	except
the question as to whether	whether
the undersigned	I
the writer	I
there are not very many	few
this is a subject that	this subject
this is to inform you	DELETE
to a certain extent	in part
to a large degree	largely
to be sure	AVOID
to summarize the above	in sum; in summary
under date of	dated; on

under separate cover	separately
under the circumstances	because
until such time as	until
we are not in a position to	we cannot
we regret to say	we are sorry
we wish to acknowledge	thank you for
we would like to ask	please; would you
whether or not	whether
will you be kind enough	please
window of opportunity	opportunity
wish to bring to your attention	notice that; note that; please note
with reference to	about
with respect to	about
with the exception of	except
with the result that	so that
with this in mind, it is clear that	therefore; clearly
within the realm of possibility	possible; possibly

Example of a Query Letter

This is a model letter, not an actual letter. It is provided as an example of what a query letter looks like to guide you in preparing your own queries.

JOHN Q. SMYTH

May 4, 20XX
Mary S. Reader
Editor, River City Gazette
25 Main Street
River City, VA 52525

Dear Ms. Reader:

The sound of rustling petticoats, when no one is there. An icy cold spot in a room with a roaring fireplace. A feeling of not being alone in an empty attic; different hotel guests staying at different times in a particular room in a hotel, all returning to their room to find nothing else disturbed but their hair brushes have been moved.

A new M. Night Shyamalan movie? Nope. All taking place right here in River City.

With Halloween just five months away I thought you might be interested in a feature article of 1,500 to 2,000 words, working title: *Meet Your Neighborhood Ghost*, for your biweekly *About Our Town* section.

I propose to interview and gather anecdotes from at least three of the seven owners of haunted properties I've identified in River City. The article will be written in a light, tongue-in-cheek style suitable for the family nature of your readership. I'm an experienced photographer and can provide 35mm photographs to support the article if you like.

Other sources I plan to interview include Dr. Fergus M. McFergus, chairman of the Paranormal Phenomenon Department at State University, who will provide context on paranormal activities, and Milo J. "Spookman" Feebers, national president, Ghost Finders International, who will discuss similar happenings around the USA.

If you like, I can do a sidebar on famous haunted houses in the South, and can also produce a 500 word version of the main article for your *Kids Page* section.

I've published a number of articles which, while not directly on point, are indicative of my ability to write this piece for you. I'll be happy to furnish clips upon request.

I think this article will give your readers a smile, as well as be fun for both of us to work on. I eagerly await your response.

Sincerely,

John Q. Smyth

1313 Anywhere Drive • River City, VA • 52525
Phone: (o) 555-555-5555 • (H): 555-555-555
JohnQ/q@aol.com

Annotated Bibliography

There is a wealth of books and other resources available to help you with your writing. This should not be considered an all-inclusive list. The books listed below are simply those I've found particularly useful.

Reference Books

General Writing Reference

The Elements Of Style, Fourth Edition by William Strunk, Jr. and E. B. White, (Longman, 1999), ISBN 020530902X, often referred to as simply Strunk and White, is the best guideline on writing that you will find anywhere. All bookstores carry it. Any version will do, but get the most current one if you can. It's a small book but packed with terrific advice. I recommend reading it from cover to cover.

Thesaurus

The most useful thesaurus I've found is *The Synonym Finder* by J.I. Rodale (Grand Central Publishing, 1986), ISBN 0446370290. I find it much quicker to use than *Roget's Thesaurus* and it suits my needs 95 percent of the time. If I'm really having trouble finding the right word, then I'll consult another source such as *Roget's*.

Desk References

Have a small one and a big one. The small one for quick look-ups and the big one when there's a less common issue to research.

Grammar Guides–There are many grammar and writing guides on the market. The writing guide I keep on my desk for quick reference is *Write Right! A Desktop Digest of Punctuation, Grammar, and Style, Fourth Edition* by Jan Venolia (Ten Speed Press, 2001), ISBN 1580083285.

In quick reference grammar guides, I prefer the shorter ones that have a sense of humor. The one I use most often is *Nitty-Gritty Grammar: A Not-So-Serious Guide to Clear Communication* by Edith H. Fine and Judith P. Josephson (Ten Speed Press, 1998), ISBN 0898159660. Another is *The Deluxe Transitive Vampire: A Handbook of Grammar for the Innocent, the Eager and the Doomed, Revised Edition* by Karen Elizabeth Gordon (Pantheon, 1993), ISBN 0679418601. *The Writer's Digest*

Grammar Desk Reference by Gary Lutz and Diane Stevenson (Writer's Digest Books, 2005), ISBN 1582973350, is a larger and more serious grammar reference. It's spiral bound, so it lays open easily on your desk.

Writers' Guides–writers' guides are thorough, all-inclusive references on standard use of grammar, punctuation, abbreviation, usage, and just about anything else you might want to know about writing. There are several good ones on the market. The one I see most often used in business is *The Gregg Reference Manual, 10th Edition* by William A. Sabin, (Career Education, 2004), ISBN 0072936533. One that I have found useful is the *New York Public Library Writer's Guide to Style and Usage* by Andrea Sutcliffe (Collins, 1994), ISBN 0062700642. And, you won't go wrong with any of the several writers guides written by Diana Hacker. Look her name up at the library or bookstore and you'll find several of them, all good.

Revising Your Writing

If you need more help with the revision process here are some good books:

Self Editing For Fiction Writers, Second Edition: How To Edit Yourself Into Print by Renni Browne and Dave King (Collins, 2004), ISBN 0060545690.

Make Your Words Work: Proven Techniques for Effective Writing— for Fiction and Nonfiction by Gary Provost (Writer's Digest Books, 1990), ISBN 0-89879-418-8. Any of Provost's books about writing are worth taking a look at.

Fiction First Aid: Instant Remedies for Novels, Stories and Scripts by Raymond Obstfeld (F & W Publications, 2002), ISBN 158297117X.

Revision: How To Find And Fix What Isn't Working In Your Story And Strengthen What Is To Build Compelling, Successful Fiction (Elements of Fiction Writing Series) by Kit Reed (Writer's Digest Books, 1989), ISBN 0898793505.

Writer's Voice

It's usually best to simply let your voice develop on its own, but if developing your writer's voice is of concern to you, here's a good book on that subject: *Finding Your Voice: How to Put Personality in Your Writing* by Les Edgerton (Writer's Digest Books, 2003), ISBN 1582971730.

Punctuation

The "A Handbook of Style" which can be found in the back of *Merriam-Webster's Collegiate Dictionary* will answer most of your punctuation questions. It is a superior dictionary to boot. For an excellent perspective on how punctuation can actually add to the drama of your writing, check out *A Dash Of Style: The Art and Mastery of Punctuation* by Noah Lukeman (W.W. Norton, 2006), ISBN 0393329803. I never imagined I would enjoy reading from cover to cover a book about punctuation, but Lukeman's book is fascinating because it covers the dramatic, dynamic, and artistic uses of punctuation. You'll be amazed at how much punctuation can do.

Writing Techniques

Dramatic Structure

A terrific and easy to read book on creating stories is *How to Tell A Story: The Secrets of Writing Captivating Tales* by Peter Rubie and Gary Provost (Writer's Digest Books, 1998), 089878094. Highly recommended for writing fiction and drama.

Aristotle's Poetics for Screenwriters: Storytelling Secrets from the Greatest Mind in Western Civilization by Michael Tierno (Hyperion, 2002), ISBN 0786887400, does a great job of making Aristotle's ideas, still the basis for dramatic structure, accessible to modern writers.

Developing Characters

The best book, bar nonc, on developing characters and characterization was originally written in 1942 and published in paperback in 1987: *Characters Make Your Story* by Maren Elwood (Writer, Inc., 1987), ISBN 0871160196. It's out of print, but you can find it on Amazon.com and bookfinder.com. Buy any version you can get your hands on. Highly recommended.

For the low-down on how to develop characters and characterization, written in clear and accessible language, look at *Dynamic Characters: How to create personalities that keep readers captivated* by Nancy Kress (Writer's Digest Books, 2004), ISBN 1582973199. Kress is the current fiction columnist for Writer's Digest Magazine. You'll find any of her books on writing to be worth your while.

Another good book on character development, particularly for writing drama, is *Creating Unforgettable Characters: A practical guide to character development* by Linda Seger (Owl Books, 1990), ISBN 0805011714.

Setting

*Setting: How to create and sustain a sharp sense of time and place in your fiction (Elements of Fiction Writing Series)*by Jack M. Bickham (Writer's Digest Books, 1994), ISBN 0898796350 is a useful reference on using setting in fiction.

Writing fiction

Short Fiction

Two of the best books I've found about writing short fiction were written by science fiction writers, but don't worry if you're not an SF fan; they're both broadly enough written to work for most types of short stories.

Creating Short Fiction: A Practical, Tested Approach to Unlock the Magic of Writing Within You, Revised Edition by Damon Knight (St. Martin's Griffin, 1997), ISBN 0312150946.

Notes To A Science Fiction Writer, Revised and Expanded Edition by Ben Bova (Houghton Mifflin, 1981), ISBN 0395305217.

Novels and Short Fiction

Lawrence Block is an award-winning mystery writer. For many years he was the fiction columnist for *Writer's Digest Magazine*. There are few people whose writing about the subject of fiction writing is as clear and entertaining as Block. Highly recommended.

Spider, Spin Me A Web: A Handbook for Fiction Writers by Lawrence Block (Harper Paperbacks, 1996), ISBN 0688146902.

Telling Lies For Fun & Profit: A Manual For Fiction Writers by Lawrence Block (Harper Paperbacks, 1994), ISBN 0688132286.

Writing the Novel: From Plot To Print by Lawrence Block (Writer's Digest Books, 1985), ISBN 0898792088.

For a different perspective on writing fiction take a look at the following:

On Writing: A Memoir of the Craft by Stephen King (Pocket, 2002), ISBN 0743455967.

How To Write A Damn Good Novel: A step-by-step no nonsense guide to dramatic storytelling by James N. Frey (St. Martin's Press, 1987), ISBN 0312010443.

How To Write A Damn Good Novel, II: Advanced Techniques for Dramatic Storytelling by James N. Frey (St. Martin's Press, 1994), ISBN 0312104782.

Writing Nonfiction

For article writing in general take a look at *Writer's Digest Handbook Of Magazine Article Writing: Handbook Of Magazine Article Writing* by Michelle Ruberg (Writer's Digest Books, 2005), ISBN 1582973334.

For writing feature articles, *Feminine Wiles: Creative Techniques for Writing Women's Feature Stories that Sell*, by Donna Elizabeth Boetig (Quill Driver Books, 1998), ISBN 1884956025, presents clear instruction with lots of tips. While the focus is on the major women's magazines, the writing tips are applicable to any article writing.

For writing nonfiction in general you won't go wrong with the following three books:

On Writing Well, 30th Anniversary Edition: The Classic Guide to Writing Nonfiction by William K. Zinsser (Collins, 2006), ISBN 0060891548.

The Art Of Creative Nonfiction: Writing and Selling the Literature of Reality (Wiley Books for Writers Series) by Lee Gutkind, (Wiley, 1997), ISBN 0471113565.

Creative Nonfiction: Researching and Crafting Stories of Real Life by Philip Gerard, (Waveland Press Inc., 2004), ISBN 157766339X.

Writing Poetry

Pulitzer prize-winning poet and former Poet Laureate of the United States Ted Kooser is remarkably down-to-earth in his advice to writers. *The Poetry Home Repair Manual: Practical Advice for Beginning Poetry* by Ted Kooser (Bison Books, 2007), ISBN 0803259786, is chock-full of great advice not only about poetry but writing in general. Highly recommended.

The Poet's Dictionary: a Handbook of Prosody and Poetic Devices by William Packard (Collins, 1994), ISBN 00627204577 is a good reference for anyone interested in writing poetry.

Writing Drama

Below are several good books that will give you everything you need to know to get started writing for stage, screen, or television:

The Art & Craft of Playwriting by Jeffrey Hatcher (Story Press Books, 2000), ISBN 1884910467.

Story: Substance, Structure, Style, And The Principles Of Screenwriting by Robert McKee (Harper Entertainment, 1997) ISBN 0060391685

Screenplay: The Foundations Of Screenwriting by Syd Field (Delta, 2005), ISBN 0385339038.

The Screenwriter's Bible: A Complete Guide To Writing, Formatting, and Selling Your Script, Fourth Edition by David Trottier (Sillman-James Press, 2005), ISBN 1879505843.

Making A Good Script Great by Linda Seger (Samuel French, 1994), ISBN 0573699216.

Elephant Bucks: An Insider's Guide To Writing For TV Sitcoms by Sheldon Bull, (Michael Wiese Productions, 2007), ISBN 1932907270.

Market Guides

There are several annual market guides published by Writer's Digest Books that that will help you find publishers for your work. These are updated each year and are usually available in bookstores and in libraries. The primary market guide is *Writer's Market* or *Writer's Market, Deluxe Edition* which includes everything in the regular edition plus online access to a constantly updated database. Specialty guides include:

• *Novel & Short Story Writer's Market 20XX*
• *The Guide to Literary Agents 20XX*
• *Poets Market 20XX*
• *Children's Writer's and Illustrator's Market 20XX*

Writing Book Queries and Proposals

Novels

Your Novel Proposal from Creation to Contract: The Complete Guide To Writing Query Letters, Synopses, And Proposals For Agents and Editors by Blythe Camenson and Marshall J. Cook (Writer's Digest Books,1999), ISBN 0898798752.

The Sell Your Novel Toolkit: Everything You Need To Know about Queries, Synopses, Marketing, And Breaking In, Second Edition by Elizabeth Lyon (Blue Heron Publishing, 1997), ISBN 0936085401.

Nonfiction Books

There are several good guides to writing nonfiction book proposals. If you're planning on writing a proposal for a nonfiction book I recommend reading all of them, to gain a wide perspective on the process, and owning at least one or two for easy reference.

The Fast-Track Course on How to Write a Nonfiction Book Proposal by Stephen Blake Mettee (Quill Driver Books, 2001), ISBN 188495622X.

Nonfiction Book Proposals Anybody Can Write: How to Get a Contract and Advance before Writing your Book, Second Edition by Elizabeth Lyon (Blue Heron Publishing, 2000), ISBN 0936085452.

How to Publish Your Nonfiction Book: A Complete Guide to Making the Right Publishers Say Yes (Square One Writer's Guide) by Rudy Shur (Square One Publishers, 2001), ISBN 0757000002.

How To Write A Book Proposal, Third Edition by Michael Larsen (Writer's Digest Books, 2004), ISBN 1582972516.

Write The Perfect Book Proposal: 10 That Sold and Why, 2nd Edition by Jeff Herman and Deborah Adams (John Wiley & Sons, Inc., 2001), ISBN 0471353124.

Self-Publishing

Two good resources for writers considering self-publishing are *Dan Poynter's Self-Publishing Manual: How to Write, Print and Sell Your Own Book, 15th Edition* by Dan Poynter (Para Publishing, 2006), ISBN 1568601344, and *Complete Guide to Self Publishing: Everything you need to know to write, publish, promote and sell your own book , 4th Edition* by Tom Ross and Marilyn Ross (Writer's Digest Books, 2002), ISBN 1582970912.

Poynter also has a wealth of information of use to writers, whether self-publishing or commercially publishing, at his website, parapublishing.com.

Freelance Writing

The following are three solid books that cover everything about freelancing from setting up your office to finding clients:

Six-Figure Freelancing: The Writer's Guide To Making More Money by Kelly James-Enger (Random House, 2005), ISBN 0375720952.

Handbook for Freelance Writing by Michael Perry (McGraw-Hill, 1998), ISBN 0844232564.

Secrets Of A Freelance Writer, Third Edition: How To Make $100,000 A Year Or More by Robert W. Bly (Owl Books, 2006), ISBN 0805078037.

Standard Manuscript Format

There is no single correct physical format for a manuscript, but following common format conventions, as shown here, is a good way to say to an editor: "I am a professional." Always use letterhead-sized, white paper. Always be sure the print is dark and legible. Paper clip sheets together or use a manuscript box; never staple.

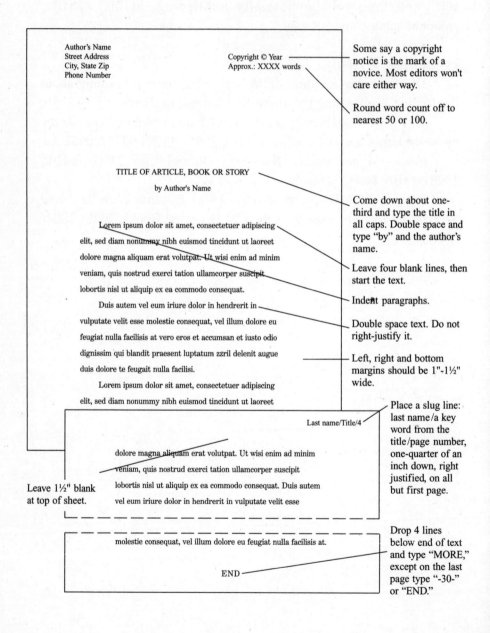

Author's Name
Street Address
City, State Zip
Phone Number

Copyright © Year
Approx.: XXXX words

Some say a copyright notice is the mark of a novice. Most editors won't care either way.

Round word count off to nearest 50 or 100.

TITLE OF ARTICLE, BOOK OR STORY

by Author's Name

Lorem ipsum dolor sit amet, consectetuer adipiscing elit, sed diam nonummy nibh euismod tincidunt ut laoreet dolore magna aliquam erat volutpat. Ut wisi enim ad minim veniam, quis nostrud exerci tation ullamcorper suscipit lobortis nisl ut aliquip ex ea commodo consequat.

Duis autem vel eum iriure dolor in hendrerit in vulputate velit esse molestie consequat, vel illum dolore eu feugiat nulla facilisis at vero eros et accumsan et iusto odio dignissim qui blandit praesent luptatum zzril delenit augue duis dolore te feugait nulla facilisi.

Lorem ipsum dolor sit amet, consectetuer adipiscing elit, sed diam nonummy nibh euismod tincidunt ut laoreet

Come down about one-third and type the title in all caps. Double space and type "by" and the author's name.

Leave four blank lines, then start the text.

Indent paragraphs.

Double space text. Do not right-justify it.

Left, right and bottom margins should be 1"-1½" wide.

Last name/Title/4

Place a slug line: last name/a key word from the title/page number, one-quarter of an inch down, right justified, on all but first page.

Leave 1½" blank at top of sheet.

dolore magna aliquam erat volutpat. Ut wisi enim ad minim veniam, quis nostrud exerci tation ullamcorper suscipit lobortis nisl ut aliquip ex ea commodo consequat. Duis autem vel eum iriure dolor in hendrerit in vulputate velit esse

molestie consequat, vel illum dolore eu feugiat nulla facilisis at.

END

Drop 4 lines below end of text and type "MORE," except on the last page type "-30-" or "END."

Index

Symbols
1and1.com 216
5B method 176

A
aar-online.org 204
Academy Award 107
accents 15, 283
acknowledgments 177
action 106, 111, 145, 156, 164
action and thriller 152
active voice 94, 96, 97
adjective 71
advance 210
adverbs 71, 130
advertisement copy writing 214
agent 64, 192, 202, 204, 205, 207-211
Alighieri, Dante 184
Amazon.com 223
American Society of Journalists and Authors 177, 221
anecdotes 52, 62, 172
antagonist 106, 115, 118, 123, 160, 164
appendices 177
Aristotle 105, 112
articles 23, 170
Asimov, Isaac 153
Association of Authors' Representatives 204
Association of Writers & Writing Programs 226
Assumed Name Certificate 215
atmosphere 111, 142, 194
audience 10, 20, 44, 45, 63, 101, 147, 152, 161, 192-194, 197, 207
author/agent relationship 204
autobiography 171
AWP Official Guide to Writing Programs, The 226

B
Bach, Richard 24
back matter 177
back story 163
Barnes & Noble (iUniverse.com) 212
Barry, Dave 59
batching 177
Bausch, Richard 167, 238
beginning 161, 162
beginnings, middles, and ends 160, 171, 172
Bible 179
biographies 25, 169, 177

biography 59, 147, 172
blog 209
blurb.com 212
Boetig, Donna 177, 241
Bond, James 111
book proposal 98
book, self-help 174
book signings 209
book tour 209
bookfinder.com 223
booklets 214
Boomers 5
boxing 176
brain-mapping 48
Bright Lights, Big City 122
Brokeback Mountain 153
browsing 176
bubbling 48
building 177
bundling 177

C
Call of the Wild, The 138
Cameron, James 109
Carol Burnett Show 227
case histories 214
category 152
cause and effect relationships 105
central idea 47, 48, 49, 52
character development 161
character driven 111
character, lead 114
character, main 114, 116
character profile 119
character sketch 116
character traits 117, 120
character, viewpoint 114, 142, 143, 155
characterization 84, 97, 111, 117, 186, 193
characters 12, 20, 23, 48, 53-55, 84, 103-107, 109, 111, 112, 114, 116, 119, 121, 123, 125, 129-136, 138-140, 142, 144, 147, 151, 152, 154-157, 159-162, 194, 197
characters, flat 115, 120
characters, rounded 115, 120
characters, supporting 115
Chekhov, Anton 142
Christie, Agatha 11
Clark, Petula 107
climax 104, 111, 157, 161
clippings 18, 177
clippings file 17, 162
clips 209, 221

clips file 17, 217
cluster 163
cluster chart 51
cluster diagram 49
clustering 48, 49, 51, 60, 178
coincidence 104, 151
coincidences 104
Coleridge, Samuel Taylor 179
colloquialisms 92, 93
column 59
comma 85, 86, 87, 127, 128
comma fault 85, 86
comma splice 85
communication 93, 180
completeness 62
complications 106
compound subjects 93
computers 32, 215
conclusion 91, 104, 112
conflict, inner 102, 103
conflict, person versus person 102
conflict with the environment 102, 103
conflicts 16, 102, 103, 160, 193
conjunction 85, 87, 88
consistency 62
content 58
contract 210
contractions 72
conversation 126, 129, 130, 131
cookbooks 169
core issue 47
correspondence courses 225
couplet 181, 182
cover letter 202
creativity 24
crisis 165

D
dedication 177
denouement 151
details 14, 17
deus ex machina ITAL 151
dialect 92, 132
dialects 93
dialog 15, 84, 97, 126-131, 133, 135, 136, 138, 139, 157, 160, 161, 163, 167, 186, 193, 194
dictating machine 33, 34
dictation services 33
dictionary 30, 31
digital voice recorder 33
domain hosting services 216
domain name 216
drafting 45, 61
drafting stage 54, 58

Dragon Naturally Speaking 32
drama 6, 114, 126, 151, 179,
    192, 196, 198
dramatic structure 105
dramatic tension 109

E
e-mail address 215
eavesdropping 15
Ed2Go (ed2go.com) 225
editing 61, 67
editor, acquisitions 204, 207
editor, freelance 205
Editorial Freelancers
    Association 205
editorial services 98
editors 21, 24, 64, 98,
    152, 170, 176, 192, 204-
    206, 208, 211
Eliot, T. S. 179
emphasis 135
end 162
ending 161, 173
enlightenment 6
essay 23, 25, 59, 189, 192
essays 169, 170, 204
Everett, David 226, 252
Everything You Need To Know
    About Writing Successf 22
examples 62
exclamation point 127, 128
exclamation points 87
expertise 23

F
fairy tale 102
fame and fortune 11, 12
Famous Writers Course 225
fantasy 152
fax machine 215
feature articles 214
feedback 65, 66, 67
fiction 6, 23, 47, 48, 52-55, 57,
    59, 63, 65, 93, 101, 103-105,
    107, 114, 126, 138, 147,
    151, 154, 160, 167, 179,
    193, 203-205, 208
fiction, historical 147
fiction, literary 152
file cabinet 34
final draft 58, 64, 72, 199
Final Draft 196
final script 58
Firm, The 105
first draf 58
first draft 56-58, 60, 72, 75, 78
first person 171
fish out of water story 163
Fitzgerald, F. Scott 122
Five Critical Cs of Writing 46
flash forward 147
flashback 145, 146, 161
focus 152
format 194
formatting 34

Forster, E. M. 104
frame story 107
Frank@writingafter50.com 228
free verse 180, 181, 184, 186,
    189
freelance writers 214, 216, 219,
    224
freelance writing 221
freewriting 48-51, 60, 178
Frey, James N. 107
front matter 177

G
genre 152, 153
glossary 177
goals 25, 27
gobbledygook 81
GoDaddy.com 216
Goodbye Mr. Chips 107
Google.com 30, 216
Gotham Writers School
    (writingclasses.com) 225
governmentese 81
grammar 63, 70,71, 73, 75, 83,
    97, 98
grammar guides 31
grammatical terms 71
Great Gatsby, The 122, 139
Grisham, John 105
guidelines 203, 213

H
haiku 180, 181, 191
Haircut, The 122
Hanssen, Robert 18
Hathaway, Robin 12, 231
Hemingway, Ernest 11, 56
heuristic interviewing 52, 53
high concept 208
Home Occupation Certificate
    216
home office 215
Hooker, Richard 24
horror and occult 152
*How to Get Control of Your Time
    and Your Life* 25
How To Tell A Story 105
*How To Write A Damn Good
    Novel II* 107
how-to 169, 173

I
iambic pentameter 182, 183
Idictate.com 33
incident 111
independent clauses 85, 87
index card case 30
index cards 52
inhouse newsletters 214
interior quote 135
Internet 11, 32, 36, 58, 141, 165,
    174, 175, 199, 216, 223, 224
Internet account 215
Internet classes 224
Internet fax account 215

intervening words 93
interview 15, 175
interviews 15, 48, 52, 62, 174,
    175, 177, 219
Into Thin Air 138
introductory hook 52
*Invented Worlds: The Psychology
    of the Arts* 4
italics 135, 136
iUniverse 212

J
jargon 92, 180
Jaws 106
Jonathan Livingston Seagull 24
journal 10, 29, 45, 189
journal, personal 8
Junger, Sebastian 11

K
key idea 47
key points 52
keyboarding 32
King, Stephen 12, 22
Kooser, Ted 140, 228
Krakauer, Jon 138

L
Lakein, Alan 25
Lardner, Ring 122
lead 57, 172
lead, anecdotal 173
lead character 121, 126, 165
lead, statistical 172
leather stores 30
Levenger.com 30
librarian, research 141
libraries 11, 32, 141, 210, 223,
    224
life goals 25
lifetime goals exercise 24
London, Jack 138
luggage stores 30
LuLu.com 212

M
M*A*S*H 24
Manos, James, Jr. 198, 246
manuals, instruction 214
manuals, technical 214
manuscripts 29, 33, 34, 62-64,
    95, 98, 202, 205, 207, 210
market guides 213
McCourt, Frank 12
McInerney, Jay 122
mechanics 63
medias res 145, 161
memoir 23, 24, 112, 147, 169,
    171
meter 186
microcassette tapes 33
Microsoft OneNote 35
Microsoft Windows 32
Microsoft Word 3, 32, 35, 216
middle 161, 162, 173

modifiers 71, 140
modifiers, misplaced 81
mood 142
Movie Magic Screenwriter 196
multiple points of view 123-125
Murphy, Eddie 163
My Heart Will Go On 108
mystery and crime 152

N
narration 156, 157, 163, 167
narrative 130, 136, 152, 161, 169, 186
narrative hook 57, 160, 206
narrative passages 52
narrative summary 60
narrator 121, 122, 130, 134, 140, 154, 155
narrator, omniscient 122
National Writers Union (nwu.org) 220, 221
New York Times 224
nonfiction 6, 23, 47, 48, 54, 57-59, 63, 65, 93, 101, 103, 112, 114, 119, 126, 138, 139, 147, 154, 168, 168, 171-173, 176, 177, 179, 192, 193, 203, 204, 206, 207
nonfiction, narrative 105
noun 71, 79
noun, plural 94
nouns 71, 79, 140, 156, 157
nouns, collective 94
nouns, concrete 157
novel 12, 23, 25, 103, 107, 125, 151, 152, 154, 160, 162, 192, 194, 206, 207
novel, contemporary 48
novel, historical 48, 138
novellas 152
nut graph 170

O
object 71
objectives 25
obstacles 106, 108, 111, 112, 161, 164, 165
office supply stores 30
op-ed pieces 19, 169
opening lines 57
opinion column 25
organizational methods 53
O'Toole, Peter 107
outline 48, 51, 54, 58, 178, 207, 20
overarching concept 47

P
Parade magazine 107
parallel construction 92
parallelism 92
Parker, Robert B. 132
passive voice 94, 95, 97
past participle 96, 97
pen stores 30

Perfect Storm, The 103, 139
perfectionism 19
period 85, 86, 128
perseverance 21
persistence 21
personality 23
phrase, prepositional 97
Picture of Dorian Gray 160
planning 45, 61
planning stage 54
plans, business 214
play format 193
playwriting101.com 199
plot 48, 53, 84, 104, 106-108, 111, 139, 142, 151, 152, 157, 165, 193
plot development 106
plot driven 111
plot lines 12
plot outline 162, 16
POD publishing. *See* print on demand
poetic form 180
poetics 112
poetry 6, 23, 24, 114, 179, 181, 183, 186, 191, 206
Poetry Home Repair Manual, The 140, 228
poetry, structured 180, 181
poetry, unstructured 180
Poets & Writers 223
point of view 121-125, 140, 152, 162, 193. *See also* viewpoint
portfolio of clips 217
practice 13
practice time 3
preposition 72
prepositional phrase 72, 96
press releases 214
prime time 5, 214
prime time generation 57, 227
prime time writers 83
prime-timer 220
Prince and the Pauper, The 163
print on demand 212, 213
printer 215
priorities 26, 27
profiles 15, 170
pronoun 71
proposals 48, 54, 208-210, 214
prose 186, 189
prose poem 180, 189
prose poetry 184
protagonist 103, 104, 106, 112, 114, 115, 118, 123, 151, 161
Proulx, Annie 153
Provost, Gary 105
publication 10, 29, 202, 204
publishers 153, 202, 204, 207-211
Publisher's Lunch 224
Publishers Weekly 224
publishersmarketplace.com/ lunch/subscribe.html 224
punch line 112

punctuation 85, 128
punctuation as signs 83
purpose statement 47
pw.com 223

Q
quatrains 181, 182
query 48, 206, 210
query letter 15, 54, 170, 207-210
question 173, 175
question mark 86, 127, 128
quilldriverbooks.com 199
quotation 173
quotation marks 127, 129, 135

R
rainbow method 52
rainbowing 51
rainbowing technique 50
Random House (Xlibris.com) 212
readability 62, 63, 95
reader-centered writing 42
readers 24, 59, 62, 70, 73, 75, 83, 86, 101-104, 112, 118, 119, 121-123, 125-127, 133-135, 140-142, 144, 146, 151, 154, 155, 157, 161, 163, 169, 170, 173, 180
readership 45
redundancy 78
redundant phrases 80, 82
reference 210
reference books 36, 70, 169, 215, 223
reference guide 75
reference library 30
reference materials 72
rejection 21
reports, annual business 214
research 23, 48, 52, 54, 141, 154, 175, 177, 219, 220
research files 34
resolution 104, 116
resources 174, 177
review stage 65, 67
revising 46
revision 57, 62, 159, 177
revision process 61, 64
rhyme 186
rhyme scheme 182, 183
Rime of the Ancient Mariner, The 179
risks 23
romance 138, 152
Room With A View, A 104
rough draft 58
royalties 210
Rubie, Peter 105
Runaway Bride 147

S
SASE (stamped, self-addressed envelope) 202, 206, 207
scansion 181, 182

scenes 52, 145, 157, 159
science fiction 25, 152
screenwriting.info 199
script 51, 193
secretarial services 33
self-discovery 6, 7
self-fulfillment 12
self-help 169
self-publishing 29, 202, 211-213
semicolon 86, 87
seminars 209
serial comma 86
sestet 181, 184
sestina 180, 184
setbacks 106
setting 12, 15, 23, 84, 97, 103,
    111, 138-142, 144, 147, 148,
    151-153, 157, 170
Shakespeare 183
shooting script 58
short stories 23, 24, 103, 125,
    151, 152, 154, 160-162, 186,
    189, 192, 194, 204
show or tell 155
slant 45
smell 15
soliloquy 193
sonnets 180-182
sound 15
speaker tags 127
speculation 220
speech patterns 132
speech tags 128, 131
spell-check 64
spelling 63
spy 152
stage business 194
stanza 181, 182, 184, 186
Star Wars 131
stories, mystery 144
story 48, 101, 103, 104, 107,
    113, 114, 121, 138-140, 144,
    146, 151, 156, 159-161
story, back 115, 116, 120
story development 162
story, frame 107
story, inner 107
story, science-fiction 138
Story to Remember, A 193
story-within-a-story 107
storyboard 51
storytellers 102
style 23, 58
style, formal 59
style guides 84
style, informal 59
subgenres 152, 153
subject 71
subject, compound 94
subject-verb agreement 94
submission guidelines 203
submissions, multiple 211
subplot 84, 116, 152
success 10, 21, 22
summary 91

summary close 174
suspense 102, 103, 109, 159, 161
syllable scheme 182
syllable sets 183
syllables 181, 182
symbolism 159
synonyms 130
synopsis 207, 208, 209

T
table of contents 177, 209
talent 21
Target, 30
taste 15
telephone line 215
Ten Commandments of Grammar
    76
tension 103, 109, 111
tension, dramatic 159
tercet 181, 184
the-efa.org 205
theme 48, 107, 152, 160
thesaurus 30, 31, 75
thesis statement 47
Titanic 107, 108, 109, 138
tone 59
touch 15
touch typing 32
Trading Places 163
Trafford Publishing
    (trafford.com) 212
transcriber, microcassette 33
transcription services 33
transition 87-91, 144
troubadours 184
true crime 147
turns of phrase 15
Twain, Mark 163
typing services 33

U
Upstairs Downstairs 139

V
vanity presses 212
verb, plural 93
verb, singular 93
verbs 71, 79, 95, 96, 130, 140,
    156
verisimilitude 126
viewpoint 121, 152. See also
    point of view
viewpoint character 122
viewpoint, objective 133
viewpoint, subjective 133, 134
vignettes 23, 123, 189
vocabulary 80, 81
voice 60
voice, active 63
voice, passive 63

W
Wal-Mart 30
wallet pens 30
Washington Post 12, 224

Web page 209
website 215, 216
Welty, Eudora 11
westerns 152
Where Angels Fear To Tread 104
WIIFM (what's in it for me) 43,
    44, 64, 170
Wikipedia 151
Wilde, Oscar 160
Will, George 59
Winner, Ellen 4
Wizard of Oz, The 163
word choices 15
word processing 35
word processing software 34
wordy phrases 80
Writer, The 223
writer-centered writing 42
writermag.com 223
Writers Bookstore, The 198
writer's conferences 226
Writer's Digest 223, 225
Writer's Digest Book Club 35
Writers Digest Books 220
Writers Digest Bookstore 199
Writers Digest Correspondence
    Course 225
Writers Digest Online 225
writer's groups 27, 98, 192, 222,
    226
writer's guidelines 211
writer's guides 31
Writers Journal, The 223
writer's magazines 205, 223
Writers Market: Where and How
    to Sell What You Write 220
Writers Store 35, 199
Writers Super Center 35
writer's voice 59
writer's workshop 66, 98
writersdigest.com 199, 223
writersdigestbookclub.com
    35, 222
writersjournal.com 223
writersstore.com 35, 198
writerssupercenter.com 35
writerswrite.net 226
writing class 153
writing courses 225
writing goals 9, 27, 29
writing materials 16, 30
writing schedule 27
writing services 11, 214, 215
writing skills 20

X
Xlibris 212

Y
Yellow Pages 216

About the Author

Following a successful career in counterintelligence and federal law enforcement and after turning fifty, Frank Milligan is living his writing dreams: publishing fiction and nonfiction, and teaching creative writing and business writing. He holds a bachelor's in psychology; a master's in business and public administration; and a master of arts in writing from Johns Hopkins University.

Acknowledgments

Many thanks to Robin Hathaway, Richard Bausch, Donna Boetig, James Manos, Jr., and David Everett who agreed to be interviewed for this book. Each a top professional writer and all willing to take time from very busy schedules to generously pass on their considerable knowledge and experience to new writers coming up behind them.

My sincere gratitude to Stephen Blake Mettee for supporting this book and opening a place at his writer's table for me, and my sincere thanks to my editor, P.J. Dempsey, whose knowledge, experience, and firm but gentle guidance made this a better book, and me a better writer.

And, my fondest appreciation to the students in my creative writing and business writing classes over the years for all that they've taught me.

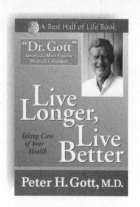
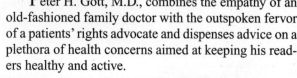
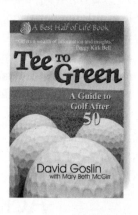
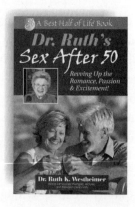

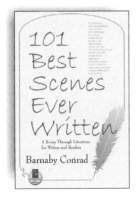